A Canticle for Leibowitz

BY WALTER M. MILLER, JR.

TRANSWORLD PUBLISHERS
LONDON

A CANTICLE FOR LEIBOWITZ

A CORGI BOOK

Originally published in
Great Britain by
Weidenfeld & Nicolson Ltd.

PRINTING HISTORY
Weidenfeld & Nicolson Edition published 1960
Bantam Edition published 1961
Corgi Edition published 1963

Corgi Books are published by Transworld Publishers Ltd.,
Park Royal Road, London, N.W.10.
Made and printed in Great Britain by
Hunt, Barnard & Co., Ltd., Aylesbury, Bucks.

THE SIMPLETONS AND THE SMART GUYS

After the Fallout, the plagues and the madness, began the bloodletting of the Simplification. "Simpletons," the mobs called themselves joyfully. And they killed without mercy all the "smart guys", the rulers, the teachers and scientists, whom they blamed for making the Earth what it was—a ghastly, barren desert.

When twelve hundred years of the darkest of dark ages had passed, human intelligence revolted against the simpletons. In a monastery cellar, students of the records left by Saint Leibowitz were cautiously, fearfully, tentatively, about to produce electric light . . .

Was man on his way to becoming too smart again?

A CANTICLE FOR LEIBOWITZ

One of the most brilliant and provocative novels of our time.

a dedication is only
a scratch where it itches—
for *ANNE*, then
in whose bosom *RACHEL* lies
muselike
guiding my clumsy song
and giggling between the lines
—with blessings, Lass

W

Acknowledgment

To all those whose assistance, in various ways,
contributed to making this book possible, the
author expresses his appreciation and gratitude,
especially and explicitly to the following: Mr.
and Mrs. W. M. Miller, Sr., Messrs. Don Congdon,
Anthony Boucher, and Alan Williams, to Dr.
Marshal Taxay, the Reverend Alvin Burggraff,
C.S.P., to Ss Francis and Clare, and to Mary, for
reasons known to each of them.

Contents

Fiat Homo

1 Brother Francis Gerard of Utah might never have discovered the blessed documents, had it not been for the pilgrim with girded loins who appeared during that young novice's Lenten fast in the desert.

Never before had Brother Francis actually seen a pilgrim with girded loins, but that this one was the bona fide article he was convinced as soon as he had recovered from the spine-chilling effect of the pilgrim's advent on the far horizon, as a wiggling iota of black caught in a shimmering haze of heat. Legless, but wearing a tiny head, the iota materialized out of the mirror glaze on the broken roadway and seemed more to writhe than to walk into view, causing Brother Francis to clutch the crucifix of his rosary and mutter an Ave or two. The iota suggested a tiny apparition spawned by the heat demons who tortured the land at high noon, when any creature capable of motion on the desert (except the buzzards and a few monastic hermits such as Francis) lay motionless in its burrow or hid beneath a rock from the ferocity of the sun. Only a thing monstrous, a thing preternatural, or a thing with addled wits would hike purposefully down the trail at noon this way.

Brother Francis added a hasty prayer to Saint Raul the Cyclopean, patron of the misborn, for protection against the Saint's unhappy protégés. (For who did not then know that there were monsters in the earth in those days? That which was born alive was, by the law of the Church and

1

the law of Nature, suffered to live, and helped to maturity if possible, by those who had begotten it. The law was not always obeyed, but it was obeyed with sufficient frequency to sustain a scattered population of adult monsters, who often chose the remotest of deserted lands for their wanderings, where they prowled by night around the fires of prairie travelers.) But at last the iota squirmed its way out of the heat risers and into clear air, where it manifestly became a distant pilgrim; Brother Francis released the crucifix with a small Amen.

The pilgrim was a spindly old fellow with a staff, a basket hat, a brushy beard, and a waterskin slung over one shoulder. He was chewing and spitting with too much relish to be an apparition, and he seemed too frail and lame to be a successful practitioner of ogre-ism or highwaymanship. Nevertheless, Francis slunk quietly out of the pilgrim's line of sight and crouched behind a heap of rubbled stone where he could watch without being seen. Encounters between strangers in the desert, while rare, were occasions of mutual suspicion, and marked by initial preparations on both sides for an incident that might prove either cordial or warlike.

Seldom more than thrice annually did any layman or stranger travel the old road that passed the abbey, in spite of the oasis which permitted that abbey's existence and which would have made the monastery a natural inn for wayfarers if the road were not a road from nowhere, leading nowhere, in terms of the modes of travel in those times. Perhaps, in earlier ages, the road had been a portion of the shortest route from the Great Salt Lake to Old El Paso; south of the abbey it intersected a similar strip of broken stone that stretched east- and westward. The crossing was worn by time, but not by Man, of late.

The pilgrim approached within hailing distance, but the novice stayed behind his mound of rubble. The pilgrim's loins were truly girded with a piece of dirty burlap, his only clothing except for hat and sandals. Doggedly he plodded ahead with a mechanical limp while assisting his crippled leg with the heavy staff. His rhythmic gait was that of a man with a long road behind him and a long way yet to go. But, upon entering the area of the ancient ruins, he broke his stride and paused to reconnoiter.

Francis ducked low.

There was no shade amid the cluster of mounds where a group of age-old buildings once had been, but some of the larger stones could, nevertheless, provide cooling refreshment to select portions of the anatomy for travelers as wise in the way of the desert as the pilgrim soon proved himself to be. He searched briefly for a rock of suitable proportions. Approvingly, Brother Francis noted that he did not grasp the stone and rashly tug, but instead, stood at a safe distance from it and, using his staff as a lever and a smaller rock for a fulcrum, he jostled the weightier one until the inevitable buzzing creature crawled forth from below. Dispassionately the traveler killed the snake with his staff and flipped the still-wriggling carcass aside. Having dispatched the occupant of the cool cranny beneath the stone, the pilgrim availed himself of the cool cranny's ceiling by the usual method of overturning the stone. Thereupon, he pulled up the back of his loincloth, sat with his withered buttocks against the stone's relatively chilly underside, kicked off his sandals, and pressed the soles of his feet against what had been the sandy floor of the cool cranny. Thus refreshed, he wiggled his toes, smiled toothlessly and began to hum a tune. Soon he was singing a kind of crooning chant in a dialect not known to the novice. Weary of crouching, Brother Francis shifted restlessly.

While he sang, the pilgrim unwrapped a biscuit and a bit of cheese. Then his singing paused, and he stood for a moment to cry out softly in the vernacular of the region: "Blest be *Adonoi Elohim*, King of All, who maketh bread to spring forth from the earth," in a sort of nasal bleat. The bleat being finished, he sat again, and commenced eating.

The wanderer had come a long way indeed, thought Brother Francis, who knew of no adjacent realm governed by a monarch with such an unfamiliar name and such strange pretensions. The old man was making a penitential pilgrimage, hazarded Brother Francis—perhaps to the "shrine" at the abbey, although the "shrine" was not yet officially a shrine, nor was its "saint" yet officially a saint. Brother Francis could think of no alternate explanation of the presence of an old wanderer on this road leading to nowhere.

The pilgrim was taking his time with the bread and cheese, and the novice grew increasingly restless as his own anxiety waned. The rule of silence for the Lenten fast days did not permit him to converse voluntarily with the old man, but if he left his hiding place behind the rubble heap before the old man departed, he was certain to be seen or heard by the pilgrim, for he had been forbidden to leave the vicinity of his hermitage before the end of Lent.

Still slightly hesitant, Brother Francis loudly cleared his throat, then straightened into view.

"Whup!"

The pilgrim's bread and cheese went flying. The old man grabbed his staff and bounded to his feet.

"Creep up on me, will you!"

He brandished the staff menacingly at the hooded figure which had arisen from beyond the rock pile. Brother Francis noticed that the thick end of the staff was armed with a spike. The novice bowed courteously, thrice, but the pilgrim overlooked this nicety.

"Stay back there now!" he croaked. "Just keep your distance, sport. I've got nothing you're after—unless it's the cheese, and you can have that. If it's meat you want, I'm nothing but gristle, but I'll fight to keep it. Back now! *back!*"

"Wait—" The novice paused. Charity, or even common courtesy, could take precedence over the Lenten rule of silence, when circumstances demanded speech, but to break silence on his own decision always left him slightly nervous.

"I'm not a sport, good simpleton," he continued, using the polite address. He tossed back his hood to show his monastic haircut and held up his rosary beads. "Do you understand these?"

For several seconds the old man remained in catlike readiness for combat while he studied the novice's sun-blistered, adolescent face. The pilgrim's had been a natural mistake. Grotesque creatures who prowled the fringes of the desert often wore hoods, masks, or voluminous robes to hide deformity. Among them were those whose deformity was not limited to the body, those who sometimes looked on travelers as a dependable source of venison.

After a brief scrutiny, the pilgrim straightened.

"Oh—one of *them.*" He leaned on his staff and scowled. "Is that the Leibowitz Abbey down yonder?" he asked, pointing toward the distant cluster of buildings to the south.

Brother Francis bowed politely and nodded at the ground.

"What are you doing out here in the ruins?"

The novice picked up a chalklike fragment of stone. That the traveler might be literate was statistically unlikely, but Brother Francis decided to try. Since the vulgar dialects of the people had neither alphabet nor orthography, he chalked the Latin words for "Penance, Solitude, and Silence," on a large flat stone, and wrote them again below in ancient English, hoping, in spite of his unacknowledged yearning for someone to talk to, that the old man would understand and leave him to his lonely Lenten vigil.

The pilgrim smiled wryly at the inscription. His laugh seemed less a laugh than a fatalistic bleat. "Hmmm-hnnnl Still writing things backward," he said; but if he understood the inscription, he did not condescend to admit it. He laid aside his staff, sat on the rock again, picked his bread and cheese out of the sand, and began scraping them clean. Francis moistened his lips hungrily, but looked away. He had eaten nothing but cactus fruit and one handful of parched corn since Ash Wednesday; the rules of fast and abstinence were rather strict for vocational vigils.

Noticing his discomfort, the pilgrim broke his bread and cheese; he offered a portion to Brother Francis.

In spite of his dehydrated condition, caused by his meager water supply, the novice's mouth flooded with saliva. His eyes refused to move from the hand that offered the food. The universe contracted; at its exact geometric center floated that sandy tidbit of dark bread and pale cheese. A demon commanded the muscles of his left leg to move his left foot half a yard forward. The demon then possessed his right leg to move the right foot ahead of the left, and it somehow forced his right pectorals and biceps to swing his arm until his hand touched the hand of the pilgrim. His fingers felt the food; they seemed even to taste the food. An involuntary shudder passed over his half-starved body. He closed his eyes and saw the Lord Abbot glaring at him and brandishing a bullwhip. Whenever the novice tried to visualize the Holy Trinity, the countenance of God the Father always became confused with the face of the abbot, which was normally, it seemed to Francis, very angry. Behind the abbot a bonfire raged, and from the midst of the flames the eyes of the Blessed Martyr Leibowitz gazed in death-agony upon his fasting protégé, caught in the act of reaching for cheese.

The novice shuddered again. "*Apage Satanas!*" he hissed as he danced back and dropped the food. Without warning, he spattered the old man with holy water from a tiny phial sneaked from his sleeve. The pilgrim had become indistinguishable from the Archenemy, for a moment, in the somewhat sun-dazed mind of the novice.

This surprise attack on the Powers of Darkness and Temptation produced no immediate supernatural results, but the natural results seemed to appear *ex opere operato.* The pilgrim-Beelzebub failed to explode into sulfurous smoke, but he made gargling sounds, turned a bright shade of red, and lunged at Francis with a bloodcurdling yell. The novice kept tripping on his tunic as he fled from flailing of the pilgrim's spiked staff, and he escaped without nail holes only because the pilgrim had forgotten his sandals. The old man's limping charge became a skippity hop. He seemed suddenly mindful of scorching rocks under his bare soles. He stopped and became preoccupied. When Brother Francis glanced over his shoulder, he gained the distinct impression that the pilgrim's retreat to his cool spot was being accomplished by the feat of hopping along on the tip of one great toe.

Ashamed of the odor of cheese that lingered on his fingertips, and repenting his irrational exorcism, the novice slunk back to his self-appointed labors in the old ruins, while the pilgrim cooled his feet and satisfied his wrath by flinging an occasional rock at the youth whenever the latter moved into view among the rubble mounds. When his arm at last grew weary, he flung more feints than stones, and merely grumbled over his bread and cheese when Francis ceased to dodge.

The novice was wandering to and fro throughout the ruins, occasionally staggering toward some focal point of his work with a rock, the size of his own chest, locked in a painful embrace. The pilgrim watched him select a stone, estimate its dimensions in hand-spans, reject it, and carefully select another, to be pried free from the rock jam of the rubble, to be hoisted by Francis and stumblingly hauled away. He dropped one stone after a few paces, and, suddenly sitting, placed his head between his knees in an apparent effort to avoid fainting. After panting awhile, he arose again and finished by rolling the stone end-over-end toward its destination. He continued this activity while the pilgrim, no longer glaring, began to gape.

The sun blazed its midday maledictions upon the parched land, laying its anathema on all moist things. Francis labored on in spite of the heat.

When the traveler had washed down the last of his sandy bread and cheese with a few squirts from his waterskin, he slipped feet into sandals, arose with a grunt, and hobbled through the ruins toward the site of the novice's labors. Noticing the old man's approach, Brother Francis scurried to a safe distance. Mockingly, the pilgrim brandished his spiked cudgel at him, but seemed more curious about the youth's masonry than he seemed eager for revenge. He paused to inspect the novice's burrow.

There, near the east boundary of the ruins, Brother Francis had dug a shallow trench, using a stick for a hoe and hands for a shovel. He had, on the first day of Lent, roofed it over with a heap of brush, and used the trench by night as refuge from the desert's wolves. But as the days of his fasting grew in number, his presence had increased his spoor in the vicinity until the nocturnal lupine prowlers seemed unduly attracted to the area of the ruins and even scratched around his brush heap when the fire was gone.

Francis had first attempted to discourage their nightly digging by increasing the thickness of the brush pile over his trench, and by surrounding it with a ring of stones set tightly in a furrow. But on the previous night, something had leaped to the top of his brush pile and howled while Francis lay shivering below, whereupon he had determined to fortify the burrow, and, using the first ring of stones as a foundation, had begun to build a wall. The wall tilted inward as it grew; but since the enclosure was roughly an oval in shape, the stones in each new layer crowded against adjacent stones to prevent an inward collapse. Brother Francis now hoped that by a careful selection of rocks and a certain amount of juggling, dirt-tamping, and pebble-wedging, he would be able to complete a dome. And, a single span of unbuttressed arch, somehow defying gravity, stood there over the burrow as a token of this ambition. Brother Francis yelped like a puppy when the pilgrim rapped curiously at this arch with his staff.

Solicitous for his abode, the novice had drawn nearer during the pilgrim's inspection. The pilgrim answered his yelp with a flourish of the cudgel and a bloodthirsty howl. Brother Francis promptly tripped on the hem of his tunic and sat down. The old man chuckled.

"Hmmm-hnnn! You'll need a strange shape of a rock to fit *that* gap," he said, and rattled his staff back and forth in a vacant space in the highest tier of stones.

The youth nodded and looked away. He continued to sit in the sand, and, by silence and by his lowered gaze, he hoped to tell the old man that he was neither free to converse nor free to accept willingly another's presence in his place of Lenten solitude. The novice began writing with a dry twig in the sand: *Et ne nos inducas in . . .*

"I've not offered to change these stones into bread for you yet, have I?" the old traveler said crossly.

Brother Francis glanced up quickly. So! the old man *could* read, and read Scripture, at that. Furthermore, his remark implied that he had understood both the novice's impulsive use of holy water and his reason for being here as well. Aware now that the pilgrim was teasing him, Brother Francis lowered his eyes again and waited.

"Hmmm-hnnn! So you're to be left alone, are you? Well, then, I'd best be on my way. Tell me, will your brothers at the abbey let an old man rest a bit in their shade?"

Brother Francis nodded. "They'll give you food and water too," he added softly, in charity.

The pilgrim chuckled. "For that, I'll find you a rock to fit that gap before I go. God with you."

But you need not—The protest died unspoken. Brother Francis watched him hobbling slowly away. The pilgrim wandered in and about among the rubble mounds. He paused occasionally to inspect a stone or pry at one with his staff. His search would surely prove fruitless, the novice thought, for it was a repetition of a search which the youth himself had been making since mid-morning. He had decided at last that it would be easier to remove and rebuild a section of the highest tier than to find a keystone that approximated the hourglass shape of the gap in that tier. But, surely, the pilgrim would soon exhaust his patience and wander on his way.

Meanwhile, Brother Francis rested. He prayed for the recovery of that inward privacy which the purpose of his vigil demanded that he seek: a clean parchment of the spirit whereon the words of a summons might be written in his solitude—if that other Immensurable Loneliness which was God stretched forth Its hand to touch his own tiny human loneliness and to mark his vocation there. The *Little Book,* which Prior Cheroki had left with him on the preceding Sunday, served as a guide to his meditation. It was centuries old, and it was called *Libellus Leibowitz,* although only an uncertain tradition attributed its authorship to the Beatus himself.

"*Parum equidem te diligebam, Domine, juventute mea; quare doleo nimis . . .* Too little, O Lord, did I love Thee in the time of my youth; wherefore I grieve exceedingly in

the time of my age. In vain did I flee from Thee in those
days. . . ."

"*Hoy!* Over here!" came a shout from beyond the rubble
mounds.

Brother Francis glanced up briefly, but the pilgrim was not
in sight. His eyes fell again to the page.

"*Repugnans tibi, ausus sum quaerere quidquid doctius
mihi fide, certius spe, aut dulcius caritate visum esset. Quis
itaque stultior me . . .*"

"Hey *boy!*" the cry came again. "I found you a stone, one
likely to fit."

This time when Brother Francis looked up, he caught a
glimpse of the pilgrim's staff waving signals to him beyond
the top of a rubble heap. Sighing, the novice returned to his
reading.

"*O inscrutabilis Scrutator animarum, cui patet omne cor,
si me vocaveras, olim a te fugeram. Si autem nunc velis
vocare me indignum . . .*"

And, irritably from beyond the rubble mound: "All right,
then, suit yourself. I'll mark the rock and set a stake by it.
Try it or not, as you please."

"Thank you," the novice sighed, but doubted that the old
man heard him. He toiled on with the text:

"*Libera me, Domine, ab vitiis meis, ut solius tuae
voluntatis mihi cupidus sim, et vocationis . . .*"

"There, then!" the pilgrim shouted. "It's staked and
marked. And may you find your voice soon, boy. *Olla
allay!*"

Soon after the last shout faded and died, Brother Francis
caught a glimpse of the pilgrim trudging away on the trail
that led toward the abbey. The novice whispered a swift
blessing after him, and a prayer for safe wayfaring.

His privacy having been restored, Brother Francis returned the book to his burrow and resumed his haphazard
stonemasonry, not yet troubling himself to investigate the
pilgrim's find. While his starved body heaved, strained,
and staggered under the weight of the rocks, his mind,
machinelike kept repeating the prayer for the certainty of
his vocation:

"*Libere me, Domine, ab vitiis meis* . . . Set me free, O
Lord, from my own vices, so that in my own heart I may be
desirous of only Thy will, and be aware of Thy summons
if it come . . . *ut solius tuae voluntatis mihi cupidus sim,
et vocationis tuae conscius si digneris me vocare. Amen.*

"Set me free, O Lord, from my own vices, so that in my own heart . . ."

A sky-herd of cumulus clouds, on their way to bestow moist blessings on the mountains after cruelly deceiving the parched desert, began blotting out the sun and trailing dark shadow-shapes across the blistered land below, offering intermittent but welcome respite from the searing sunlight. When a racing cloud-shadow wiped its way over the ruins, the novice worked rapidly until the shadow was gone, then rested until the next bundle of fleece blotted out the sun.

It was quite by accident that Brother Francis finally discovered the pilgrim's stone. While wandering thereabouts, he stumbled over the stake which the old man had driven into the ground as a marker. He found himself on his hands and knees staring at a pair of marks freshly chalked on an ancient stone: ⅗

The marks were so carefully drawn that Brother Francis immediately assumed them to be symbols, but minutes of musing over them left him still bemused. With markings perhaps? But no, the old man had called: "God-with-you," as a witch would not. The novice pried the stone free from the rubble and rolled it over. As he did so, the rock mound rumbled faintly from within; a small stone clattered down the slope. Francis danced away from a possible avalanche, but the disturbance was momentary. In the place where the pilgrim's rock had been wedged, however, there now appeared a small black hole.

Holes were often inhabited.

But this hole seemed to have been so tightly corked by the pilgrim's stone that scarcely a flea could have entered it before Francis had overturned the rock. Nevertheless, he found a stick and gingerly thrust it into the opening. The stick encountered no resistance. When he released it, the stick slid into the hole and vanished, as if into a larger underground cavity. He waited nervously. Nothing slithered forth.

He sank to his knees again and cautiously sniffed at the hole. Having noticed neither an animal odor nor any hint of brimstone, he rolled a bit of gravel into it and leaned closer to listen. The gravel bounced once, a few feet below the opening, and then kept rattling its way downward, struck something metallic in passing, and finally came to rest somewhere far below. Echoes suggested an underground opening the size of a room.

Brother Francis climbed unsteadily to his feet and looked around. He seemed alone, as usual, except for his companion buzzard which, soaring on high, had been watching him with such interest lately that other buzzards occasionally left their territories near the horizons and came to investigate.

The novice circled the rubble heap, but found no sign of a second hole. He climbed an adjacent heap and squinted down the trail. The pilgrim had long since vanished. Nothing moved along the old roadway, but he caught a fleeting glimpse of Brother Alfred crossing a low hill a mile to the east in search of firewood near his own Lenten hermitage. Brother Alfred was deaf as a post. There was no one else in view. Francis foresaw no reason whatever to scream for help, but to estimate in advance the probable results of such a scream, if the need should arise, seemed only an exercise of prudence. After a careful scrutiny of the terrain, he climbed down from the mound. Breath needed for screaming would be better used for running.

He thought of replacing the pilgrim's stone to cork the hole as before, but the adjacent stones had shifted slightly so that it no longer fit its previous place in the puzzle. Besides, the gap in the highest tier of his shelter wall remained unfilled, and the pilgrim was right: the stone's size and shape suggested a probable fit. After only brief misgivings, he hoisted the rock and staggered back to his burrow.

The stone slipped neatly into place. He tested the new wedge with a kick; the tier held fast, even though the jolt caused a minor collapse a few feet away. The pilgrim's marks, though blurred by his handling of the stone, were still clear enough to be copied. Brother Francis carefully redrew them on another rock, using a charred stick as a stylus. When Prior Cheroki made his Sabbath tour of the hermitages, perhaps the priest would be able to say whether the marks had meaning, either as charm or curse. To fear the pagan cabals was forbidden, but the novice was curious at least to learn what sign would be overhanging his sleeping pit, in view of the weight of the masonry on which the sign was written.

His labors continued through the heat of the afternoon. A corner of his mind kept reminding him of the hole—the interesting, and yet fearsome, little hole—and the way the rattle of gravel had caused faint echoes from somewhere below ground. He knew that the ruins all about him here were very old. He knew also, from tradition, that the ruins had been gradually eroded into these anomalous heaps of stone by generations of monks and occasional strangers, men seeking a load of stone or looking for the bits of rusty steel which could be found by shattering the larger sections of columns and slabs to extract the ancient strips of that metal, mysteriously planted in the rocks by men of an age almost forgotten to the world. This human erosion had all but obliterated the resemblance to buildings, which tradition ascribed to the ruins in an earlier period, although the abbey's present master-builder still took pride in his ability to sense and to point out the vestige of a floor plan here and there. And there was still metal to be found, if anyone cared to break enough rock to find it.

The abbey itself had been built of these stones. That several centuries of stonemasons might have left anything of interest still to be discovered in the ruins, Francis regarded as improbable fancy. And yet, he had never heard anyone mention buildings with basements or underground rooms. The master-builder, he recalled at last, had been quite specific in saying that the buildings at this site had had aspects of hasty construction, lacked deep foundations, and had rested for the most part on flat surface slabs.

With his shelter approaching completion, Brother Francis ventured back to the hole and stood looking down at it; he was unable to put off the desert-dweller's conviction that wherever a place exists to hide from the sun, something is already hiding in it. Even if the hole was now uninhabited, something would certainly slither into it before tomorrow's dawn. On the other hand, if something already lived in the hole, Francis thought it safer to make its acquaintance by day than by night. There seemed to be no tracks in the vicinity except his own, the pilgrim's, and the tracks of the wolves.

Making a quick decision, he began clearing rubble and sand away from the hole. After half an hour of this, the hole was no larger, but his conviction that it opened into a subterranean pit had become a certainty. Two small boulders, half buried, and adjoining the opening, were obviously jammed together by the force of too much mass crowding the mouth of a shaft; they seemed caught in a bottleneck.

When he pried one stone toward the right, its neighbor rolled left, until no further motion was possible. The reverse effect occurred when he pried in the opposing direction, but he continued to jostle at the rock-jam.

His lever spontaneously leaped from his grasp, delivered a glancing blow to the side of his head, and disappeared in a sudden cave-in. The sharp blow sent him reeling. A flying stone from the rockslide struck him in the back and he fell gasping, uncertain whether or not he was falling into the pit until the instant his belly hit solid ground and he hugged it. The roar of the rockfall was deafening but brief.

Blinded by dust, Francis lay gasping for breath and wondering whether he dared to move, so sharp was the pain in his back. Having recovered a little breath, he managed to get one hand inside his habit and groped for the place between his shoulders where a few crushed bones might be. The place felt rough, and it stung. His fingers came away damp and red. He moved, but groaned and lay quietly again.

There was a soft beating of wings. Brother Francis glanced up in time to see the buzzard preparing to alight on a rubble heap a few yards away. The bird took wing again at once, but Francis imagined that it had eyed him with a sort of motherly concern in the manner of a worried hen. He rolled over quickly. A whole black heavenly host of them had gathered, and they circled at a curiously low altitude. Just skimming the mounds. They soared higher when he moved. Suddenly ignoring the possibility of chipped vertebrae or a crushed rib, the novice climbed shakily to his feet. Disappointed, the black sky-horde rode back to altitude on their invisible elevators of hot air, then disbanded and dispersed toward their remoter aerial vigils. Dark alternatives to the Paraclete whose coming he awaited, the birds seemed eager at times to descend in place of the Dove; their sporadic interest had been unnerving him of late, and he promptly decided, after some experimental shrugging, that the sharp rock had done no more than bruise and scrape.

A dust column which had plumed up from the site of the cave-in was tapering away on the breeze. He hoped someone would see it from the abbey's watchtowers and come to investigate. At his feet, a square opening yawned in the earth, where one flank of the mound had collapsed into the pit below. Stairs led downward, but only the top steps remained unburied by the avalanche which had paused for

six centuries in mid-fall to await the assistance of Brother
Francis before completing its roaring descent.

On one wall of the stair well a half-buried sign remained
legible. Mustering his modest command of pre-Deluge English, he whispered the words haltingly:

FALLOUT SURVIVAL SHELTER
Maximum Occupancy: 15

Provision limitations, single occupant: 180 days; divide by
actual number of occupants. Upon entering shelter, see that
First Hatch is securely locked and sealed, that the intruder
shields are electrified to repel contaminated persons attempting entry, that the warning lights are *ON* outside the enclosure. . . .

The rest was buried, but the first word was enough for
Francis. He had never seen a "Fallout," and he hoped he'd
never see one. A consistent description of the monster had
not survived, but Francis had heard the legends. He crossed
himself and backed away from the hole. Tradition told that
the Beatus Leibowitz himself had encountered a Fallout, and
had been possessed by it for many months before the
exorcism which accompanied his Baptism drove the fiend
away.

Brother Francis visualized a Fallout as half-salamander,
because, according to tradition, the thing was born in the
Flame Deluge, and as half-incubus who despoiled virgins in
their sleep, for, were not the monsters of the world still
called "children of the Fallout"? That the demon was capable
of inflicting all the woes which descended upon Job was
recorded fact, if not an article of creed.

The novice stared at the sign in dismay. Its meaning was
plain enough. He had unwittingly broken into the abode
(deserted, he prayed) of not just one, but fifteen of the
dreadful beings! He groped for his phial of holy water.

2

"A spiritu fornicationis,
  Domine, libera nos.
From the lightning and the tempest,
  O Lord, deliver us.

From the scourge of the earthquake,
  O Lord, deliver us.
From plague, famine, and war,
  O Lord, deliver us.

"From the place of ground zero,
  O Lord, deliver us.
From the rain of the cobalt,
  O Lord, deliver us.
From the rain of the strontium,
  O Lord, deliver us.
From the fall of the cesium,
  O Lord, deliver us.

"From the curse of the Fallout,
  O Lord, deliver us.
From the begetting of monsters,
  O Lord, deliver us.
From the curse of the Misborn,
  O Lord, deliver us.
A morte perpetua,
  Domine, libera nos.

"Peccatores,
  te rogamus, audi nos.
That thou wouldst spare us,
  we beseech thee, hear us.
That thou wouldst pardon us,
  we beseech thee, hear us.
That thou wouldst bring us truly to penance,
  te rogamus, audi nos."

Snatches of such versicles from the Litany of the Saints came whispering on each panting breath as Brother Francis lowered himself gingerly into the stair well of the ancient Fallout Shelter, armed as he was only with holy water and an improvised torch lighted from the banked embers of last night's fire. He had waited more than an hour for someone from the abbey to come investigate the dust plume. No one had come.

To abandon his vocational vigil even briefly, unless seriously ill or unless ordered to return to the abbey, would be regarded as an *ipso facto* renunciation of his claim of a true vocation to life as a monk of the Albertian Order of Leibowitz. Brother Francis would have preferred death. He was faced, therefore, with the choice of investigating the fearsome pit before sunset, or of spending the night in his burrow in ignorance of whatever might lurk in the shelter and might reawaken to prowl in darkness. As a nocturnal hazard, the wolves already made trouble enough, and the wolves were merely creatures of flesh and blood. Creatures of less solid substance, he preferred to meet by the light of day; although, to be sure, scant daylight fell into the pit below, the sun now being low in the west.

The debris which had crashed down into the shelter formed a hill with its crest near the head of the stairs, and there was only a narrow squeezeway between the rocks and the ceiling. He went through it feet first and found himself forced to continue feet first, because of the steepness of the slope. Thus confronting the Unkown face-to-backside, he groped for footholds in the loose heap of broken stone and gradually worked his way downward. Occasionally, when his torch flickered low, he paused to tilt its flame downward, letting the fire spread further along the wood; during such pauses, he tried to appraise the danger about him and below. There was little to be seen. He was in an underground room, but at least one third of its volume was filled by the mound of debris that had fallen through the stair well. The cascade of stone had covered all the floor, crushed several pieces of furniture that he could see, and perhaps had completely buried others. He saw battered metal lockers leaning awry, waist-deep in rubble. At the far end of the room was a metal door, hinged to swing toward him, and tightly sealed by the avalanche. Still legible in flaking paint on the door were the stenciled letters:

INNER HATCH
SEALED ENVIRONMENT

Evidently the room into which he was descending was only an antechamber. But whatever lay beyond INNER HATCH was sealed there by several tons of rock against the door. Its environment was SEALED indeed, unless it had another exit.

Having made his way to the foot of the slope, and after assuring himself that the antechamber contained no obvious menace, the novice went cautiously to inspect the metal door at closer range by torchlight. Printed under the stenciled letters of INNER HATCH was a smaller rust-streaked sign:

WARNING: This hatch must not be sealed before all personnel have been admitted, or before all steps of safety procedure prescribed by Technical Manual CD-Bu-83A have been accomplished. When Hatch is sealed, air within shelter will be pressurized 2.0 p.s.i. above ambient barometric level to minimize inward diffusion. Once sealed, the hatch will be automatically unlocked by the servomonitor system when, but not before, any of the following conditions prevail: (1) when the exterior radiation count falls below the danger level, (2) when the air and water repurification system fails, (3) when the food supply is exhausted, (4) when the internal power supply fails. See CD-Bu-83A for further instructions.

Brother Francis found himself slightly confused by the Warning, but he intended to heed it by not touching the door at all. The miraculous contraptions of the ancients were not to be carelessly tampered with, as many a dead excavator-of-the-past had testified with his dying gasp.

Brother Francis noticed that the debris which had been lying in the antechamber for centuries was darker in color and rougher in texture than the debris which had weathered under the desert sun and in the sandy wind before today's cave-in. One could tell by a glance at the stones that Inner Hatch had been blocked not by today's rockslide but by one more ancient than the abbey itself. If Fallout Shelter's Sealed Environment contained a Fallout, the demon had obviously not opened Inner Hatch since the time of the Flame Deluge, before the Simplification. And, if it had been sealed beyond the metal door for so many centuries, there was small reason, Francis told himself, to fear that it might come bursting through the hatch before Holy Saturday.

His torch burned low. Having found a splintered chair leg, he set it ablaze with his waning flame, then began gathering bits of broken furniture with which to build a dependable fire, meanwhile pondering the meaning of that ancient sign: FALLOUT SURVIVAL SHELTER.

As Brother Francis readily admitted, his mastery of pre-Deluge English was far from masterful yet. The way nouns could sometimes modify other nouns in that tongue had always been one of his weak points. In Latin, as in most simple dialects of the region, a construction like *servus puer* meant about the same thing as *puer servus,* and even in English *slave boy* meant *boy slave.* But there the similarity ended. He had finally learned that *house cat* did not mean *cat house,* and that a dative of purpose or possession, as in *mihi amicus,* was somehow conveyed by *dog food* or *sentry box* even without inflection. But what of a triple appositive like *fallout survival shelter?* Brother Francis shook his head. The Warning on Inner Hatch mentioned food, water, and air; and yet surely these were not necessities for the fiends of Hell. At times, the novice found pre-Deluge English more perplexing than either Intermediate Angelology or Saint Leslie's theological calculus.

He built his fire on the slope of the rubble pile, where it could brighten the darker crannies of the antechamber. Then he went to explore whatever might remain uncovered by debris. The ruins above ground had been reduced to archaeological ambiguity by generations of scavengers, but this underground ruin had been touched by no hand but the hand of impersonal disaster. The place seemed haunted by the presences of another age. A skull, lying among the rocks in a darker corner, still retained a gold tooth in its grin—clear evidence that the shelter had never been invaded by wanderers. The gold incisor flickered when the fire danced high.

More than once in the desert had Brother Francis encountered, near some parched arroyo, a small heap of human bones, picked clean and whitening in the sun. He was not especially squeamish, and one expected such things. He was, therefore, not startled when he first noticed the skull in the corner of the antechamber, but the flicker of gold in its grin kept catching his eye while he pried at the doors (locked or stuck) of the rusty lockers and tugged at the drawers (also stuck) of a battered metal desk. The desk might prove to be a priceless find, if it contained documents or a small book or two that had survived the angry bonfires of the Age of Simplification. While he kept trying to open the drawers, the fire burned low; he fancied that the skull began emitting a faint glow of its own. Such a phenomenon was not especially uncommon, but in the gloomy crypt, Brother Francis found it somehow most disturbing. He gathered more wood for the fire, returned to jerk and tug at the desk, and tried to ignore the skull's flickering grin. While a little wary yet of lurking Fallouts, Francis had sufficiently recovered from his initial fright to realize that the shelter, notably the desk and the lockers, might well be teeming with rich relics of an age which the world had, for the most part, deliberately chosen to forget.

Providence had bestowed a blessing here. To find a bit of

the past which had escaped both the bonfires and the looting scavengers was a rare stroke of luck these days. There was, however, always a risk involved. Monastic excavators, alert for ancient treasures, had been known to emerge from a hole in the ground, triumphantly carrying a strange cylindrical artifact, and then—while cleaning it or trying to ascertain its purpose—press the wrong button or twist the wrong knob, thereby ending the matter without benefit of clergy. Only eighty years ago the Venerable Boedullus had written with obvious delight to his Lord Abbot that his small expedition had uncovered the remains of, in his own words, "the site of an intercontinental launching pad, complete with several fascinating subterranean storage tanks." No one at the abbey ever knew what the Venerable Boedullus meant by "intercontinental launching pad," but the Lord Abbot who had reigned at that time sternly decreed that monastic antiquarians must, on pain of excommunication, avoid such "pads" thenceforth. For his letter to the abbot was the last that anyone ever saw of the Venerable Boedullus, his party, his "launching pad" site, and the small village which had grown up over that site; an interesting lake now graced the landscape where the village had been, thanks to some shepherds who diverted the course of a creek and caused it to flow into the crater to store water for their flocks in time of drought. A traveler who had come from that direction about a decade ago reported excellent fishing in that lake, but the shepherds thereabouts regarded the fish as the souls of the departed villagers and excavators; they refused to fish there because of Bo'dollos, the giant catfish that brooded in the deep.

"... nor shall any other excavation be initiated which does not have as its primary purpose the augmentation of the Memorabilia," the Lord Abbot's decree had added—meaning that Brother Francis should search the shelter only for books and papers, not tampering with interesting hardware.

The gold-capped tooth kept winking and glittering at the corner of his eye while Brother Francis heaved and strained at the desk drawers. The drawers refused to budge. He gave the desk a final kick and turned to glare impatiently at the skull: *Why don't you grin at something else for a change?*

The grin remained. The gold-toothed residuum lay with its head pillowed between a rock and a rusty metal box. Quitting the desk, the novice picked his way across the debris at last for a closer inspection of the mortal remains. Clearly, the person had died on the spot, struck down by the torrent of stones and half buried by the debris. Only the skull and the bones of one leg had not been covered. The femur was broken, the back of the skull was crushed.

Brother Francis breathed a prayer for the departed, then very gently lifted the skull from its resting place and turned it around so that it grinned toward the wall. Then his eye fell on the rusty box.

The box was shaped like a satchel and was obviously a carrying case of some kind. It might have served any number of purposes, but it had been rather badly battered by flying stones. Gingerly he worked it loose from the rubble and carried it closer to the fire. The lock seemed to be broken, but the lid had rusted shut. The box rattled when he shook it. It was not an obvious place to look for books or papers, but—obviously too—it was designed to be opened and closed, and might contain a scrap or two of information for the Memorabilia. Nevertheless, remembering the fate of Brother Boedullus and others, he sprinkled it with holy water before attempting to pry it open, and he handled the ancient relic as reverently as was possible while battering at its rusty hinges with a stone.

At last he broke the hinges, and the lid fell free. Small metal tidbits bounced from trays, spilled among the rocks, some of them falling irretrievably into crevices. But, in the bottom of the box in the space beneath the trays, he beheld —papers! After a quick prayer of thanksgiving, he regathered as many of the scattered tidbits as he could, and, after loosely replacing the lid, began climbing the hill of debris toward the stair well and the thin patch of sky, with the box hugged tightly under one arm.

The sun was blinding after the darkness of the shelter. He scarcely bothered to notice that it was sinking dangerously low in the west, but began at once to search for a flat slab on which the contents of the box could be spread for examination without risk of losing anything in the sand.

Minutes later, seated on a cracked foundation slab, he began removing the tidbits of metal and glass that filled the trays. Most of them were small tubular things with a wire whisker at each end of each tube. These, he had seen before. The abbey's small museum had a few of them, of various size, shape and color. Once he had seen a shaman of the hill-pagan people wearing a string of them as a ceremonial necklace. The hill people thought of them as "parts of the body of the

god"—of the fabled *Machina analytica*, hailed as the wisest
of their gods. By swallowing one of them, a shaman could
acquire "Infallibility," they said. He certainly acquired In-
disputability that way, among his own people—unless he
swallowed one of the poison kind. The similar tidbits in the
museum were connected together too—not in the form of a
necklace, but as a complex and rather disorderly maze in the
bottom of a small metal box, exhibited as: "Radio Chassis:
Application Uncertain."

Inside the lid of the carrying case, a note had been glued;
the glue had powdered, the ink had faded, and the paper
was so darkened by rusty stains that even good handwriting
would have been hard enough to read, but this was written
in a hasty scrawl. He studied it intermittently while emptying
the trays. It seemed to be English, of a sort, but half an hour
passed before he deciphered most of the message:

CARL—
    Must grab plane for [*undecipherable*] in twenty minutes.
For God's sake, keep Em there till we know if we're at war.
Please! try to get her on the alternate list for the shelter. Can't
get her a seat my plane. Don't tell her why I sent her over
with this box of junk, but try to keep her there till we know
[*undecipherable*] at worst, one of the alternates not show.
                                                    I.E.L.
P.S. I put the seal on the lock and put TOP SECRET on the
lid just to keep Em from looking inside. First tool box I happened to grab. Shove it in my locker or something.

The note seemed hasty gibberish to Brother Francis, who
was at the moment too excited to concentrate on any single
item more than the rest. After a final sneer at the note-
writer's hasty scrawl, he began the task of removing the tray-
racks to get at the papers in the bottom of the box. The trays
were mounted on a swinging linkage which was obviously
meant to swing the trays out of the box in stair-step array,
but the pins were rusted fast, and Francis found it necessary to pry them out with a short steel tool from one of the
tray compartments.

When Brother Francis had removed the last tray, he
touched the papers reverently: only a handful of folded documents here, and yet a treasure; for they had escaped the
angry flames of the Simplification, wherein even sacred
writings had curled, blackened, and withered into smoke
while ignorant mobs howled and hailed it a triumph. He

handled the papers as one might handle holy things, shielding them from the wind with his habit, for all were brittle and cracked from age. There was a sheaf of rough sketches and diagrams. There were hand-scribbled notes, two large folded papers, and a small book entitled *Memo*.

First he examined the jotted notes. They were scrawled by the same hand that had written the note glued to the lid, and the penmanship was no less abominable. *Pound pastrami,* said one note, *can kraut, six bagels—bring home for Emma*. Another reminded: *Remember—pick up Form 1040, Uncle Revenue*. Another was only a column of figures with a circled total from which a second amount was subtracted and finally a percentage taken, followed by the word *damn!* Brother Francis checked the figures; he could find no fault with the abominable penman's arithmetic, at least, although he could deduce nothing about what the quantities might represent.

Memo, he handled with special reverence, because its title was suggestive of "Memorabilia." Before opening it, he crossed himself and murmured the Blessing of Texts. But the small book proved a disappointment. He had expected printed matter, but found only a hand-written list of names, places, numbers and dates. The dates ranged through the latter part of the fifth decade, and earlier part of the sixth decade, twentieth century. Again it was affirmed!—the contents of the shelter came from the twilight period of the Age of Enlightenment. An important discovery indeed.

Of the larger folded papers, one was tightly rolled as well, and it began to fall apart when he tried to unroll it; he could making out the words *RACING FORM*, but nothing more. After returning it to the box for later restorative work, he turned to the second folded document; its creases were so brittle that he dared inspect only a little of it, by parting the folds slightly and peering between them.

A diagram, it seemed, but—a diagram of white lines on dark paper!

Again he felt the thrill of discovery. It was clearly a blueprint!—and there was not a single original blueprint left at the abbey, but only inked facsimiles of several such prints. The originals had faded long ago from overexposure to light. Never before had Francis seen an original, although he had seen enough hand-painted reproductions to recognize it as a blueprint, which, while stained and faded, remained legible after so many centuries because of the total darkness and low humidity in the shelter. He turned the document over—and felt brief fury. What idiot had desecrated the priceless paper? Someone had sketched absent-minded geometrical figures and childish cartoon faces all over the back. What thoughtless vandal—

The anger passed after a moment's reflection. At the time of the deed, blueprints had probably been as common as weeds, and the owner of the box the probable culprit. He shielded the print from the sun with his own shadow while trying to unfold it further. In the lower right-hand corner was a printed rectangle containing, in simple block letters, various titles, dates, "patent numbers," reference numbers, and names. His eye traveled down the list until it encountered: "CIRCUIT DESIGN BY: *Leibowitz, I. E.*"

He closed his eyes tightly and shook his head until it seemed to rattle. Then he looked again. There it was, quite plainly:

CIRCUIT DESIGN BY: *Leibowitz, I. E.*

He flipped the paper over again. Among the geometric figures and childish sketches, clearly stamped in purple ink, was the form:

The name was written in a clear feminine hand, not in the hasty scrawl of the other notes. He looked again at the initialed signature of the note in the lid of the box: *I. E. L.*—and again at "CIRCUIT DESIGN BY . . ." And the same initials appeared elsewhere throughout the notes.

There had been argument, all highly conjectural, about

whether the beatified founder of the Order, if finally canonized, should be addressed as Saint Isaac or as Saint Edward. Some even favored Saint Leibowitz as the proper address, since the Beatus had, until the present, been referred to by his surname.

"*Beate Leibowitz, ora pro me!*" whispered Brother Francis. His hands were trembling so violently that they threatened to ruin the brittle documents.

He had uncovered relics of the Saint.

Of course, New Rome had not yet proclaimed that Leibowitz was a saint, but Brother Francis was so convinced of it that he made bold to add: "*Sancte Leibowitz, ora pro me!*"

Brother Francis wasted no idle logic in leaping to his immediate conclusion: he had just been granted a token of his vocation by Heaven itself. He had found what he had been sent into the desert to find, as Brother Francis saw it. He was called to be a professed monk of the Order.

Forgetting his abbot's stern warning against expecting a vocation to come in any spectacular or miraculous form, the novice knelt in the sand to pray his thanks and to offer a few decades of the rosary for the intentions of the old pilgrim who had pointed out the rock leading to the shelter. *May you find your Voice soon, boy*, the wanderer had said. Not until now did the novice suspect that the pilgrim meant *Voice* with a capital V.

"*Ut solius tuae voluntatis mihi cupidus sim, et vocationis tuae conscius, si digneris me vocare . . .*"

It would be left to the abbot to think that his "voice" was speaking the language of circumstances and not the language of cause and effect. It would be left to the *Promotor Fidei* to think that "Leibowitz," perhaps, was not an uncommon name before the Flame Deluge, and that *I. E.* could as easily represent "Ichabod Ebenezer" as "Isaac Edward." For Francis, there was only one.

From the distant abbey, three bell notes rang out across the desert, a pause, then the three notes were followed by nine.

"*Angelus Domini nuntiavit Mariae*," the novice dutifully responded glancing up in surprise to see that the sun had become a fat scarlet ellipse that already touched the western horizon. The rock barrier around his burrow was not yet complete.

As soon as the Angelus was said, he hastily repacked the papers in the rusty old box. A call from Heaven did not necessarily involve charismata for subduing wild beasts or befriending hungry wolves.

By the time twilight had faded and the stars had appeared, his makeshift shelter was as well fortified as he could make it; whether it was wolf-proof remained to be tested. The test would not be long in coming. He had already heard a few howls from the west. His fire was rekindled, but there was no light left outside the circle of firelight to permit the gathering of his daily collection of purple cactus fruit—his only source of nourishment except on Sundays, when a few handfuls of parched corn were sent from the abbey after a priest had made his rounds with the Holy Sacrament. The letter of the rule for a Lenten vocational vigil was not so strict as its practical application. As applied, the rule amounted to simple starvation.

Tonight, however, the gnawing of hunger was less trouble-some to Francis than his own impatient urge to run back to the abbey and announce the news of his discovery. To do so would be to renounce his vocation no sooner than it had come to him; he was here for the duration of Lent, vocation or no vocation, to continue his vigil as if nothing extraor-dinary had occurred.

Dreamily, from near the fire, he gazed into the darkness in the direction of Fallout Survival Shelter and tried to vis-ualize a towering basilica rising from the site. The fantasy was pleasant, but it was difficult to imagine anyone choos-ing this remote stretch of desert as the focal point of a fu-ture diocese. If not a basilica, then a smaller church—The Church of Saint Leibowitz of the Wilderness—surrounded by a garden and a wall, with a shrine of the Saint attracting rivers of pilgrims with girded loins out of the north. "Father" Francis of Utah conducted the pilgrims on a tour of the ruins, even through "Hatch Two" into the splendors of "Sealed Environment" beyond, the catacombs of the Flame Deluge where . . . where . . . well, afterwards, he would offer Mass for them on the altar stone which enclosed a relic of the church's name-saint—a bit of burlap? fibers from the hang-man's noose? fingernail clippings from the bottom of the rusty box?—or perhaps *RACING FORM*. But the fantasy withered. The chances of Brother Francis becoming a priest were slight—not being a missionary Order, the Brothers of Leibow-itz needed only enough priests for the abbey itself and a few smaller communities of monks in other locations. Furthermore, the "Saint" was still only a Beatus officially, and would never be formally declared a saint unless he wrought a few more good solid miracles to underwrite his own beatification, which was not an infallible proclamation, as canonization would be, although it permitted the monks of the Leibowitz Order formally to venerate their founder and patron, outside of the Mass and the Office. The proportions of the fantasy church dwindled to the size of a wayside shrine; the river of pilgrims shrank to a trickle. New Rome was busy with other matters, such as the petition for a formal definition on the question of the Preternatural Gifts of the Holy Virgin, the Dominicans holding that the Immaculate Conception implied not only indwelling grace, but *also* that the Blessed Mother had had the preternatural powers which were Eve's before the Fall; some theologians of other Orders, while admitting this to be pious conjecture, denied that it was necessarily the case, and contended that a "creature" might be "originally innocent" but not endowed with preternatural gifts. The Dominicans bowed to this, but contended that the belief had always been implicit in other dogma—such as the Assumption (preternatural immortality) and the Preservation from Actual Sin (implying preternatural integrity) and still other examples. While attempting to settle this dispute, New Rome had seemingly left the case for the canonization of Leibowitz to gather dust on the shelf.

Contenting himself with a small shrine of the Beatus and a casual trickle of pilgrims, Brother Francis drowsed. When he awoke, the fire was reduced to glowing embers. Something seemed amiss. Was he quite alone? He blinked around at the encompassing darkness.

From beyond the bed of reddish coals, the dark wolf blinked back.

The novice yelped and dived for cover.

The yelp, he decided as he lay trembling within his den of stones and brush, had been only an involuntary breach of the rule of silence. He lay hugging the metal box and praying that the days of Lent might pass swiftly, while padded feet scratched about his enclosure.

3 "... and then, Father, I almost took the bread and cheese."

"But you didn't take it?"

"No."

"Then there was no sin by deed."

"But I wanted it so badly, I could taste it."

"Willfully? Did you deliberately enjoy the fantasy?"

"No."

"You tried to get rid of it."

"Yes."

"So there was not culpable gluttony of thought either. Why are you confessing this?"

"Because then I lost my temper and splashed him with holy water."

"You what? *Why?*"

Father Cheroki, wearing his stole, stared at the penitent who knelt in profile before him in the scorching sunlight on the open desert; the priest kept wondering how it was possible for such a youth (not particularly intelligent insofar as he could determine) to manage to find occasions or near-occasions of sin while completely isolated on barren desert, far from any distraction or apparent source of temptation. There should be very little trouble a boy could get into out here, armed as he was with only a rosary, a flint, a penknife, and a prayerbook. So it seemed to Father Cheroki. But this confession was taking up quite a lot of time; he wished the boy would get on with it. His arthritis was bothering him again, but because of the presence of the Holy Sacrament on the portable table which he took with him on his rounds, the priest preferred to stand, or to stay on his knees along with the penitent. He had lighted a candle before the small golden case which contained the Hosts, but the flame was invisible in the sun-glare, and the breeze might even have blown it out.

"But exorcism is permissible these days, without any specific higher authorization. What are you confessing—being angry?"

"That too."

27

"At whom did you become angry? At the old man—or at yourself for almost taking the food?"

"I—I'm not sure."

"Well, make up your mind," Father Cheroki said impatiently. "Either accuse yourself, or else not."

"I accuse myself."

"Of what?" Cheroki sighed.

"Of abusing a sacramental in a fit of temper."

" 'Abusing'? You had no rational reason to suspect diabolic influence? You just became angry and squirted him with it? Like throwing the ink in his eye?"

The novice squirmed and hesitated, sensing the priest's sarcasm. Confession was always difficult for Brother Francis. He could never find the right words for his misdeeds, and in trying to remember his own motives, he became hopelessly confused. Nor was the priest helping matters by taking the "either-you-did-or-else-you-didn't" stand—even though, obviously, either Francis had or else he *hadn't*.

"I think I lost my senses for a moment," he said finally.

Cheroki opened his mouth, apparently meaning to pursue the matter, then thought better of it. "I see. What next, then?"

"Gluttonous thoughts," Francis said after a moment.

The priest sighed. "I thought we were through with that. Or is this another time?"

"Yesterday. There was this lizard, Father. It had blue and yellow stripes, and such magnificent hams—thick as your thumb and plump, and I kept thinking how it would taste like chicken, roasted all brown and crisp outside, and—"

"All right," the priest interrupted. Only a hint of revulsion crossed his aged face. After all, the boy was spending a lot of time in the sun. "You took pleasure in these thoughts? You didn't try to get rid of the temptation?"

Francis reddened. "I—I tried to catch it. It got away."

"So, not merely thought—deed as well. Just that one time?"

"Well—yes, just that."

"All right, in thought and deed, willfully meaning to eat meat during Lent. Please be as specific as you can after this. I thought you had examined your conscience properly. Is there anything else?"

"Quite a lot."

The priest winced. He had several hermitages to visit; it was a long hot ride, and his knees were hurting. "Please get on with it as quickly as you can," he sighed.

"Impurity, once."

"Thought, word, or deed?"

"Well, there was this succubus, and she—"

"Succubus? Oh—nocturnal. You were asleep?"

"Yes, but—"

"Then why confess it?"

"Because afterwards."

"Afterwards what? When you woke up?"

"Yes. I kept thinking about her. Kept imagining it all over again."

"All right, concupiscent thought, deliberately entertained. You're sorry? Now, what next?"

All this was the usual sort of thing that one kept hearing time after endless time from postulant after postulant, novice after novice, and it seemed to Father Cheroki that the least Brother Francis could do would be to bark out his self-accusations *one, two, three,* in a neat orderly manner, without all this prodding and prompting. Francis seemed to find difficulty in formulating whatever he was about to say; the priest waited.

"I think my vocation has come to me, Father, but—" Francis moistened his cracked lips and stared at a bug on a rock.

"Oh, has it?" Cheroki's voice was toneless.

"Yes, I think—but would it be a sin, Father, if when I first got it, I thought rather scornfully of the handwriting? I mean?"

Cheroki blinked. Handwriting? Vocation? What kind of a question was— He studied the novice's serious expression for a few seconds, then frowned.

"Have you and Brother Alfred been passing notes to each other?" he asked ominously.

"Oh, no, Father!"

"Then whose handwriting are you talking about?"

"The Blessed Leibowitz."

Cheroki paused to think. Did there, or did there not, exist in the abbey's collection of ancient documents, any manuscript penned personally by the founder of the Order?—an original copy? After a moment's reflection, he decided in the affirmative; yes, there were a few scraps of it left, carefully kept under lock and key.

"Are you talking about something that happened back at the abbey? Before you came out here?"

"No, Father. It happened right over there—" He nodded

toward the left. "Three mounds over, near the tall cactus."

"Involving your vocation, you say?"

"Y-yes, but—"

"Of *course*," Cheroki said sharply, "you could NOT POS-SIBLY be trying to say that—you have received—from the Blessed Leibowitz, dead now, lo, the last six hundred years—a handwritten invitation to profess your solemn vows? And you, uh, deplored his handwriting?—Forgive me, but that's the impression I was getting."

"Well, it's *some*thing like that, Father."

Cheroki sputtered. Becoming alarmed, Brother Francis produced a scrap of paper from his sleeve and handed it to the priest. It was brittle with age and stained. The ink was faded.

"*Pound pastrami,*" Father Cheroki pronounced, slurring over some of the unfamiliar words, "*can kraut, six bagels—bring home for Emma.*" He stared fixedly at Brother Francis for several seconds. "This was written by whom?"

Francis told him.

Cheroki thought it over. "It's not possible for you to make a good confession while you're in *this* condition. And it wouldn't be proper for me to absolve you when you're not in your right mind." Seeing Francis wince, the priest touched him reassuringly on the shoulder. "Don't worry, son, we'll talk it over after you're better. I'll hear your confession then. For the present—" He glanced nervously at the vessel containing the Eucharist. "I want you to gather up your things and return to the abbey at once."

"But, Father, I—"

"I command you," the priest said tonelessly, "to return to the abbey at once."

"Y-yes, Father."

"Now, I'm *not* going to absolve you, but you might make a good act of contrition and offer two decades of the rosary as penance anyhow. Would you like my blessing?"

The novice nodded, fighting tears. The priest blessed him, arose, genuflected before the Sacrament, recovered the golden vessel, and reattached it to the chain around his neck. Having pocketed the candle, collapsed the table, and strapped it in place behind the saddle, he gave Francis a last solemn nod, then mounted and rode away on his mare to complete his circuit of the Lenten hermitages. Francis sat in the hot sand and wept.

It would have been simple if he could have taken the priest

to the crypt to show him the ancient room, if he could have displayed the box and all its contents, and the mark the pilgrim had made on the rock. But the priest was carrying the Eucharist, and could not have been induced to climb down into a rock-filled basement on his hands and knees, or to paw through the contents of the old box and enter into archaeological discussions; Francis had known better than to ask. Cheroki's visit was necessarily solemn, as long as the locket he was wearing contained a single Host; although, after it was empty, he might be amenable to some informal listening. The novice could not blame Father Cheroki for leaping to the conclusion that he had gone out of his mind. He *was* a little groggy from the sun, and he had stammered quite a bit. More than one novice had turned up with addled wits after a vocational vigil.

There was nothing to do but obey the command to return.

He walked to the shelter and glanced into it once again, to reassure himself that it was really there; then he went to get the box. By the time he had it repacked and was ready to leave, the dust plume had appeared in the southeast, heralding the arrival of the supply carrier with water and corn from the abbey. Brother Francis decided to wait for his supplies before starting the long trek home.

Three donkeys and one monk ambled into view at the head of the dust streamer. The lead donkey plodded under the weight of Brother Fingo. In spite of the hood, Francis recognized the cook's helper from his hunched shoulders and from the long hairy shins that dangled on either side of the donkey so that Brother Fingo's sandals nearly dragged the ground. The animals that followed came loaded with small bags of corn and skins of water.

"*Sooooee* pig-pig-pig! *Sooee* pig!" Fingo called, cupping his hands to his mouth and broadcasting the hog-call across the ruins as if he had not seen Francis waiting for him beside the trail. "*Pig pig pig!*—Oh, *there* you are, Francisco! I mistook you for a bone pile. Well, we'll have to fatten you up for the wolves. There you are, help yourself to the Sunday slops. How goes the hermit trade? Think you'll make it a career? Just one waterskin, mind you, and one sack of corn. And watch Malicia's hind feet; she's in rut and feels frolicky—kicked Alfred back there, *crunch!* right in the kneecap. Careful with it!" Brother Fingo brushed back his hood and chortled while the novice and Malicia fenced for position. Fingo was undoubtedly the ugliest man alive, and when he laughed, the vast display of pink gums and huge teeth of assorted colors added little to his charm; he was a sport, but the sport could scarcely be called monstrous; it was a rather common hereditary pattern in the Minnesota country from whence he came; it produced baldness and a very uneven distribution of melanin, so that the gangling monk's hide was a patchwork of beef-liver and chocolate splashes on an albino background. However, his perpetual good humor so compensated for his appearance that one ceased to notice it after a few minutes; and after long acquaintance, Brother Fingo's markings seemed as normal as those of a painted pony. What might have seemed hideous if he were a sulking fellow, managed almost to become as decorative as clown's make-up when accompanied by exuberant good cheer. Fingo's assignment to the kitchen was punitive and probably temporary. He was a woodcarver by trade, and normally worked in the carpenter's shop. But some incident of self-assertion, in connection with a figure of the Blessed Leibowitz which he had been permitted to carve, had caused the abbot to order him transferred to the kitchen until he showed some signs of practicing humility. Meanwhile, the figure of the Beatus waited in the carpentry shop, half-carved.

Fingo's grin began to fade as he studied Francis' countenance while the novice unloaded his grain and water from the frisky she-ass. "You look like a sick sheep, boy," he said to the penitent. "What's the trouble? Is Father Cheroki in one of his slow rages again?"

Brother Francis shook his head. "Not that I could tell."

"Then what's wrong? Are you really sick?"

"He ordered me back to the abbey."

"Wha-a-at?" Fingo swung a hairy shin over the jackass and dropped a few inches to the ground. He towered over Brother Francis, clapped a meaty hand on his shoulder, and peered down into his face. "What is it, the jaundice?"

"No. He thinks I'm—" Francis tapped his temple and shrugged.

Fingo laughed. "Well, that's true, but we *all* knew that. Why is he sending you back?"

Francis glanced down at the box near his feet. "I found some things that belonged to the Blessed Leibowitz. I started to tell him, but he didn't believe me. He wouldn't let me explain. He—"

"You found *what?*" Fingo smiled his disbelief, then

dropped to his knees and opened the box while the novice watched nervously. The monk stirred the whiskered cylinders in the trays with one finger and whistled softly. "Hill-pagan charms, aren't they? This is old, Francisco, this is really *old*." He glanced at the note in the lid. "What's this gibberish?" he asked, squinting up at the unhappy novice.

"Pre-Deluge English."

"I never studied it, except what we sing in choir."

"It was written by the Beatus himself."

"*This?*" Brother Fingo stared from the note to Brother Francis and back to the note. He shook his head suddenly, clamped the lid back on the box, and stood up. His grin had become artificial. "Maybe Father's right. You *better* hike back and have Brother Pharmacist brew you up one of his toad-stool specials. That's the fever, Brother."

Francis shrugged. "Perhaps."

"Where did you find this stuff?"

The novice pointed. "Over that way a few mounds. I moved some rocks. There was a cave-in, and I found a basement. Go see for yourself."

Fingo shook his head. "I've got a long ride ahead."

Francis picked up the box and started toward the abbey while Fingo returned to his donkey, but after a few paces the novice stopped and called back.

"Brother Spots—could you take two minutes?"

"Maybe," answered Fingo. "What for?"

"Just walk over there and look in the hole."

"Why?"

"So you can tell Father Cheroki if it's really there."

Fingo paused with one leg half across his donkey's back. "Ha!" He withdrew the leg. "All right. If it's not there, I'll tell *you*."

Francis watched for a moment while the gangling Fingo strode out of sight among the mounds; then he turned to shuffle down the long dusty trail toward the abbey, intermittently munching corn and sipping from the waterskin. Occasionally he glanced back. Fingo was gone much longer than two minutes. Brother Francis had ceased to watch for his reappearance by the time he heard a distant bellow from the ruins far behind him. He turned. He could make out the distant figure of the woodcarver standing atop one of the mounds. Fingo was waving his arms and vigorously nodding his head in affirmation. Francis waved back, then hiked wearily on his way.

Two weeks of near-starvation had exacted their tribute. After two or three miles he began to stagger. When still nearly a mile from the abbey, he fainted beside the road. It was late afternoon before Cheroki, riding back from his rounds, noticed him lying there, hastily dismounted, and bathed the youth's face until he gradually brought him around. Cheroki had encountered the supply donkeys on his way back and had paused to hear Fingo's account, confirming Brother Francis' find. Although he was not prepared to believe that Francis had discovered anything of real importance, the priest regretted his earlier impatience with the boy. Having noticed the box lying nearby with its contents half-spilled in the road, and having glanced briefly at the note in the lid, while Francis sat groggy and confused at the edge of the trail, Cheroki found himself willing to regard the boy's earlier babblings as the result of romantic imagination rather than of madness or delirium. He had neither visited the crypt nor closely examined the contents of the box, but it was obvious, at least, that the boy had been misinterpreting real events rather than confessing hallucinations.

"You can finish your confession as soon as we get back," he told the novice softly, helping him to climb up behind the saddle on the mare. "I think I can absolve you if you don't insist on personal messages from the saints. Eh?"

Brother Francis was too weak at the moment to insist on anything.

4   "You did the right thing," the abbot grunted at last. He had been slowly pacing the floor of his study for perhaps five minutes, his wide peasant face wearing a thick-furrowed muscular glower, while Father Cheroki sat nervously on the edge of his chair. Neither priest had spoken since Cheroki had entered the room in answer to his ruler's summons; Cheroki jumped slightly when Abbot Arkos finally grunted out the words.

"You did the right thing," the abbot said again, stopping in the center of the room and squinting at his prior, who finally began to relax. It was nearly midnight and Arkos had been preparing to retire for an hour or two of sleep before Matins and Lauds. Still damp and disheveled from a recent plunge in the bathing barrel, he reminded Cheroki of a were-bear only incompletely changed into a man. He was wearing a coyote-skin robe, and the only hint of his office was the pectoral cross that nestled in the black fur on his chest and flashed with candlelight whenever he turned toward the desk. His wet hair hung over his forehead, and with his short jutting beard and his coyote skins, he looked, at the moment, less like a priest than a military chieftain, full of restrained battle-anger from a recent assault. Father Cheroki, who came of baronial stock from Denver, tended to react formally to men's official capacities, tended to speak courteously to the badge of office while not allowing himself to see the man who wore it, in this respect following the Court customs of many ages. Thus Father Cheroki had always maintained a formally cordial relationship with the ring and the pectoral cross, with the office, of his abbot, but permitted himself to see as little as possible of Arkos the man. This was rather difficult under present circumstances, the Reverend Father Abbot being fresh out of his bath, and padding around his study in his bare feet. He had apparently just trimmed a corn and cut too deep; one great toe was bloody. Cheroki tried to avoid noticing it, but felt very ill at ease.

"You *do* know what I'm talking about?" Arkos growled impatiently.

Cheroki hesitated. "Would you mind, Father Abbot, being specific—in case it's connected with something I might have heard about only in confession?"

"Hah? Oh! Well, I'm bedeviled! You did hear his confession, I clean forgot. Well, get him to tell you again, so you can talk—though Heaven knows, it's all over the abbey anyhow. No, don't go see him now. *I'll* tell *you*, and don't answer on whatever's sealed. You've seen that stuff?" Abbot Arkos waved toward his desk where the contents of Brother Francis' box had been emptied for examination.

Cheroki nodded slowly. "He dropped it beside the road when he fell. I helped gather it up, but I didn't look at it carefully."

"Well, you know what he claims it is?"

Father Cheroki glanced aside. He seemed not to hear the question.

"All right, all right," the abbot growled, "never mind

what he *claims* it is. Just go look it over carefully yourself and decide what *you* think it is."

Cheroki went to bend over the desk and scrutinize the papers carefully, one at a time, while the abbot paced and kept talking, seemingly to the priest but half to himself.

"It's impossible! You did the right thing to send him back before he uncovered more. But of course that's not the *worst* part. The worst part is the old man he babbles about. It's getting too thick. I don't know anything that could damage the case worse than a whole flood of improbable 'miracles.' A few real incidents, certainly! It has to be established that the intercession of the Beatus has brought about the miraculous—before canonization can occur. But there can be too much! Look at the Blessed Chang—beatified two centuries ago, but never canonized—so far. And *why?* His Order got too eager, that's why. Every time somebody got over a cough, it was a miraculous cure by the Beatus. Visions in the basement, evocations in the belfry; it sounded more like a collection of ghost stories than a list of miraculous incidents. Maybe two or three incidents were really valid, but when there's that much chaff—well?"

Father Cheroki looked up. His knuckles had whitened on the edge of the desk and his face seemed strained. He seemed not to have been listening. "I beg your pardon, Father Abbot?"

"Well, the same thing could happen here, that's what," said the abbot, and resumed his slow padding to and fro. "Last year there was Brother Noyon and his miraculous hangman's noose. Ha! And the year before that, Brother Smirnov gets mysteriously cured of the gout—*how?*—by touching a probable relic of our Blessed Leibowitz, the young louts say. And now this Francis, he meets a pilgrim—wearing *what?*—wearing for a kilt the *very* burlap cloth they hooded Blessed Leibowitz with before they hanged him. And with what for a belt? A rope. What rope? Ahh, the very same—" He paused, looking at Cheroki. "I can tell by your blank look that you haven't heard this yet? No? All right, so you can't say. No, no, Francis didn't say *that*. All he said was—" Abbot Arkos tried to inject a slightly falsetto quality into his normally gruff voice. "All Brother Francis said was—'I met a little old man, and I thought he was a pilgrim heading for the abbey because he was going that way, and he was wearing an old burlap sack tied around with a piece of rope. And he made a mark on the rock, and the mark looked like *this*.'"

Arkos produced a scrap of parchment from the pocket of his fur robe and held it up toward Cheroki's face in the candle-glow. Still trying, with only slight success, to imitate Brother Francis: "'And I couldn't figure out what it meant. Do *you* know?'"

Cheroki stared at the symbols צֿל and shook his head.

"I wasn't asking *you*," Arkos gruffed in his normal voice. "That's what Francis said. I didn't know either."

"You do now?"

"I do now. Somebody looked it up. *That* is a *lamedh*, and that is a *sadhe*. Hebrew letters."

"*Sadhe lamedh?*"

"No. Right to left. *Lamedh sadhe*. An ell, and a tee-ess sound. If it had vowel marks, it might be 'loots,' 'lots,' 'lets,' 'lets,' 'latz,' 'litz'—anything like that. If it had some letters between those two, it might sound like *Lllll*—guess-who."

"Leibo— Ho, *no!*"

"Ho, yes! Brother *Francis* didn't think of it. Somebody else thought of it. Brother *Francis* didn't think of the burlap hood and the hangman's rope; one of his chums did. So what happens? By tonight, the whole novitiate is buzzing with the sweet little story that Francis met the Beatus himself out there, and the Beatus escorted our boy over to where *that* stuff was and told him he'd find his vocation."

A perplexed frown crossed Cheroki's face. "Did Brother Francis say that?"

"*NOO!*" Arkos roared. "Haven't you been listening? Francis said no such things. I wish he had, by gum; then I'd *HAVE* the rascal! But *he* tells it sweet-and-simple, rather stupidly, in fact, and lets the others read in the meanings. I haven't talked to him myself. I sent the Rector of the Memorabilia to get his story."

"I think I'd better talk to Brother Francis," Cheroki murmured.

"*Do!* When you first came in, I was still wondering whether to roast you alive or not. For sending him in, I mean. If you had let him stay out there on the desert, we wouldn't have this fantastic twaddle going around. But, on the other hand, if he'd stayed out there, there's no telling what *else* he might have dug out of that cellar. I think you did the right thing, to send him in."

Cheroki, who had made the decision on no such basis, found silence to be the appropriate policy.

"See him," growled the abbot. "Then send him to me."

It was about nine on a bright Monday morning when Brother Francis rapped timidly at the door of the abbot's study. A good night's sleep on the hard straw pallet in his old familiar cell, plus a small bite of unfamiliar breakfast, had not perhaps done any wonders for starved tissue or entirely cleared the sun-daze from his brain, but these relative luxuries had at least restored him to sufficient clarity of mind to perceive that he had cause to be afraid. He was, in fact, terrified, so that his first tap at the abbot's door went unheard. Not even Francis could hear it. After several minutes, he mustered the courage to knock again.

"*Benedicamus Domino.*"

"*Deo? gratias?*" asked Francis.

"Come in, my boy, come *in!*" called an affable voice, which, after some seconds of puzzling, he recognized with amazement to have been that of his sovereign abbot.

"You twist the little *knob,* my son," said the same friendly voice after Brother Francis had stood frozen on the spot for some seconds, with his knuckles still in position for knocking.

"Y-y-yes—" Francis scarcely touched the knob, but it seemed that the accursed door opened anyway; he had hoped that it would be tightly stuck.

"The Lord Abbot s-s-sent for—*me?*" squawked the novice.

Abbot Arkos pursed his lips and nodded slowly. "Mmmm-yes, the Lord Abbot sent for—*you. Do* come in and shut the door."

Brother Francis got the door closed and stood shivering in the center of the room. The abbot was toying with some of the wire-whiskered things from the old toolbox.

"Or perhaps it would be more fitting," said Abbot Arkos, "if the Reverend Father Abbot were sent for *by you.* Now that you have been so favored by Providence and have become so famous, eh?" He smiled soothingly.

"Heh heh?" Brother Francis laughed inquiringly. "Oh n-n-no, m'Lord."

"You do not dispute that you have won overnight fame? That Providence elected you to discover *THIS—*" he gestured sweepingly at the relics on the desk "—this *JUNK* box, as its previous owner no doubt rightly called it?"

The novice stammered helplessly, and somehow managed to wind up wearing a grin.

"You are seventeen and plainly an idiot, are you not?"

"That is undoubtedly true, m'Lord Abbot."

"What excuse do you propose for believing yourself called to Religion?"

"No excuse, Magister meus."

"*Ah?* So? Then you feel that you have no vocation to the Order?"

"Oh, I *do!*" the novice gasped.

"But you propose no excuse?"

"None."

"You little cretin, I am asking your reason. Since you state none, I take it you are prepared to deny that you met anyone in the desert the other day, that you stumbled on this—this *JUNK* box with no help, and that what I have been hearing from others is only—feverish raving?"

"Oh, no, Dom Arkos!"

"Oh, no, what?"

"I cannot deny what I saw with my own eyes, Reverend Father."

"So, you *did* meet an angel—or was it a saint?—or perhaps not yet a saint?—and he showed you where to look?"

"I never said he was—"

"And *this* is your excuse for believing yourself to have a true vocation, is it not? That this, this—shall we call him a 'creature'?—spoke to you of finding a voice, and marked a rock with his initials, and told you it was what you were looking for, and when you looked under it—there *THIS* was. Eh?"

"Yes, Dom Arkos."

"What is your opinion of your own execrable vanity?"

"My execrable vanity is unpardonable, m'Lord'n'Teacher."

"To imagine yourself important enough to be *unpardonable* is an even vaster vanity," roared the sovereign of the abbey.

"M'Lord, I am indeed a worm."

"Very well, you need only deny the part about the pilgrim. No one *else* saw such a person, you know. I understand he was supposed to have been headed in this direction? That he even said he might stop here? That he inquired about the abbey? Yes? And where would he have disappeared to, if he ever existed? No such person came past here. The brother on duty at that time in the watchtower didn't see him. Eh? Are you now ready to admit that you imagined him?"

"If there are not really two marks on that rock where he—then maybe I might—"

The abbot closed his eyes and sighed wearily. "The marks are there—faintly," he admitted. "You might have made them yourself."

"No, m'Lord."

"Will you admit that you imagined the old creature?"

"No, m'Lord."

"Very well, do you know what is going to happen to you now?"

"Yes, Reverend Father."

"Then prepare to take it."

Trembling, the novice gathered up his habit about his waist and bent over the desk. The abbot withdrew a stout hickory ruler from the drawer, tested it on his palm, then gave Francis a smart whack with it across the buttocks.

"*Deo gratias!*" the novice dutifully responded, gasping slightly.

"Care to change your mind, my boy?"

"Reverend Father, I can't deny—"

WHACK!

"*Deo gratias!*"

WHACK!

"*Deo gratias!*"

Ten times was this simple but painful litany repeated, with Brother Francis yelping his thanks to Heaven for each scorching lesson in the virtue of humility, as he was expected to do. The abbot paused after the tenth whack. Brother Francis was on tip-toe and bouncing slightly. Tears squeezed from the corners of clenched eyelids.

"My dear Brother Francis," said the Abbot Arkos, "are you *quite* sure you saw the old man?"

"certain," he squeaked, steeling himself for more.

Abbot Arkos glanced clinically at the youth, then walked round his desk and sat down with a grunt. He glowered for a time at the slip of parchment bearing the letters צל.

"Who do you suppose he could have been?" Abbot Arkos muttered absently.

Brother Francis opened his eyes, causing a brief shed of water.

"Oh, you've convinced me, boy, worse luck for *you*."

Francis said nothing, but prayed silently that the need to

convince his sovereign of his veracity would not often arise. In response to an irritable gesture from the abbot, he lowered his tunic.

"You may sit down," said the abbot, becoming casual if not genial.

Francis moved toward the indicated chair, lowered himself halfway into it, but then winced and stood up again. "If it's all the same to the Reverend Father Abbot—"

"All right, then *stand*. I won't keep you long anyhow. You're to go out and finish your vigil." He paused, noticing the novice's face brighten a little. "Oh no you don't!" he snapped. "You're not going back to the same place. You'll trade hermitages with Brother Alfred, and not go near those ruins again. Furthermore, I command you not to discuss the matter with anyone, except your confessor or with me, although, Heaven knows, the damage is already done. Do you know what you've started?"

Brother Francis shook his head. "Yesterday being Sunday, Reverend Father, we weren't required to keep silent, and at recreation I just answered the fellows' questions. I thought—"

"Well, your *fellows* have cooked up a very cute explanation, dear son. Did you know that it was the Blessed Leibowitz himself you met out there?"

Francis looked blank for a moment, then shook his head again. "Oh, no, m'Lord Abbot. I'm sure it couldn't have been. The Blessed Martyr wouldn't do such a thing."

"Wouldn't do such-a-*what* thing?"

"Wouldn't chase after somebody and try to hit him with a stick that had a nail in one end."

The abbot wiped his mouth to hide an involuntary smile. He managed to appear thoughtful after a moment. "Oh, I don't know about that, now. It was *you* he was chasing, wasn't it? Yes, I thought so. You told your fellow novices about that part too? Yes, eh? Well, you see, *they* didn't think that would exclude the possibility of his being the Beatus. Now I doubt if there are very *many* people that the Beatus would chase with a stick, but—" He broke off, unable to suppress laughter at the expression on the novice's face. "All right, son—but who do you suppose he could have been?"

"I thought perhaps he was a pilgrim on his way to visit our shrine, Reverend Father."

"It isn't a shrine yet, and you're not to call it that. And anyway he wasn't, or at least, he didn't. And he didn't pass our gates, unless the watch was asleep. And the novice on watch denies being asleep, although he admitted feeling drowsy that day. So what do *you* suggest?"

"If the Reverend Father Abbot will forgive me, I've been on watch a few times myself."

"And?"

"Well, on a bright day when there's nothing moving but the buzzards, after a few hours you just start looking up at the buzzards."

"Oh you *do*, do you? When you're supposed to be watching the trail!"

"And if you stare at the sky too long, you just kind of blank-out—not really asleep, but, sort of, preoccupied."

"So that's what you do when you're on watch, do you?" the abbot growled.

"Not necessarily. I mean, no, Reverend Father, I wouldn't know it if I had, I don't think. Brother Je—I mean—a brother I relieved once was like that. He didn't even know it was time for the watch to change. He was just sitting there in the tower and staring up at the sky with his mouth open. In a daze."

"Yes, and the first time you go stupefied that way, along'll come a heathen war-party out of the Utah country, kill a few gardeners, tear up the irrigating system, spoil our crops, and dump stones in the well before we can start defending ourselves. Why are you looking so—oh, I forgot—you were Utah-born before you ran away, weren't you? But never mind, you could, just possibly, be right about the watch—how he could have missed seeing the old man, that is. You're sure he was just an *ordinary* old man—not anything more? Not an angel? Not a beatus?"

The novice's gaze drifted ceilingward in thought, then fell quickly to his ruler's face. "Do angels or saints cast shadows?"

"Yes—I mean no. I mean—how should I know! He did cast a shadow, didn't he?"

"Well—it was such a small shadow you could hardly see it."

"*What?*"

"Because it was almost noon."

"Imbecile! *I'm* not asking *you* to tell me *what* he was. I know very well what he was, if you saw him at all." Abbot Arkos thumped repeatedly on the table for emphasis. "I want to know if you—*You!*—are *sure beyond a doubt* that he was just an ordinary old man!"

This line of questioning was puzzling to Brother Francis. In his own mind, there was no neat straight line separating the Natural from the Supernatural order, but rather, an intermediate twilight zone. There were things that were *clearly* natural, and there were Things that were *clearly* supernatural, but between these extremes was a region of confusion (his own)—the preternatural—where things made of mere earth, air, fire, or water tended to behave disturbingly like *Things*. For Brother Francis, this region included whatever he could see but not understand. And Brother Francis was never "sure beyond a doubt," as the abbot was asking him to be, that he properly understood much of anything. Thus, by raising the question at all, Abbot Arkos was unwittingly throwing the novice's pilgrim into the twilight region, into the same perspective as the old man's first appearance as a legless black strip that wriggled in the midst of a lake of heat illusion on the trail, into the same perspective as he had occupied momentarily when the novice's world had contracted until it contained nothing but a hand offering him a particle of food. If some creature more-than-human chose to disguise itself as human, how was *he* to penetrate its disguise, or suspect there was one? If such a creature did not wish to be suspected, would it not remember to cast a shadow, leave footprints, eat bread and cheese? Might it not chew spice-leaf, spit at a lizard, and remember to imitate the reaction of a mortal who forgot to put on his sandals before stepping on hot ground? Francis was not prepared to estimate the intelligence or ingenuity of hellish or heavenly beings, or to guess the extent of their histrionic abilities, although he assumed such creatures to be either hellishly or divinely clever. The abbot, by raising the question at all, had formulated the nature of Brother Francis' answer, which was: to entertain the question itself, although he had not previously done so.

"Well, boy?"

"M'Lord Abbot, you don't suppose he *might* have been—"

"I'm asking you *not* to suppose. I'm asking you to be flatly certain. *Was* he, or was he *not*, an ordinary flesh-and-blood person?"

The question was frightening. That the question was dignified by coming from the lips of so exalted a person as his sovereign abbot made it even more frightening, though he could plainly see that his ruler stated it merely because he wanted a *particular* answer. He wanted it rather badly. If he wanted it that badly, the question must be important. If the question was important enough for an abbot, then it was *far* too important for Brother Francis who *dared not* be wrong.

"I—I think he was flesh and blood, Reverend Father, but not exactly 'ordinary.' In some ways, he was rather *extra*ordinary."

"*What* ways?" Abbot Arkos asked sharply.

"Like—how straight he could spit. And he could *read*, I think."

The abbot closed his eyes and rubbed his temples in apparent exasperation. How easy it would have been flatly to have told the boy that his pilgrim was only an old tramp of some kind, and then to have commanded him not to think otherwise. But by allowing the boy to see that a question was possible, he had rendered such a command ineffective before he uttered it. Insofar as thought could be governed at all, it could only be commanded to follow what reason affirmed anyhow; command it otherwise, and it would not obey. Like any wise ruler, Abbot Arkos did not issue orders vainly, when to disobey was possible and to enforce was not possible. It was better to look the other way than to command ineffectually. He had asked a question that he himself could not answer by reason, having never seen the old man, and had thereby lost the right to make the answer mandatory.

"Get out," he said at last, without opening his eyes.

5   Somewhat mystified by the commotion at the abbey, Brother Francis returned to the desert that same day to complete his Lenten vigil in rather wretched solitude. He had expected some excitement about the relics to arise, but the excessive interest which everyone had taken in the old wanderer surprised him. Francis had spoken of the old man, simply because of the part he had played, either by accident or by design of Providence, in the monk's stumbling upon the crypt and its relics. The pilgrim was only a minor ingredient, as far as Francis was concerned, in a mandala design at whose center rested a relic of a saint. But his fellow novices had seemed more interested in the pilgrim than in the relic, and even the abbot had summoned him, not to ask about the box, but to ask about the old man. They had asked him a hundred questions about the pilgrim to which he could reply only: "I didn't notice," or "I wasn't looking right then," or "If he said, I don't remember," and some of the questions were a little weird. And so he questioned himself: *Should I have noticed? Was I stupid not to watch what he did? Wasn't I paying enough attention to what he said? Did I miss something important because I was dazed?*

He brooded on it in the darkness while the wolves prowled about his new encampment and filled the nights with their howling. He caught himself brooding on it during times of the day that were assigned as proper for the prayers and spiritual exercises of the vocational vigil, and he confessed as much to Prior Cheroki the next time the priest rode his Sunday circuit. "You shouldn't let the romantic imaginations of the *others* bother you; you have enough trouble with your *own*," the priest told him, after chiding him for neglecting the exercises and prayers. "They don't think up questions like that on the basis of what *might be true;* they concoct the questions on the basis of what *might be sensational* if it just happened to be true. It's ridiculous! I can tell you that the Reverend Father Abbot has ordered the entire novitiate to drop the subject." After a moment, he unfortunately added: "There really *wasn't* anything about the old man to suggest the supernatural—*was* there?" with only the faintest trace of hopeful wonder in his tone.

Brother Francis wondered too. If there had been a suggestion of the supernatural, he had not noticed it. But then too, judging by the number of questions he had been unable to answer, he had not noticed very much. The profusion of the questions had made him feel that his failure to observe had been, somehow, culpable. He had become grateful to the pilgrim upon discovering the shelter. But he had not interpreted events entirely in terms of his own interests, in accordance with his own longing for some shred of evidence that the dedication of his lifetime to the labors of the monastery was born not so much of his own will as it was of grace, empowering the will, but not compelling it, rightly to choose. Perhaps the events had a vaster significance that he had missed, during the totality of his self-absorption.

What is your opinion of your own execrable vanity?

My execrable vanity is like that of the fabled cat who studied ornithology, m'Lord.

His desire to profess his final and perpetual vows—was it not akin to the motive of the cat who became an ornithologist?—so that he might glorify his own ornithophagy, esoterically devouring *Penthestes atricapillus* but never eating chickadees. For, as the cat was called by Nature to be an ornithophage, so was Francis called by his own nature hungrily to devour such knowledge as could be taught in those days, and, because there were no schools but the monastic schools, he had donned the habit first of a postulant, later of a novice. But to suspect that God as well as Nature had beckoned him to become a professed monk of the Order?

What else could he do? There was no returning to his homeland, the Utah. As a small child, he had been sold to a shaman, who would have trained him as his servant and acolyte. Having run away, he could not return, except to meet grisly tribal "justice." He had stolen a shaman's property (Francis' own person), and while thievery was an honorable profession among the Utah, getting caught was a capital crime when the thief's victim was the tribal warlock. Nor would he have cared to lapse back into the relatively primitive life of an illiterate shepherd people, after his schooling at the abbey.

But what else? The continent was lightly settled. He thought of the wall-map in the abbey's library, and of the sparse distribution of the crosshatched areas, which were regions—if not of civilization—then of civil order, where some form of lawful sovereignty, transcending the tribal, held sway. The rest of the continent was populated, very thinly, by the people of the forest and the plain, who were, for the most part, not savages, but simple clanfolk loosely organized into small communities here and there, who lived by hunting, gathering, and primitive agriculture, whose birth rate was barely high enough (discounting monster-births and sports) to sustain the population. The principal industries of the continent, excepting a few seacoast regions, were hunting, farming, fighting, and witchcraft—the last being the most promising "industry" for any youth with a choice of careers and having in mind as primary ends, maximum wealth and prestige.

The schooling which Francis had been given at the abbey prepared him for nothing which was of practical value in a dark, ignorant, and workaday world, where literacy was non-

existent and a literate youth, therefore, seemed of no worth
to a community unless he could also farm, fight, hunt or
show some special talent for inter-tribal theft, or for the
divining of water and workable metal. Even in the scattered
domains where a form of civil order existed, the fact of
Francis' literacy would help him not at all, if he must lead a
life apart from the Church. It was true that petty barons
sometimes employed a scribe or two, but such cases were
rare enough to be negligible, and were as often filled by
monks as by monastery-schooled laymen.

The only demand for scribes and secretaries was created
by the Church herself, whose tenuous hierarchic web was
stretched across the continent (and occasionally to far-dis-
tant shores, although the diocesans abroad were virtually
autonomous rulers, subject to the Holy See in theory but
seldom in practice, being cut off from New Rome less by
schism than by oceans not often crossed) and could be held
together only by a communication network. The Church had
become, quite coincidentally and without meaning to be,
the only means whereby news was transmitted from place
to place across the continent. If plague came to the northeast, the southwest would soon hear of it, as a coincidental
effect of tales told and retold by messengers of the Church,
coming and going from New Rome.

If the nomadic infiltration in the far northwest threatened
a Christian diocese, an encyclical letter might soon be read
from pulpits far to the south and east, warning of the threat
and extending the apostolic benediction to "men of any
station, so long as they be skilled at arms, who, having
the means to make the journey, may be piously disposed
to do so, in order to swear fealty to Our beloved son, N.,
lawful ruler of that place, for such a period of time as may
seem necessary for the maintenance of standing armies there
for defense of Christians against the gathering heathen
horde, whose ruthless savagery is known to many and who,
to Our deepest grief, tortured, murdered, and devoured those
priests of God which We Ourselves sent to them with the
Word, that they might enter as lambs into the fold of the
Lamb, of whose flock on Earth We are the Shepherd; for,
while We have never despaired nor ceased to pray that these
nomadic children of the darkness may be led into the Light
and enter Our realms in peace (for it is not to be thought
that peaceful strangers should be repelled from a land so
vast and empty; nay, they should be welcomed who come

peacefully, even should they be strangers to the visible Church and its Divine Founder, so long as they hearken to that Natural Law which is written in the hearts of all men, binding them to Christ in spirit, though they be ignorant of His Name), it is nevertheless meet and fitting and prudent that Christendom, while praying for peace and the conversion of the heathen, should gird itself for defense in the Northwest, where the hordes gather and the incidents of heathen savagery have lately increased, and upon each of you, beloved sons, who can bear arms and shall travel to the Northwest to join forces with those who prepare rightfully to defend their lands, homes, and churches, We extend, and hereby bestow, as a sign of Our special affection, the Apostolic Benediction."

Francis had thought briefly of going to the northwest, if he failed to find a vocation to the Order. But, although he was strong and skillful enough with blade and bow, he was rather short and not very heavy, while—according to rumor —the heathen was nine feet tall. He could not testify as to the truth of the rumor, but saw no reason to think it false.

Besides dying in battle, there was very little that he could think of to do with his lifetime—little that seemed worth the doing—if he could not devote it to the Order.

His certainty of his vocation had not been broken, but only slightly bent, by the scorching administered to him by the abbot, and by the thought of the cat who became an ornithologist when called only by Nature to become an ornithophage. The thought made him unhappy enough to permit him to be overcome by temptation, so that, on Palm Sunday, with only six days of starvation remaining until the end of Lent, Prior Cheroki heard from Francis (or from the shriveled and sun-scorched residuum of Francis, wherein the soul remained somehow encysted) a few brief croaks which constituted what was probably the most succinct confession that Francis ever made or Cheroki ever heard:

"Bless me, Father; I ate a lizard."

Prior Cheroki, having for many years been confessor to fasting penitents, found that custom had, with him, as with a fabled gravedigger, given it all "a property of easiness," so that he replied with perfect equanimity and not even a blink: "Was it an abstinence day, and was it artificially prepared?"

Holy Week would have been less lonely than the earlier

weeks of Lent, had the hermits not been, by then, past caring; for some of the Passiontide liturgy was carried outside the abbey walls to touch the penitents at their vigil sites; twice the Eucharist came forth, and on Maundy Thursday the abbot himself made the rounds, with Cheroki and thirteen monks, to perform the Mandatum at each hermitage. Abbot Arkos' vestments were concealed under a cowl, and the lion almost managed to seem humble kitten as he knelt, and washed and kissed the feet of his fasting subjects with maximum economy of movement and a minimum of flourish and display, while the others chanted the antiphons. *"Mandatum novum do vobis: ut diligatis invicem . . ."* On Good Friday a Procession of the Cross brought out a veiled crucifix, stopping at each hermitage to unveil it gradually before the penitent, lifting the cloth inch by inch for the Adoration, while the monks chanted the Reproaches:

"My people, what have I done to thee? or in what have I grieved thee? Answer . . . I exalted thee with virtuous power; and thou hangest me from the gibbet of a cross. . . ."

And then, Holy Saturday.

The monks carried them in one at a time—famished and raving. Francis was thirty pounds lighter and several degrees weaker than he had been on Ash Wednesday. When they set him on his feet in his own cell, he staggered, and before he reached the bunk, he fell. The brothers hoisted him into it, bathed him, shaved him, and anointed his blistered skin, while Francis babbled deliriously about something in a burlap loincloth, addressing it at times as an angel and again as a saint, frequently invoking the name of Leibowitz and trying to apologize.

His brethren, forbidden by the abbot to speak of the matter, merely exchanged significant glances or nodded mysteriously among themselves.

Reports filtered to the abbot.

"Bring him here," he grunted at a recorder, as soon as he heard that Francis could walk. His tone sent the recorder scurrying.

"Do you deny saying these things?" Arkos growled.

"I don't remember saying them, m'Lord Abbot," said the novice, eying the abbot's ruler. "I may have been raving."

"Assuming that you *were* raving—would you say it again now?"

"About the pilgrim being the Beatus? Oh, no, Magister meus!"

"Then assert the contrary."

"I don't *think* the pilgrim was the *Beatus*."

"Why not just a straightforward: *He was not?*"

"Well, never having seen the Blessed Leibowitz personally, I wouldn't—"

"*Enough!*" the abbot ordered. "*Too* much! That's *all* I want to see of you and hear of you for a long, long time! *Out!* But just one thing—*DON'T* expect to profess your vows with the others this year. You won't be permitted."

For Francis it was like a blow in the stomach with the end of a log.

6   As topic for conversation, the pilgrim remained forbidden subject matter in the abbey; but with respect to the relics and the fallout shelter the prohibition was, of necessity, gradually relaxed—except for their discoverer who remained under orders not to discuss them, and preferably to think of the matter as little as possible. Still, he could not avoid hearing things now and again, and he knew that in one of the abbey's workshops, monks were at work on the documents, not only his own but some others that had been found in the ancient desk, before the abbot ordered that the shelter be closed.

Closed! The news jolted Brother Francis. The shelter scarcely had been touched. Beyond his own adventure, there had been no attempt to penetrate further into the secrets of the shelter except to open the desk which he had tried to open, with no success, before he noticed the box. *Closed!* With no attempt to discover what might lie beyond the inner door marked "Hatch Two" nor to investigate "Sealed Environment." Without even removing the stones or the bones. *Closed!* The investigation abruptly choked off, without apparent cause.

Then there began a rumor.

"*Emily had a gold tooth. Emily had a gold tooth. Emily had a gold tooth.*" It was, in fact, quite true. It was one of those historical trivialities that manage somehow to outlive important facts which someone should have bothered to remember but which went unrecorded until some monastic historian was forced to write: "Neither the contents of the Memorabilia nor any archaeological source yet uncovered disclose the name of the ruler who occupied the White Palace during the middle and late sixties, although Fr. Barcus has claimed, not without supporting evidence, that his name was—"

And yet, it was clearly recorded in the Memorabilia that Emily had worn a gold tooth.

It was not surprising that the Lord Abbot commanded that the crypt be sealed forthwith. Remembering how he had lifted the ancient skull and turned it to face the wall, Brother Francis suddenly feared the wrath of Heaven. Emily Leibowitz had vanished from the face of the Earth at the beginning of the Flame Deluge, and only after many years would her widower admit that she was dead.

It was said that God, in order to test mankind which had become swelled with pride as in the time of Noah, had commanded the wise men of that age, among them the Blessed Leibowitz, to devise great engines of war such as had never before been upon the Earth, weapons of such might that they contained the very fires of Hell, and that God had suffered these magi to place the weapons in the hands of princes, and to say to each prince: "Only because the enemies have such a thing have we devised this for thee, in order that they may know that thou hast it also, and fear to strike. See to it, m'Lord, that thou fearest them as much as they shall now fear thee, that none may unleash this dread thing which we have wrought."

But the princes, putting the words of their wise men to naught, thought each to himself: If I but strike quickly enough, and in secret, I shall destroy those others in their sleep, and there will be none to fight back; the earth shall be mine.

Such was the folly of princes, and there followed the Flame Deluge.

Within weeks—some said days—it was ended, after the first unleashing of the hell-fire. Cities had become puddles of glass, surrounded by vast acreages of broken stone. While nations had vanished from the earth, the lands littered with bodies, both men and cattle, and all manner of beasts, together with the birds of the air and all things that flew, all things that swam in the rivers, crept in the grass, or burrowed in holes; having sickened and perished, they covered the land, and yet where the demons of the Fallout covered the countryside, the bodies for a time would not decay, except in contact with fertile earth. The great clouds of wrath engulfed the forests and the fields, withering trees and causing the crops to die. There were great deserts where once life was, and in those places of the Earth where men still lived, all were sickened by the poisoned air, so that, while some escaped death, none was left untouched; and many died even in those lands where the weapons had not struck, because of the poisoned air.

In all parts of the world men fled from one place to other places, and there was a confusion of tongues. Much wrath was kindled against the princes and the servants of the princes and against the magi who had devised the weapons. Years passed, and yet the Earth was not cleansed. So it was clearly recorded in the Memorabilia.

From the confusion of tongues, the intermingling of the remnants of many nations, from fear, the hate was born. And the hate said: *Let us stone and disembowel and burn the ones who did this thing. Let us make a holocaust of those who wrought this crime, together with their hirelings and their wise men; burning, let them perish, and all their works, their names, and even their memories. Let us destroy them all, and teach our children that the world is new, that they may know nothing of the deeds that went before. Let us make a great simplification, and then the world shall begin again.*

So it was that, after the Deluge, the Fallout, the plagues, the madness, the confusion of tongues, the rage, there began the bloodletting of the Simplification, when remnants of mankind had torn other remnants limb from limb, killing rulers, scientists, leaders, technicians, teachers, and whatever persons the leaders of the maddened mobs said deserved death for having helped to make the Earth what it had become. Nothing had been so hateful in the sight of these mobs as the man of learning, at first because they had served the princes, but then later because they refused to join in the bloodletting and tried to oppose the mobs, calling the crowds "bloodthirsty simpletons."

Joyfully the mobs accepted the name, took up the cry: *Simpletons! Yes, yes! I'm a simpleton! Are you a simpleton? We'll build a town and we'll name it Simple Town, because by then all the smart bastards that caused all this, they'll be dead! Simpletons! Let's go! This ought to show 'em! Anybody here not a simpleton? Get the bastard, if there is!*

To escape the fury of the simpleton packs, such learned people as still survived fled to any sanctuary that offered itself. When Holy Church received them, she vested them in monks' robes and tried to hide them in such monasteries and convents as had survived and could be reoccupied, for the religious were less despised by the mob except when they openly defied it and accepted martydrom. Sometimes such sanctuary was effective, but more often it was not. Monasteries were invaded, records and sacred books were burned, refugees were seized and summarily hanged or burned. The Simplification had ceased to have plan or purpose soon after it began, and became an insane frenzy of mass murder and destruction such as can occur only when the last traces of social order are gone. The madness was transmitted to the children, taught as they were—not merely to forget—but to hate, and surges of mob fury recurred sporadically even through the fourth generation after the Deluge. By then, the fury was directed not against the learned, for there were none, but against the merely literate.

Isaac Edward Leibowitz, after a fruitless search for his wife, had fled to the Cistercians where he remained in hiding during the early post-Deluge years. After six years, he had gone once more to search for Emily or her grave, in the far southwest. There he had become convinced at last of her death, for death was unconditionally triumphant in that place. There in the desert he quietly made a vow. Then he went back to the Cistercians, took their habit, and after more years became a priest. He gathered a few companions about him and made some quiet proposals. After a few more years, the proposals filtered to "Rome," which was no longer Rome (which was no longer a city), having moved elsewhere, moved again, and still again—in less than two decades, after staying in one place for two millennia. Twelve years after the proposals were made, Father Isaac Edward Leibowitz had won permission from the Holy See to found a new community of religious, to be named after Albertus Magnus, teacher of Saint Thomas, and patron of men of science. Its task, unannounced, and at first only vaguely defined, was to preserve human history for the great-great-great-grandchildren of the children of the simpletons who wanted it destroyed. Its earliest habit was burlap rags and bindlestiffs—the uniform of the simpleton mob. Its members were either "bookleggers" or "memorizers," according to the tasks assigned. The bookleggers smuggled books to the southwest desert and buried them there in kegs. The memorizers committed to rote memory entire volumes of history, sacred writings, literature, and science, in case some unfortunate book smuggler was caught, tortured, and forced to reveal the location of the kegs. Meanwhile, other members of the new Order located a water hole about three days' journey from the book cache and began the building of a monastery. The project, aimed at saving a small remnant of human culture from the remnant of humanity who wanted it destroyed, was then underway.

Leibowitz, while taking his own turn at booklegging, was caught by a simpleton mob; a turncoat technician, whom the priest swiftly forgave, identified him as not only a man of learning, but also a specialist in the weapons field. Hooded in burlap, he was martyred forthwith, by strangulation with a hangman's noose not tied for neck-breaking, at the same time being roasted alive—thus settling a dispute in the crowd concerning the method of execution.

The memorizers were few, their memories limited.

Some of the book kegs were found and burned, as well as several other bookleggers. The monastery itself was attacked thrice before the madness subsided.

From the vast store of human knowledge, only a few kegs of original books and a pitiful collection of hand-copied texts, rewritten from memory, had survived in the possession of the Order by the time the madness had ended.

Now, after six centuries of darkness, the monks still preserved this Memorabilia, studied it, copied and recopied it, and patiently waited. At the beginning, in the time of Leibowitz, it had been hoped—and even anticipated as probable—that the fourth or fifth generation would begin to want its heritage back. But the monks of the earliest days had not counted on the human ability to generate a new cultural inheritance in a couple of generations if an old one is utterly destroyed, to generate it by virtue of lawgivers and prophets, geniuses or maniacs; through a Moses, or through a Hitler, or an ignorant but tyrannical grandfather, a cultural inheritance may be acquired between dusk and dawn, and many have been so acquired. But the new "culture" was an inheritance of darkness, wherein "simpleton" meant the same thing as "citizen" meant the same thing as "slave." The monks waited. It mattered not at all to them that the knowledge they saved was useless, that much of it was not really knowledge now, was as inscrutable to the monks in some instances as it would be to an illiterate wild-boy from the hills; this knowledge was empty of content, its subject matter long since gone. Still, such knowledge had a symbolic structure that was peculiar to itself, and at least the symbol-interplay could be observed. To observe the way a knowledge-system is knit together is to learn at least a minimum knowledge-of-knowledge, until someday—someday, or some century—an Integrator would come, and things would be fitted together again. So time mattered not at all. The Memorabilia was there, and it was given to them by duty to preserve, and preserve it they would if the darkness in the world lasted ten more centuries, or even ten thousand years, for they, though born in that darkest of ages, were still the very bookleggers and memorizers of the Beatus Leibowitz; and when they wandered abroad from their abbey, each of them, the professed of the Order—whether stable-hand or Lord Abbot—carried as part of his habit a book, usually a Breviary these days, tied up in a bindlestiff.

After the shelter was closed, the documents and relics which had been taken from it were quietly rounded up, one at a time and in an unobtrusive manner, by the abbot. They became unavailable for inspection, presumably locked in Arkos' study. For all practical purposes, they had vanished. Anything which vanished at the level of the abbot's study was not safe subject matter for public discussion. It was something to be whispered about in quiet corridors. Brother Francis seldom heard the whispers. Eventually, they stopped, only to be revived when a messenger from New Rome muttered with the abbot in the refectory one night. An occasional snatch of their muttering reached adjacent tables. The whispers lasted for a few weeks after the messenger's departure, then subsided again.

Brother Francis Gerard of Utah returned to the desert the following year and fasted again in solitude. Once more he returned, weak and emaciated, and soon was summoned into the presence of Abbot Arkos, who demanded to know whether he claimed further conferences with members of the Heavenly Hosts.

"Oh, no, m'Lord Abbot. Nothing by day but buzzards."

"By night?" Arkos asked suspiciously.

"Only wolves," said Francis, adding cautiously: "I think."

Arkos did not choose to belabor the cautious amendment, but merely frowned. The abbot's frown, Brother Francis had come to observe, was the causative source of radiant energy which traveled through space with finite velocity and which was as yet not very well understood except in terms of its withering effect upon whatever thing absorbed it, that thing usually being a postulant or novice. Francis had absorbed a five-second burst of the stuff by the time the next question was put to him.

"Now what about last year?"

The novice paused to swallow. "The—old—man?"

"The old man."

"Yes, Dom Arkos."

Trying to keep any hint of a question mark out of his tone, Arkos droned: "Just an old man. Nothing more. We're sure of that now."

"I *think* it was just an old man, too."

Father Arkos reached wearily for the hickory ruler.

WHACK!

"Deo gratias!"

WHACK!

"Deo . . ."

As Francis returned to his cell, the abbot called after him down the corridor: "By the way, I intended to mention . . ."

"Yes, Reverend Father?"

"No vows this year," he said absently, and vanished into his study.

7   Brother Francis spent seven years in the novitiate, seven Lenten vigils in the desert, and became highly proficient in the imitation of wolf calls. For the amusement of his brethren, he summoned the pack to the vicinity of the abbey by howling from the walls after dark. By day, he served in the kitchen, scrubbed the stone floors, and continued his classroom study of antiquity.

Then one day a messenger from a seminary in New Rome came riding to the abbey on an ass. After a long conference with the abbot, the messenger sought out Brother Francis. He seemed surprised to find that youth, now fully a man, still wearing the habit of a novice and scrubbing the kitchen floor.

"We have been studying the documents you discovered, for some years now," he told the novice. "Quite a few of us are convinced they're authentic."

Francis lowered his head. "I'm not permitted to mention the matter, Father," he said.

"Oh, that." The messenger smiled and handed him a scrap of paper bearing the abbot's seal, and written in the ruler's hand: *Ecce Inquisitor Curiae. Ausculta et obsequere. Arkos, AOL, Abbas.*

"It's all right," he added hastily, noticing the novice's sudden tension. "I'm not speaking to you officially. Someone else from the court will take your statements later. You know, don't you, that your papers have been in New Rome for some time now? I just brought some of them back."

Brother Francis shook his head. He knew less, perhaps, than anyone, concerning high-level reactions to his discovery of the relics. He noticed that the messenger wore the white habit of the Dominicans, and he wondered with a certain uneasiness about the nature of the "court" whereof the Black Friar had spoken. There was an inquisition against Catharism in the Pacific Coast region, but he could not imagine how *that* court could be concerned with relics of the Beatus. *Ecce Inquisitor Curiae*, the note said. Probably the abbot meant "investigator." The Dominican seemed a rather mild-humored man, and was not carrying any visible engines of torture.

"We expect the case for canonization of your founder to be reopened soon," the messenger explained. "Your Abbot Arkos is a very wise and prudent man." He chuckled. "By turning the relics over to another Order for examination, and by having the shelter sealed before it was fully explored — Well, you do understand, don't you?"

"No, Father. I had supposed he thought the whole thing too trivial to spend any time on."

The Black Friar laughed. "Trivial? I think not. But if *your* Order turns up evidence, relics, miracles, and whatever, the court has to consider the source. *Every* religious community is eager to see its founder canonized. So your abbot very wisely told you: 'Hands off the shelter.' I'm sure it's been frustrating for all of you, but—better for the cause of your founder to let the shelter be explored with other witnesses present."

"You're going to open it again?" Francis asked eagerly.

"No, not I. But when the court is ready, it will send observers. Then anything that is found in the shelter that might affect the case will be safe, in case the opposition questions its authenticity. Of course, the only reason for suspecting that the contents of the shelter *might* affect the cause is— Well, the things you found."

"May I ask how that is, Father?"

"Well, one of the embarrassments at the time of the beatification was the early life of Blessed Leibowitz—before he became a monk and a priest. The advocate for the other side kept trying to cast doubt on the early period, pre-Deluge. He was trying to establish that Leibowitz never made a careful search—that his wife might even have been alive at the time of his ordination. Well, it wouldn't be the first time, of course; sometimes dispensations have been granted —but that's beside the point. The *advocatus diaboli* was just trying to cast doubt on your founder's character. Trying to suggest that he had accepted Holy Orders and taken vows before being certain his family responsibility was ended. The opposition failed, but it may try again. And if those human remains you found really *are*—" He shrugged and smiled.

Francis nodded. "It would pinpoint the date of her death."

"At the very beginning of the war that nearly ended everything. And in my own opinion—well, that handwriting in the box, it's either that of the Beatus or a very clever counterfeit."

Francis reddened.

"I'm not suggesting that *you* were involved in any counterfeit scheme," the Dominican added hastily, upon noticing the blush.

The novice, however, had only been remembering his own opinion of the scrawl.

"Tell me, how did it happen?—how you located the site, I mean. I'll need the whole story of it."

"Well, it started because of the wolves."

The Dominican began taking notes.

A few days after the messenger's departure from the abbey, Abbot Arkos called for Brother Francis. "Do you still feel that your vocation is with us?" Arkos asked pleasantly.

"If m'Lord Abbot will pardon my execrable vanity—"

"Oh, let's ignore your execrable vanity for a moment. Do you or don't you?"

"Yes, Magister meus."

The abbot beamed. "Well, now, my son. I think we're convinced of it too. If you're ready to commit yourself for all time, I think the time's ripe for you to profess your solemn vows." He paused for a moment, and, watching the novice's face, seemed disappointed not to detect any change of expression. "What's this? You're not glad to hear it? You're not—? Ho! what's wrong?"

While Francis' face had remained a politely attentive mask, the mask gradually lost color. His knees buckled suddenly.

Francis had fainted.

Two weeks later, the novice Francis, having perhaps set an endurance record for survival time on desert vigils, left the ranks of the novitiate and, vowing perpetual poverty, chastity, obedience, together with the special pledges peculiar to the community, received blessings and a bindlestiff in the abbey, and became forever a professed monk of the Albertian Order of Leibowitz, chained by chains of his own forging to the foot of the Cross and the rule of the Order. Thrice the ritual inquired of him: "If God calleth thee to be His Booklegger, wilt thou suffer death before betraying thy brethren?" And thrice Francis responded: "Aye, Lord."

"Then arise Brother Bookleggers and Brother Memorizers and receive the kiss of brotherhood. *Ecce quam bonum, et quam jucundum . . .*"

Brother Francis was transferred from the kitchen and assigned to less menial labor. He became apprentice copyist to an aged monk named Horner, and, if things went well for him, he might reasonably look forward to a lifetime in the copyroom, where he would dedicate the rest of his days to such tasks as the hand-copying of algebra texts and illuminating their pages with olive leaves and cheerful cherubim surrounding tables of logarithms.

Brother Horner was a gentle old man, and Brother Francis liked him from the start. "Most of us do better work on the assigned copy," Horner told him, "if we have our own project too. Most of the copyists become interested in some particular work from the Memorabilia and like to spend a little time at it on the side. For example, Brother Sarl over there—his work was lagging, and he was making mistakes. So we let him spend an hour a day on a project he chose for himself. When the work gets so tedious that he starts making errors in copy, he can put it aside for a while and work on his own project. I allow everyone to do the same. If you finish your assigned work before the day's over but don't have your own project, you'll have to spend the extra time on our perennials."

"Perennials?"

"Yes, and I don't mean plants. There's a perennial demand from the whole clergy for various books—Missals, Scripture, Breviaries, the *Summa*, encyclopaediae, and the like. We sell quite a lot of them. So when you don't have a pet project, we'll put you on the perennials when you finish early. You've plenty of time to decide."

"What project did Brother Sarl pick?"

The aged overseer paused. "Well, I doubt if you'd even understand it. I don't. He seems to have found a method for restoring missing words and phrases to some of the old fragments of original text in the Memorabilia. Perhaps the left-hand side of a half-burned book is legible, but the right edge of each page is burned, with a few words missing at the end of each line. He's worked out a mathematical method for finding the missing words. It's not foolproof, but it works to some degree. He's managed to restore four whole pages since he began the attempt."

Francis glanced at Brother Sarl, who was an octogenarian and nearly blind. "How long did it take him?" the apprentice asked.

"About forty years," said Brother Horner. "Of course he's only spent about five hours a week at it, and it *does* take considerable arithmetic."

Francis nodded thoughtfully. "If one page per decade could be restored, maybe in a few centuries—"

"Even less," croaked Brother Sarl without looking up from his work. "The more you fill in, the faster the remainder goes. I'll get the next page done in a couple of years. After that, God willing, maybe—" His voice tapered off into a numble. Francis frequently noticed that Brother Sarl talked to himself while working.

"Suit yourself," said Brother Horner. "We can always use more help on the perennials, but you can have your own project when you want one."

The idea came to Brother Francis in an unexpected flash.

"May I use the time," he blurted, "to make a copy of the Leibowitz blueprint I found?"

Brother Horner seemed momentarily startled. "Well—I don't know, son. Our Lord Abbot is, well—just a little *sensitive* on that subject. And the thing may not belong in the Memorabilia. It's in the tentative file now."

"But you *know* they fade, Brother. And it's been handled a lot in the light. The Dominicans had it in New Rome for so long—"

"Well—I suppose it would be a rather *brief* project. If Father Arkos doesn't object, but—" He waggled his head in doubt.

"Perhaps I could include it as one of a set," Francis hastily offered. "What few recopied blueprints we have are so old they're brittle. If I made several duplicates—of some of the others—"

Horner smiled wryly. "What you're suggesting is, that by including the Leibowitz blueprint in a set, you might escape detection."

Francis reddened.

"Father Arkos might not even notice, eh?—if he happened to wander through."

Francis squirmed.

"All right," said Horner, his eyes twinkling slightly. "You may use your unassigned time to make duplicates of any of the recopied prints that are in bad condition. If anything else gets mixed up in the lot, I'll try not to notice."

Brother Francis sent several months of his unassigned time in redrawing some of the older prints from the Memorabilia's files before daring to touch the Leibowitz print. If the old drawings were worth saving at all, they needed to be recopied every century or two anyhow. Not only did the original copies fade, but often the redrawn versions became nearly illegible after a time, due to the impermanence of the inks employed. He had not the slightest notion why the ancients had used white lines and lettering on a dark background, in preference to the reverse. When he roughly re-sketched a design in charcoal, thereby reversing the background, the rough sketch appeared more realistic than the white-on-dark, and the ancients were immeasurably wiser than Francis; if they had taken the trouble to put ink where blank paper would ordinarily be, and leave slivers of white paper where an inked line would appear in a straightforward drawing, then they must have had their reasons. Francis recopied the documents to appear as nearly like the originals as possible—even though the task of spreading blue ink around tiny white letters was particularly tedious, and quite wasteful of ink, a fact which caused Brother Horner to grumble.

He copied an old architectural print, then a drawing for a machine part whose geometry was apparent but whose purpose was vague. He redrew a mandala abstraction, titled "STATOR WNDG MOD 73-A 3-PH 6-P 1800-RPM 5-HP CL-A SQUIRREL CAGE," which proved completely incomprehensible, and not at all capable of imprisoning a squirrel. The ancients were often subtle; perhaps one needed a special set of mirrors in order to see the squirrel. He painstakingly redrew it anyhow.

Only after the abbot, who occasionally passed through the copyroom, had seen him working at another blueprint at least three times (twice Arkos had paused for a quick look at Francis' work), did he summon the courage to venture to the Memorabilia files for the Leibowitz blueprint, nearly a year after beginning his free-time project.

The original document had already been subjected to a certain amount of restorative work. Except for the fact that it bore the name of the Beatus, it was disappointingly like most of the others he had redrawn.

The Leibowitz print, another abstraction, appealed to nothing, least of all to reason. He studied it until he could see the whole amazing complexity with his eyes closed, but knew no more than he had known before. It appeared to be no more than a network of lines connecting a patchwork of doohickii, squiggles, quids, laminulae, and thingumbob. The lines were mostly horizontal or vertical, and crossed each other with either a little jump-mark or a dot; they made right-angle turns to get around doohickii, and they never stopped in mid-space but always terminated at a squiggle, quiggle, quid, or thingumbob. It made so little sense that a long period of staring at it produced a stupefying effect. Nevertheless he began work at duplicating every detail, even to the copying of a central brownish stain which he thought might be the blood of the Blessed Martyr, but which Brother Jeris suggested was only the stain left by a decayed apple core.

Brother Jeris, who had joined the apprentice copyroom at the same time as Brother Francis, seemed to enjoy teasing him about the project. "What, pray," he asked, squinting over Francis' shoulder, "is the meaning of 'Transistorized Control System for Unit Six-B,' learned Brother?"

"Clearly, it is the title of the document," said Francis, feeling slightly cross.

"Clearly. But what does it mean?"

"It is the *name* of the diagram which lies before your eyes, Brother Simpleton. What does 'Jeris' mean?"

"Very little, I'm sure," said Brother Jeris with mock humility. "Forgive my density, please. You have successfully defined the name by pointing to the creature named, which is truly the meaning of the name. But now the creature-diagram itself represents something, does it not? What does the diagram represent?"

"The transistorized control system for unit six-B, obviously."

Jeris laughed. "Quite clear! Eloquent! If the creature is the name, then the name is the creature. 'Equals may be substituted for equals,' or 'The order of an equality is reversible,' but may we proceed to the next axiom? If 'Quantities equal to the same quantity may substitute for each other' is true, then is there not some 'same quantity' which *both* name and diagram represent? Or is it a closed system?"

Francis reddened. "I would imagine," he said slowly, after pausing to stifle his annoyance, "that the diagram represents an abstract concept, rather than a concrete *thing*. Perhaps the ancients had a systematic method for depicting a pure thought. It's clearly not a recognizable picture of an object."

"Yes, yes, it's *clearly* unrecognizable!" Brother Jeris agreed with a chuckle.

"On the other hand, perhaps it *does* depict an object, but only in a very formal stylistic way—so that one would need special training or—"

"Special eyesight?"

"In my opinion, it's a high abstraction of perhaps transcendental value expressing a thought of the Beatus Leibowitz."

"Bravo! Now what was he thinking about?"

"Why—'Circuit Design,'" said Francis, picking the term out of the block of lettering at the lower right.

"Hmmm, what discipline does *that* art pertain to, Brother? What is its genus, species, property, and difference? Or is it only an 'accident'?"

Jeris was becoming pretentious in his sarcasm, Francis thought, and decided to meet it with a soft answer. "Well, observe this column of figures, and its heading: 'Electronics Parts Numbers.' There *was* once, an art or science, called Electronics, which might belong to both Art and Science."

"Uh-*huh!* Thus settling 'genus' and 'species.' Now as to 'difference,' if I may pursue the line. What was the subject matter of Electronics?"

"That too is written," said Francis, who had searched the Memorabilia from high to low in an attempt to find clues which might make the blueprint slightly more comprehensible—but to very small avail. "The subject matter of Electronics was the electron," he explained.

"So it is written, indeed. I am impressed. I know so little of these things. What, pray, was the 'electron'?"

"Well, there is one fragmentary source which alludes to it as a 'Negative Twist of Nothingness.'"

"What! How did they negate a nothingness? Wouldn't that make it a somethingness?"

"Perhaps the negation applies to 'twist.'"

"Ah! Then we would have an 'Untwisted Nothing,' eh? Have you discovered how to untwist a nothingness?"

"Not yet," Francis admitted.

"Well keep at it, Brother! How clever they must have been, those ancients—to know how to untwist nothing. Keep at it, and you may learn how. Then we'd have the 'electron' in our midst, wouldn't we? Whatever would we do with it? Put it on the altar in the chapel?"

"All right," Francis sighed, "I don't know. But I have a certain faith that the 'electron' existed at one time, although I don't know how it was constructed or what it might have been used for."

"How touching!" chuckled the iconoclast, and returned to his work.

The sporadic teasing of Brother Jeris saddened Francis, but did nothing to lessen his devotion to his project.

The exact duplication of every mark, blotch, and stain proved impossible, but the accuracy of his facsimile proved sufficient for the deception of the eye at a distance of two paces, and therefore adequate for display purposes, so that the original might be sealed and packed away. Having completed the facsimile, Brother Francis found himself disappointed. The drawing was too stark. There was nothing about it to suggest at first glance that it might be a holy relic. The style was terse and unpretentious—fittingly enough, perhaps, for the Beatus himself, and yet—

A copy of the relic was not enough. Saints were humble people who glorified not themselves but God, and it was left to others to portray the inward glory of the saintly by outward, visible signs. The stark copy was not enough: it was coldly unimaginative and did not commemorate the saintly qualities of the Beatus in any visible way.

Glorificemus, thought Francis, while he worked on the perennials. He was copying pages of the Psalms at the moment for later rebinding. He paused to regain his place in the text, and to notice meaning in the words—for after hours of copying, he had ceased to read at all, and merely allowed his hand to retrace the letters which his eyes encountered. He noticed that he had been copying David's prayer for pardon, the fourth penitential psalm, *"Miserere mei, Deus . . .* for I know my iniquity, and my sin is always before me." It was a humble prayer, but the page before his eyes was not written in a humble style to match. The *M* in *Miserere* was gold-leaf inlay. A flourishing arabesque of interwoven gold and violet filaments filled the margins and grew into nests around the splendid capitals at the beginning of each verse. However humble the prayer itself, the page was magnificent. Brother Francis was copying only the body of the text onto new parchment, leaving spaces for the splendid capitals and margins as wide as the text lines. Other craftsmen would fill in riots of color around his simply inked copy and would construct the pictorial capitals. He was learning to illuminate, but was not yet proficient enough to be trusted at gold-inlay work on the perennials.

Glorificemus. He was thinking of the blueprint again.

Without mentioning the idea to anyone, Brother Francis began to plan. He found the finest available lambskin and spent several weeks of his spare time at curing it and stretching it and stoning it to a perfect surface, which he eventually bleached to a snowy whiteness and carefully stored away. For months afterward, he spent every available minute of his free time looking through the Memorabilia, again seeking clues to the meaning of the Leibowitz print. He found nothing resembling the squiggles in the drawing, nor anything else to help him interpret its meaning, but after a long time he stumbled across a fragment of a book which contained a partially destroyed page whose subject matter was blueprinting. It seemed to be a piece of an encyclopaedia. The reference was brief and some of the article was missing, but after reading it several times, he began to suspect that he

—and many earlier copyists—had wasted a lot of time and ink. The white-on-dark effect seemed not to have been a particularly desirable feature, but one which resulted from the peculiarities of a certain cheap reproduction process. The original drawing from which the blueprint had been made had been black-on-white. He had to resist a sudden impulse to beat his head against the stone floor. All that ink and labor to copy an accident! Well, perhaps Brother Horner need not be told. It would be a work of charity to say nothing about it, because of Brother Horner's heart condition.

The knowledge that the color scheme of blueprints was an accidental feature of those ancient drawings lent impetus to his plan. A glorified copy of the Leibowitz print could be made without incorporating the accidental feature. With the color scheme reversed, no one would recognize the drawing at first. Certain other features could obviously be modified. He dared change nothing that he did not understand, but surely the parts tables and the block-lettered information could be spread symmetrically around the diagram on scrolls and shields. Because the meaning of the diagram itself was obscure, he dared not alter its shape or plan by a hair; but since its color scheme was unimportant, it might as well be beautiful. He considered gold inlay for the squiggles and doohickii, but the thingumbob was too intricate for goldwork, and a gold quid would seem ostentatious. The quiggles just *had* to be done jet black, but that meant that the lines should be off-black, to assert the quiggles. While the unsymmetrical design would have to stay as it was, he could think of no reason why its meaning would be altered by using it as a trellis for a climbing vine, whose branches (carefully dodging the quiggles) might be made to furnish an impression of symmetry or render asymmetry natural. When Brother Horner illuminated a capital M, transmuting it into a wonderful jungle of leaves, berries, branches, and perhaps a wily serpent, it nevertheless remained legible as M. Brother Francis saw no reason for supposing that the same would not apply to the diagram.

The general shape, over-all, with a scrolled border, might well become a shield, rather than the stark rectangle which enclosed the drawing in the print. He made dozens of preliminary sketches. At the very top of the parchment would be a representation of the Triune God, and at the very bottom —the coat of arms of the Albertian Order, with, just above it the image of the Beatus.

But there was no accurate likeness of the Beatus in existence, so far as Francis knew. There were several fanciful portraits, but none dating back to the Simplification. There was, as yet, not even a conventional representation, although tradition told that Leibowitz had been rather tall and somewhat stooped. But perhaps when the shelter was reopened—

Brother Francis' preliminary sketchwork was interrupted one afternoon by his sudden awareness that the presence which loomed behind him and cast its shadow across his copy-table was that of—was that of— *No! Please! Beate Leibowitz, audi me! Mercy, Lord! Let it be anybody but—*

"Well, what have we here?" rumbled the abbot, glancing over his designs.

"A drawing, m'Lord Abbot."

"So I notice. But what is it?"

"The Leibowitz blueprint."

"That one you found? What? It doesn't look much like it. Why the changes?"

"It's going to be—"

"Speak louder!"

"*—AN ILLUMINATED COPY!*" Brother Francis involuntarily shrieked.

"Oh."

Abbot Arkos shrugged and wandered away.

Brother Horner, a few seconds later, while wandering past the apprentice's desk was surprised to notice that Francis had fainted.

8 To the amazement of Brother Francis, Abbot Arkos no longer objected to the monk's interest in the relics. Since the Dominicans had agreed to examine the matter, the abbot had relaxed; and since the cause for the canonization had resumed some progress in New Rome, he appeared at times to forget entirely that anything special had happened during the vocational vigil of one Francis Gerard, AOL, formerly of Utah, presently of the scriptorium and copyroom. The incident was eleven years old. The preposterous whisperings in the novitiate concerning the pilgrim's identity had long since died away. The novitiate of Brother Francis' time was not the novitiate of today. The newest of the new crop of youngsters had never heard of the affair.

The affair had cost Brother Francis seven Lenten vigils among the wolves, however, and he never fully trusted the subject as safe. Whenever he mentioned it, he would dream that night of wolves and of Arkos; in the dream, Arkos kept flinging meat to the wolves, and the meat was Francis.

The monk found, however, that he might continue his project without being molested, except by Brother Jeris who continued to tease. Francis began the actual illumination of the lambskin. The intricacies of scrollwork and the excruciating delicacy of the gold-inlay work would, because of the brevity of his spare-project time, make it a labor of many years; but in a dark sea of centuries wherein nothing seemed to flow, a lifetime was only brief eddy, even for the man who lived it. There was a tedium of repeated days and repeated seasons; then there were aches and pains, finally Extreme Unction, and a moment of blackness at the end—or at the beginning, rather. For then the small shivering soul who had endured the tedium, endured it badly or well, would find itself in a place of light, find itself absorbed in the burning gaze of infinitely compassionate eyes as it stood before the Just One. And then the King would say: "Come," or the King would say: "Go," and only for that moment had the tedium of years existed. It would be hard to believe differently during such an age as Francis knew.

Brother Sarl finished the fifth page of his mathematical restoration, collapsed over his desk, and died a few hours later. Never mind. His notes were intact. Someone, after a century or two, would come along and find them interesting, would perhaps complete his work. Meanwhile, prayers ascended for the soul of Sarl.

Then there was Brother Fingo and his woodcarving. He had been returned to the carpentry shop a year or two ago and was permitted occasionally to chisel and scrape at his half-finished image of the Martyr. Like Francis, Fingo had only an hour now and then to work at his chosen task; the woodcarving progressed at a rate that was almost imperceptible unless one looked at the carving only after intervals of several months. Francis saw it too frequently to notice the growth. He found himself charmed by Fingo's easygoing exuberance, even while realizing that Fingo had adopted his affable manner to compensate for his ugliness, and he liked to spend idle minutes, whenever he could find them, watching Fingo work.

The carpentry shop was rich with the odors of pine, cedar, spruce shavings, and human sweat. Wood was not easy to obtain at the abbey. Except for fig trees and a couple of cottonwoods in the immediate vicinity of the water hole, the region was treeless. It was a three-day ride to the nearest stand of scrub that passed for timber, and the woodgatherers often were gone from the abbey for a week at a time before they came back with a few donkeyloads of branches for making pegs, spokes, and an occasional chair leg. Sometimes they dragged back a log or two for replacing a rotting beam. But with such a limited wood supply, carpenters were necessarily woodcarvers and sculptors as well.

Sometimes, while watching Fingo carve, Francis would sit on a bench in the corner of the workshop and sketch, trying to visualize details of the carving which were, as yet, only roughly hewn in the wood. The vague outlines of the face were there, but still masked by splinters and chisel-marks. With his sketches, Brother Francis tried to anticipate the features before they emerged from the grain. Fingo glanced at his sketches and laughed. But as the work progressed, Francis could not escape the feeling that the face of the carving was smiling a vaguely familiar smile. He sketched it thus, and the feeling of familiarity increased. Still, he could not place the face, or recall who had smiled so wryly.

"Not bad, really. Not bad at all," said Fingo of his sketches.

The copyist shrugged. "I can't get over the feeling that I've seen him before."

"Not around here, Brother. Not in my time."

Francis fell ill during Advent, and several months had passed before he visited the workshop again.

"The face is nearly finished, Francisco," said the woodcarver. "How do you like it now?"

"I know him!" Francis gasped, staring at the merry-but-sad wrinkled eyes, the hint of a wry smile at the corners of the mouth—somehow almost too familiar.

"You do? Who is it then?" wondered Fingo.

"It's—well, I'm not sure. I *think* I know him. But—"

Fingo laughed. "You're just recognizing your own sketches," he offered in explanation.

Francis was not so certain. Still, he could not quite place the face.

Hmm-hnnn! the wry smile seemed to say.

The abbot found the smile irritating, however. While he allowed the work to be completed, he declared that he would never permit it to be used for the purpose originally planned —as an image to be placed in the church if the canonization of the Beatus were ever accomplished. Many years later, when the whole figure was completed, Arkos caused it to be set up in the corridor of the guesthouse, but later transferred it to his study after it had shocked a visitor from New Rome.

Slowly, painfully, Brother Francis was making the lambskin a blaze of beauty. Word of his project spread beyond the copyroom, and the monks often gathered around his table to watch the work and murmur admiration. "Inspiration," someone whispered. "There's evidence enough. It could have been the Beatus he met out there—"

"I don't see why you don't spend your time on something useful," grumbled Brother Jeris, whose sarcastic wit had been exhausted by several years of patient answers from Brother Francis. The skeptic had been using his own free-project time for making and decorating oilskin shades for the lamps in the church, thereby winning the attention of the abbot, who soon placed him in charge of the perennials. As the account ledgers soon began to testify, Brother Jeris' promotion was justified.

Brother Horner, the old master copyist, fell ill. Within weeks, it became apparent that the well-loved monk was on his deathbed. A Mass of Burial was chanted early in Advent. The remains of the saintly old master-copyist were committed to the earth of their origin. While the community expressed its grief in prayer, Arkos quietly appointed Brother Jeris as master of the copyroom.

On the day after his appointment, Brother Jeris informed Brother Francis that he considered it appropriate for him to put away the things of a child and start doing a man's work. Obediently, the monk wrapped his precious project in parchment, protected it with heavy boards, shelved it, and began making oilskin lampshades in his spare time. He murmured no protest, but contented himself with realizing that someday the soul of dear Brother Jeris would depart by the same road as the soul of Brother Horner, to begin that life for which this world was but a staging ground—might begin it at a rather early age, judging by the extent to which he fretted, fumed, and drove himself; and afterward, God willing, Francis might be allowed to complete his beloved document.

Providence, however, took an earlier hand in the matter, without summoning the soul of Brother Jeris to its Maker. During the summer which followed his appointment as master, a prothonotary apostolic and his retinue of clerks came by way of a donkey train to the abbey from New Rome; he introduced himself as Monsignor Malfreddo Aguerra, the postulator for the Beatus Leibowitz in the canonization procedure. With him were several Dominicans. He had come to observe the reopening of the shelter and the exploration of "Sealed Environment." Also, to investigate such evidence as the abbey could produce that might have a bearing on the case, including—to the abbot's dismay—reports of an alleged apparition of the Beatus which had, so travelers said, come to one Francis Gerard of Utah, AOL.

The Saint's advocate was warmly greeted by the monks, was quartered in the rooms reserved for visiting prelates, was lavishly served by six young novices instructed to be responsive to his every whim, although, as it turned out, Monsignor Aguerra was a man of few whims, to the disappointment of would-be caterers. The finest wines were opened; Aguerra sipped them politely but preferred milk. Brother Huntsman snared plump quail and chaparral cocks for the guest's table; but after inquiring about the feeding habits of the chaparral cocks ("Corn fed, Brother?"—"No, snake-fed, Messér"), Monsignor Aguerra seemed to prefer monks-gruel in the refectory. If only he had inquired about the anonymous bits of meat in the stews, he might have preferred the truly succulent chaparral cocks. Malfreddo Aguerra insisted that life go on as usual at the abbey. But, nevertheless, the advocate was entertained each evening at recreation by fiddlers and a troupe of clowns until he began to believe that "life as usual" at the abbey must be extraordinarily lively, as lives of monastic communities go.

On the third day of Aguerra's visit, the abbot summoned Brother Francis. The relationship between the monk and his ruler, while not close, had been formally friendly, since the time the abbot permitted the novice to profess his vows, and Brother Francis was not even trembling when he knocked at the study door and asked: "You sent for me, Reverend Father?"

"Yes, I did," Arkos said, then asked evenly: "Tell me, have you ever thought about death?"

"Frequently, m'Lord Abbot."

"You pray to Saint Joseph that your death will not be an unhappy one?"

"Umm—often, Reverend Father."

"Then I suppose you'd not care to be suddenly stricken? To have someone use your guts to string a fiddle? To be fed to the hogs? To have your bones be buried in unconsecrated ground? Eh?"

"Nnn-noo, Magister meus."

"I thought not, so be very careful about what you say to Monsignor Aguerra."

"I—?"

"You." Arkos rubbed his chin and seemed lost in unhappy speculation. "I can see it too clearly. The Leibowitz cause is shelved. Poor Brother is struck down by a falling brick. There he lies, moaning for absolution. In the very midst of us, mind you. And there we stand, looking down in pity—clergy among us—watching him croak his last, without even a last blessing on the lad. Hellbound. Unblessed. Unshrived. Under our very noses. A pity, eh?"

"*M'Lord?*" Francis squawked.

"Oh, don't blame me. I'll be too busy trying to keep your brothers from carrying out their impulse to kick you to death."

"When?"

"Why not at all, we hope. Because you *are* going to be careful, aren't you?—about what you say to the monsignor. Otherwise I may *let* them kick you to death."

"Yes, but—"

"The postulator wants to see you at once. Please stifle your imagination, and be certain about what you say. Please try not to think."

"Well, I think I can."

"Out, son, out."

Francis felt fright when he first tapped at Aguerra's door, but he saw quickly that the fright was unfounded. The prothonotary was a suave and diplomatic elder who seemed keenly interested in the small monk's life.

After several minutes of preliminary amenities, he approached the slippery subject: "Now, about your encounter with the person who may have been the Blessed Founder of—"

"Oh, but I never said he was our Blessed Leibo . . ."

"Of course you didn't, my son. Of course you didn't. Now I have here an account of the incident—gathered purely from hearsay sources, of course—and I'd like for you to read it, and then either confirm it or correct it." He paused to draw a scroll from his case; he handed it to Brother Francis. "This version is based on travelers' stories," he added. "Only *you* can describe what happened—first hand—so I want you to edit it *most* scrupulously."

"Certainly, Messér. But what happened was really very simple—"

"Read, *read!* Then we'll talk about it, eh?"

The fatness of the scroll made it apparent that the hearsay account was not "really very simple." Brother Francis read with mounting apprehension. The apprehension soon grew to the proportions of horror.

"You look white, son," said the postulator. "Is something troubling you?"

"Messér, *this*—it wasn't like this *at all!*"

"No? But indirectly at least, you must have been the author of it. How could it have been otherwise? Weren't you the only witness?"

Brother Francis closed his eyes and rubbed his forehead. He had told the simple truth to fellow novices. Fellow novices had whispered among themselves. Novices had told the story to travelers. Travelers had repeated it to travelers. Until finally—*this!* Small wonder that Abbot Arkos had enjoined discussion. If only he had never mentioned the pilgrim at all!

"He only spoke a few words to me. I saw him just that once. He chased me with a stick, asked me the way to the abbey, and made marks on the rock where I found the crypt. Then I never saw him again."

"No halo?"

"No, Messér."

"No heavenly choir?"

"*No!*"

"What about the carpet of roses that grew up where he walked?"

"No, no! Nothing like that, Messér," the monk gasped.

"He didn't write his name on the rock?"

"As God is my judge, Messér, he only made those two marks. I didn't know what they meant."

"Ah, well," sighed the postulator. "Travelers' stories are always exaggerated. But I wonder how it all got started. Now suppose you tell me how it really happened."

Brother Francis told him quite briefly. Aguerra seemed saddened. After a thoughtful silence, he took the fat scroll, gave it a parting pat, and dropped it into the waste-bin. "There goes miracle number seven," he grunted.

Francis hastened to apologize.

The advocate brushed it aside. "Don't give it a second thought. We really have enough evidence. There are several spontaneous cures—several cases of instantaneous recovery from illness caused by the intercession of the Beatus. They're simple, matter of fact, and well documented. They're what cases for canonization are built on. Of course they lack the poetry of *this* story, but I'm almost glad it's unfounded—glad for your sake. The devil's advocate would have crucified you, you know."

"I never said anything like—"

"I understand, I understand! It all started because of the shelter. We reopened it today, by the way."

Francis brightened. "Did—did you find anything more of Saint Leibowitz'?"

"*Blessed* Leibowitz, please!" monsignor corrected. "No, not yet. We opened the inner chamber. Had a devil of a time getting it unsealed. Fifteen skeletons inside and many fascinating artifacts. Apparently the woman—it *was* a woman, by the way—whose remains you found was admitted to the outer chamber, but the inner chamber was already full. Possibly it would have provided some degree of protection if a falling wall hadn't caused the cave-in. The poor souls inside were trapped by the stones that blocked the entrance. Heaven knows why the door wasn't designed to swing inward."

"The woman in the antechamber, *was* she Emily Leibowitz?"

Aguerra smiled. "Can we prove it? I don't know yet. I believe she was, yes—I believe—but perhaps I'm letting hope run away with reason. We'll see what we can uncover yet; we'll see. The *other* side has a witness present. I can't jump to conclusions."

Despite his disappointment at Francis' account of the meeting with the pilgrim, Aguerra remained friendly enough. He spent ten days at the archaeological site before returning to New Rome, and he left two of his assistants behind to supervise further excavation. On the day of his departure, he visited Brother Francis in the scriptorium.

"They tell me you were working on a document to commemorate the relics you found," said the postulator. "Judging by the descriptions I've heard, I think I should very much like to see it."

The monk protested that it was really nothing, but he went immediately to fetch it, with such eagerness that his hands were trembling as he unpacked the lambskin. Joyfully he observed that Brother Jeris was looking on, while wearing a nervous frown.

The monsignor stared for many seconds. *"Beautiful!"* he exploded at last. "What glorious color! It's superb, superb. Finish it—Brother, finish it!"

Brother Francis looked up at Brother Jeris and smiled questioningly.

The master of the copyroom turned quickly away. The back of his neck grew red. On the following day, Francis unpacked his quills, dyes, gold leaf, and resumed his labor on the illuminated diagram.

9 A few months after the departure of Monsignor Aguerra, there came a second donkey train—with a full complement of clerks and armed guards for defense against highwaymen, mutant maniacs, and rumored dragons—to the abbey from New Rome. This time the expedition was headed by a monsignor with small horns and pointy fangs, who announced that he was charged with the duty of opposing the canonization of the Blessed Leibowitz, and that he had come to investigate—and perhaps fix responsibility for, he hinted —certain incredible and hysterical rumors which had filtered out of the abbey and lamentably reached even the gates of New Rome. He made it evident that he would tolerate no romantic nonsense, as a certain earlier visitor perhaps had done.

The abbot greeted him politely and offered him an iron cot in a cell with a south exposure, after apologizing for the fact that the guest suite had been recently exposed to smallpox. The monsignor was attended by his own staff, and ate mush and herbs with the monks in the refectory—quail and chaparral cocks being unaccountably scarce that season, so the huntsmen reported.

This time, the abbot did not feel it necessary to warn Francis against any too liberal exercise of his imagination. Let him exercise it, if he dared. There was small danger of the *advocatus diaboli* giving immediate credence even to the truth, without first giving it a thorough thrashing and thrusting his fingers into its wounds.

"I understand you are prone to fainting spells," said Monsignor Flaught when he had Brother Francis alone and had fixed him with what Francis decided was a malign glare. "Tell me, is there any epilepsy in your family? Madness? Mutant neural patterns?"

"None, Excellency."

"I'm not an 'Excellency,'" snapped the priest. "Now, we're going to get the *truth* out of you." *A little simple straightforward surgery should be adequate,* his tone seemed to imply, *with only a minor amputation being required.*

"Are you aware that documents can be artificially aged?" he demanded.

Brother Francis was not so aware.

"Do you realize that the name, Emily, did not appear among the papers you found?"

"Oh, but it—" He paused, suddenly uncertain.

"The name which appeared was Em, was it not?—which *might* be a diminutive for Emily?"

"I—I believe that is correct, Messér."

"But it might also be a diminutive for *Emma*, might it not? And the name Emma DID appear in the box!"

Francis was silent.

"*Well?*"

"What was the question, Messér?"

"Never mind! I just thought I'd tell you that the evidence suggests that 'Em' was for Emma, and 'Emma' was not a diminutive of Emily. What do you say to that?"

"I had no previous opinion on the subject, Messér, but—"

"But what?"

"Aren't husband and wife often careless about what they call each other?"

"*ARE YOU BEING FLIPPANT WITH ME?*"

"No, messér."

"Now, tell the truth! How did you happen to discover that

shelter, and what is this fantastic twaddle about an apparition?"

Brother Francis attempted to explain. The *advocatus diaboli* interrupted with periodic snorts and sarcastic queries, and when he was finished, the advocate raked at his story with semantic tooth and nail until Francis himself wondered if he had really seen the old man or had imagined the incident.

The cross-examining technique was ruthless, but Francis found the experience less frightening than an interview with the abbot. The devil's advocate could do no worse than tear him limb from limb this one time, and the knowledge that the operation would soon be over helped the amputee to bear the pain. When facing the abbot, however, Francis was always aware that a blunder could be punished again and again, Arkos being his ruler for a lifetime and the perpetual inquisitor of his soul.

And Monsignor Flaught seemed to find the monk's story too distressingly simple-minded to warrant full-scale attack, after observing Brother Francis' reaction to the initial onslaught.

"Well, Brother, if that's your story and you stick to it, I don't think we'll be bothered with you at all. Even if it's true—which I don't admit—it's so trivial it's silly. Do you realize that?"

"That's what *I* always thought, Messér," sighed Brother Francis, who had for many years tried to detach the importance which others had attached to the pilgrim.

"Well, it's high time you said so!" Flaught snapped.

"I always said that I *thought* he was *probably* just an old man."

Monsignor Flaught covered his eyes with his hand and sighed heavily. His experience with uncertain witnesses led him to say no more.

Before leaving the abbey, the *advocatus diaboli*, like the Saint's advocate before him, stopped at the scriptorium and asked to see the illuminated commemoration of the Leibowitz blueprint ("that dreadful incomprehensibility" as Flaught called it). This time the monk's hands trembled not with eagerness but with fear, for once again he might be forced to abandon the project. Monsignor Flaught gazed at the lambskin in silence. He swallowed thrice. At last he forced himself to nod.

"Your imagery is vivid," he admitted, "but we all knew *that*, didn't we?" He paused. "You've been working on it how long now?"

"Six years, Messér—intermittently."

"Yes, well, it would seem that you have at least as many years to go."

Monsignor Flaught's horns immediately shortened by an inch, and his fangs disappeared entirely. He departed the same evening for New Rome.

The years flowed smoothly by, seaming the faces of the young and adding gray to their temples. The perpetual labor of the monastery continued, daily storming heaven with the ever-recurring hymn of the Divine Office, daily supplying the world with a slow trickle of copied and recopied manuscript, occasionally renting clerks and scribes to the episcopate, to ecclesiastical tribunals, and to such few secular powers as would hire them. Brother Jeris developed ambitions of building a printing press, but Arkos quashed the plan when he heard of it. There was neither sufficient paper nor proper ink available, nor any demand for inexpensive books in a world smug in its illiteracy. The copyroom continued with pot and quill.

On the Feast of the Five Holy Fools, a Vatican messenger arrived with glad tidings for the Order. Monsignor Flaught had withdrawn all objections and was doing penance before an ikon of the Beatus Leibowitz. Monsignor Aguerra's case was proved; the Pope had directed that a decree be issued recommending canonization. The date for the formal proclamation was set for the coming Holy Year, and was to coincide with the calling of a General Council of the Church for the purpose of making a careful restatement of doctrine concerning the limitation of the *magisterium* to matters of faith and morals; it was a question which had been settled many times in history, but it seemed to re-arise in new forms in every century, especially in those dark periods when man's "knowledge" of wind, stars, and rain was really only belief. During the time of the council, the founder of the Albertian Order would be enrolled in the Calendar of Saints.

The announcement was followed by a period of rejoicing at the abbey. Dom Arkos, now withered by age and close to dotage, summoned Brother Francis into his presence and wheezed:

"His Holiness invites us to New Rome for the canonization. Prepare to leave."

"I, m'Lord?"

"You alone. Brother Pharmacist forbids me to travel, and it would not be well for Father Prior to leave while I am ill.

"Now don't faint on me again," Dom Arkos added querulously. "You're probably getting more credit than you deserve for the fact that the court accepted the death date of Emily Leibowitz as conclusively proved. But His Holiness invited you anyway. I suggest you thank God and claim no credit."

Brother Francis tottered. "His Holiness . . . ?"

"Yes. Now, we're sending the original Leibowitz blueprint to the Vatican. What do you think about taking along your illuminated commemoration as a personal gift to the Holy Father?"

"Uh," said Francis.

The abbot revived him, blessed him, called him a good simpleton, and sent him to pack his bindlestiff.

10 The trip to New Rome would require at least three months, perhaps longer, the time depending to some extent on the distance which Francis could cover before the inevitable band of robbers relieved him of his ass. He would be traveling alone and unarmed, carrying only his bindlestiff and begging bowl in addition to the relic and its illuminated replica. He prayed that ignorant robbers would have no use for the latter; for, indeed, among the bandits of the wayside were sometimes kindly thieves who took only what was of value to them, and permitted their victim to retain his life, carcass, and personal effects. Others were less considerate.

As a precaution, Brother Francis wore a black patch over his right eye. The peasants were a superstitious lot and could often be routed by even a hint of the evil eye. Thus armed and equipped, he set out to obey the summons of the *Sacerdos Magnus,* that Most Holy Lord and Ruler, Leo *Pappas* XXI.

Nearly two months after leaving the abbey, the monk met his robber on a heavily wooded mountain trail, far from any human settlement except the Valley of the Misborn, which lay a few miles beyond a peak to the west, where, leperlike, a colony of the genetically monstrous lived in seclusion from the world. There were some such colonies which were supervised by hospitalers of Holy Church, but the Valley of the Misborn was not among them. Sports who had escaped death at the hands of the forest tribes had congregated there several centuries ago. Their ranks were continually replenished by warped and crawling things that sought refuge from the world, but some among them were fertile and gave birth. Often such children inherited the monstrosity of the parent stock. Often they were born dead or never reached maturity. But occasionally the monstrous trait was recessive, and an apparently normal child resulted from the union of sports. Sometimes, however, the superficially "normal" offspring were blighted by some invisible deformity of heart or mind that bereft them, seemingly, of the essence of humanity while leaving them its appearances. Even within the Church, some had dared espouse the view that such creatures truly had been deprived of the *Dei imago* from conception, that their souls were but animal souls, that they might with impunity under the Natural Law be destroyed as animal and not Man, that God had visited animal issue upon the species as a punishment for the sins that had nearly destroyed humankind. Few theologians whose believe in Hell had never failed them would deprive their God of recourse to *any* form of temporal punishment, but for men to take it upon themselves to judge any creature born of woman to be lacking in the divine image was to usurp the privilege of Heaven. Even the idiot which seems less gifted than a dog, or a pig, or a goat, shall, if born of woman, be called an immortal soul, thundered the *magisterium*, and thundered it again and again. After several such pronouncements, aimed at curbing infanticide, had issued from New Rome, the luckless misborn had come to be called the "Pope's nephews," or the "Pope's children," by some.

"Let that which is born alive of human parents be suffered to live," the previous Leo had said, "in accordance with both the Natural Law and the Divine Law of Love; let it be cherished as Child and nurtured, whatever its form and demeanor, for it is a fact available to natural reason alone, unaided by Divine Revelation, that among the Natural Rights of Man the right to parental assistance in an attempt to survive is precedent to all other rights, and may not be modified legitimately by Society or State except insofar as Princes are empowered to implement that right. Not even the beasts of the Earth act otherwise."

The robber that accosted Brother Francis was not in any obvious way one of the malformed, but that he came from the Valley of the Misborn was made evident when two hooded figures arose from behind a tangle of brush on the slope that overlooked the trail and hooted mockingly at the monk from ambush, while aiming at him with drawn bows. From such a distance, Francis was not certain of his first impression that one hand grasped a bow with six fingers or an extra thumb; but there was no doubt at all that one of the robed figures was wearing a robe with two hoods, although he could make out no faces, nor could he determine whether the extra hood contained an extra head or not.

The robber himself stood in the trail directly ahead. He was a short man, but heavy as a bull, with a glazed knob of a pate and a jaw like a block of granite. He stood in the trail with his legs spread wide and his massive arms folded across his chest while he watched the approach of the small figure astride the ass. The robber, as best Brother Francis could see, was armed only with his own brawn and a knife which he did not bother to remove from his belt-thong. He beckoned Francis forward. When the monk stopped fifty yards away, one of the Pope's children unleashed an arrow; the missile whipped into the trail just behind the donkey, causing the animal to spurt ahead.

"Get off," the robber ordered.

The ass stopped in the path. Brother Francis tossed back his hood to reveal the eye patch and raised a trembling finger to touch it. He began lifting the patch slowly from his eye.

The robber tossed back his head and laughed a laugh that might have sprung, Francis thought, from the throat of Satan; the monk muttered an exorcism, but the robber appeared untouched.

"You black-sacked jeebers wore that one out years ago," he said. "Now get off."

Brother Francis smiled, shrugged, and dismounted without further protest. The robber inspected the donkey, patting its flanks, examining teeth and hooves.

"Eat? Eat?" cried one of the robed creatures on the hillside.

"Not this time," barked the robber. "Too scrawny."

Brother Francis was not entirely convinced that they were talking about the donkey.

"Good day to you, sir," the monk said pleasantly. "You may take the ass. Walking will improve my health, I think." He smiled again and started away.

An arrow slashed into the trail at his feet.

"Stop that!" howled the robber, then to Francis: "Now strip. And let's see what's in that roll and in the package."

Brother Francis touched his begging bowl and made a gesture of helplessness, which brought only another scornful laugh from the robber.

"I've seen that alms-pot trick before too," he said. "The last man with a bowl had half a heklo of gold hidden in his boot. Now strip."

Brother Francis, who was not wearing boots, hopefully displayed his sandals, but the robber gestured impatiently. The monk untied his bindlestiff, spread its contents for display, and began to undress. The robber searched his clothing, found nothing, and tossed the clothing back to its owner, who breathed his gratitude; he had been expecting to be left naked on the trail.

"Now let's see inside that *other* package."

"It contains only documents, sir," the monk protested. "Of value to no one except the owner."

"Open it."

Silently Brother Francis untied the package and unwrapped the original blueprint and the illuminated commemoration thereof. The gold-leaf inlay and the colorful design flashed brilliantly in the sunlight that filtered through the foliage. The robber's craggy jaw dropped an inch. He whistled softly.

"What a pretty! Now wouldn't the woman like *that* to hang on the cabin wall!"

Francis went sick inside.

"*Gold!*" the robber shouted to his robed accomplices on the hill.

"*Eat? Eat?*" came the gurgling and chortling reply.

"We'll eat, never fear!" called the robber, then explained conversationally to Francis: "They get hungry after a couple of days just sitting there. Business is bad. Traffic's light these days."

Francis nodded. The robber resumed his admiration of the illuminated replica.

Lord, if Thou hast sent him to test me, then help me to die like a man, that he may take it only over the dead body of Thy servant. Holy Leibowitz, see this deed and pray for me—

"What is it?" the robber asked. "A charm?" He studied the two documents together for a time. "Oh! One is a ghost of the other. What magic is this?" He stared at Brother Francis with suspicious gray eyes. "What is it called?"

"Uh—Transistorized Control System for Unit Six-B," the monk stammered.

The robber, who had been looking at the documents upside down, could nevertheless see that one diagram involved a figure-background reversal of the other—an effect which seemed to intrigue him as much as the gold leaf. He traced out the similarities in design with a short and dirty forefinger, leaving a faint smudge on the illuminated lambskin. Francis held back tears.

"Please!" the monk gasped. "The gold is so thin, it's worth nothing to speak of. Weigh it in your hand. The whole thing weighs no more than the paper itself. It's of no use to you. Please, sir, take my clothing instead. Take the donkey, take my bindlestiff. Take whatever you will, but leave me these. They mean nothing to you."

The robber's gray gaze was meditative. He watched the monk's agitation and rubbed his jaw. "I'll let you keep your clothes and your donkey and everything *except* this," he offered. "I'll just take the charms, then."

"For the love of God, sir, then kill me too!" Brother Francis wailed.

The robber snickered. "We'll see. Tell me what they're for."

"Nothing. One is a memento of a man long dead. An ancient. The other is only a copy."

"What good are they to you?"

Francis closed his eyes for a moment and tried to think of a way to explain. "You know the forest tribes? How they venerate their ancestors?"

The gray eyes of the robber flashed angrily for a moment. *"We despise* our ancestors," he barked. "Cursed be they who gave us birth!"

"Cursed, cursed!" echoed one of the shrouded archers on the hillside.

"You know who we are? Where we are from?"

Francis nodded. "I meant no offense. The ancient whose relic this is—he is not our ancestor. He was our teacher of old. We venerate his memory. This is only like a keepsake, no more."

"What about the copy?"

"I made it myself. Please, sir, it took me fifteen years. It's nothing to you. Please—you wouldn't take fifteen years of a man's life—for no reason?"

"Fifteen *years?*" The robber threw back his head and howled with laughter. "You spent fifteen years making *that?*"

"Oh, but—" Francis was suddenly silent. His eyes swung toward the robber's stubby forefinger. The finger was tapping the original blueprint.

"*That* took you fifteen years? And it's almost ugly beside the other." He slapped his paunch and between guffaws kept pointing at the relic. "Ha! Fifteen years! So that's what you do way out there! *Why?* What is the dark ghost-image good for? Fifteen years to make that! Ho ho! What a woman's work!"

Brother Francis watched him in stunned silence. That the robber should mistake the sacred relic itself for the copy of the relic left him too shocked to reply.

Still laughing, the robber took both documents in his hands and prepared to rip them both in half.

"*Jesus, Mary, Joseph!*" the monk screamed and went to his knees in the trail. "For the love of God, sir!"

The robber tossed the papers on the ground. "I'll wrestle you for them," he offered sportingly. "Those against my blade."

"Done," said Francis impulsively, thinking that a contest would at least afford Heaven a chance to intervene in an unobtrusive way. *O God, Thou who strengthened Jacob so that he overcame the angel on the rock . . .*

They squared off. Brother Francis crossed himself. The robber took his knife from his belt-thong and tossed it after the papers. They circled.

Three seconds later, the monk lay groaning on the flat of his back under a short mountain of muscle. A sharp rock seemed to be severing his spine.

"Heh-heh," said the robber, and arose to reclaim his knife and roll up the documents.

Hands folded as if in prayer, Brother Francis crept after

him on his knees, begging at the top of his lungs. "Please, then, take only one, *not both!* Please!"

"You've got to *buy* it back now," the robber chortled. "I won them fair enough."

"I have nothing, I am *poor!*"

"That's all right, if you want them that bad, you'll get gold. Two heklos of gold, that's the ransom. Bring it here any time. I'll tuck your things in my shanty. You want them back, just bring the gold."

"Listen, they're important to other people, not to me. I was taking them to the Pope. Maybe they'll pay you for the important one. But let me have the other one just to *show* them. It's of no importance at all."

The robber laughed over his shoulder. "I believe you'd kiss a boot to get it back."

Brother Francis caught up with him and fervently kissed his boot.

This proved too much for even such a fellow as the robber. He shoved the monk away with his foot, separated the two papers, and flung one of them in Francis' face with a curse. He climbed aboard the monk's donkey and started riding it up the slope toward the ambush. Brother Francis snatched up the precious document and hiked along beside the robber, thanking him profusely and blessing him repeatedly while the robber guided the ass toward the shrouded archers.

"*Fifteen years!*" the robber snorted, and again shoved Francis away with his foot. "Begone!" He waved the illuminated splendor aloft in the sunlight. "Remember—two heklos of gold'll ransom your keepsake. And tell your Pope I won it fair."

Francis stopped climbing. He sent a glowing cross of benediction after the departing bandit and quietly praised God for the existence of such selfless robbers, who could make such an ignorant mistake. He fondled the original blueprint lovingly as he hiked away down the trail. The robber was proudly displaying the beautiful commemoration to his mutant companions on the hill.

"*Eat! Eat!*" said one of them, petting the donkey.

"Ride, ride," corrected the robber. "Eat later."

But when Brother Francis had left them far behind, a great sadness gradually engulfed him. The taunting voice still rang in his ears. *Fifteen years! So that's what you do over there! Fifteen years! What a woman's work! Ho ho ho ho . . .*

The robber had made a mistake. But the fifteen years were gone anyhow, and with it all the love and torment that had gone into the commemoration.

Cloistered as he had been, Francis had become unaccustomed to the ways of the outside world, to its harsh habits and curt attitudes. He found his heart deeply troubled by the robber's mockery. He thought of Brother Jeris' gentler mockery of earlier years. Maybe Brother Jeris had been right.

His head hung low in his hood as he traveled slowly on.

At least there was the original relic. At least.

11 The hour had come. Brother Francis, in his simple monk's habit, had never felt less important than at that moment, as he knelt in the majestic basilica before the beginning of the ceremony. The stately movements, the vivid swirls of color, the sounds which accompanied the ceremonious preparations for ceremony, already seemed liturgical in spirit, making it difficult to bear in mind that nothing of importance was happening yet. Bishops, monsignori, cardinals, priests, and various lay-functionaries in elegant, antiquated dress moved to and fro in the great church, but their comings and goings were graceful clockwork which never paused, stumbled, or changed its mind to rush in the other direction. A *sampetrius* entered the basilica; so grandly was he attired that Francis at first mistook the cathedral workman for a prelate. The *sampetrius* carried a footstool. He carried it with such casual pomp that the monk, if he had not been kneeling, might have genuflected as the object drifted by. The *sampetrius* dropped to one knee before the high altar, then crossed to the papal throne where he substituted the new footstool for one which seemed to have a loose leg; thereupon, he departed by the same route as he had come. Brother Francis marveled at the studied elegance of movement that accompanied even the trivial. No one hurried. No one minced or fumbled. No motion occurred which did not quietly contribute to the dignity and overpowering beauty of this ancient place, even as the motionless statues and paintings contributed to it. Even the whisper of one's breathing seemed to echo faintly from distant apses.

Terribilis est locus iste: hic domus Dei est, et porta caeli; terrible indeed, House of God, Gate of Heaven!

Some of the statues were alive, he observed after a time. A suit of armor stood against the wall a few yards to his left. Its mailed fist held the staff of a gleaming battle-ax. Not even the plume of its helmet had stirred during the time Brother Francis had been kneeling there. A dozen identical suits of armor stood at intervals along the walls. Only after seeing a horsefly crawl through the visor of the "statue" on his left did he suspect that the warlike husk contained an occupant. His eye could detect no motion, but the armor emitted a few metallic creaks while it harbored the horsefly. These, then, must be the papal guard, so renowned in knightly battle: the small private army of God's First Vicar.

A captain of the guard was making a stately tour of his men. For the first time, the statue moved. It lifted its visor in salute. The captain thoughtfully paused and used his kerchief to brush the horsefly from the forehead of the expressionless face inside the helmet before passing on. The statue lowered its visor and resumed its immobility.

The stately décor of the basilica was briefly marred by the entrance of pilgrim throngs. The throngs were well organized and efficiently ushered, but they were patently strangers to this place. Most of them seemed to tread on tiptoe to their stations, cautious to create no sound and as little movement as possible, unlike the *sampetrii* and New Roman clergy who made sound and motion eloquent. Here and there among the pilgrims someone stifled a cough or stumbled.

Suddenly the basilica became warlike, as the guard was strengthened. A new troop of mailed statues tramped into the sanctuary itself, dropped to one knee, and tilted their pike-staffs, saluting the altar before taking their posts. Two of them stood flanking the papal throne. A third fell to his knees at the throne's right hand; he remained kneeling there with the sword of Peter lying across his upraised palms. The tableau became motionless again, except for occasional dancing of flame among the altar candles.

Upon the hallowed silence burst a sudden peal of trumpets.

The sound's intensity mounted until the throbbing *Ta-ra Ta-ra-raa* could be felt upon one's face and grew painful to the ears. The voice of the trumpets was not musical but annunciatory. The first notes began in mid-scale, then climbed slowly in pitch, intensity, and urgency, until the monk's scalp crawled, and there seemed to be nothing at all in the basilica but the explosion of the tubas.

Then, dead silence—followed by the cry of a tenor:·

FIRST CANTOR: *"Appropinquat agnis pastor et ovibus pascendis."*
SECOND CANTOR: *"Genua nunc flectantur omnia."*
FIRST CANTOR: *"Jussit olim Jesus Petrum pascere gregem Domini."*
SECOND CANTOR: *"Ecce Petrus Pontifex Maximus."*
FIRST CANTOR: *"Gaudeat igitur populus Christi, et gratias agat Domino."*
SECOND CANTOR: *"Nam docebimur a Spiritu sancto."*
CHOIR: *"Alleluia, alleluia—"*

The crowd arose and then knelt in a slow wave that followed the movement of the chair containing the frail old man in white who gestured his blessings to the people as the gold, black, purple, and red procession moved him slowly toward the throne. Breath kept choking up in the throat of the small monk from a distant abbey in a distant desert. It was impossible to see everything that was happening, so overwhelming was the tide of music and motion, drowning one's senses and sweeping the mind along willy-nilly toward that which was soon to come.

The ceremony was brief. Its intensity would have become unendurable had it been longer. A monsignor—Malfreddo Aguerra, the Saint's advocate himself, Brother Francis observed—approached the throne and knelt. After a brief silence, he voiced his plea in plain chant.

"Sancte pater, ab Sapientia summa petimus ut ille Beatus Leibowitz cujus miracula mirati sunt multi . . ."

The request called upon Leo to enlighten his people by solemn definition concerning the pious belief that the Beatus Leibowitz was indeed a saint, worthy of the *dulia* of the Church as well as the veneration of the faithful.

"Gratissima Nobis causa, fili," the voice of the old man in white sang in response, explaining that his own heart's desire was to announce by solemn proclamation that the blessed Martyr was among the saints, but also that it was by divine guidance alone, *sub ducatu sancti Spiritus*, that he might comply with Aguerra's request. He asked all to pray for that guidance.

Again the thunder of the choir filled the basilica with the

Litany of the Saints: "Father-of-Heaven, God, have mercy on us. Son, Repurchaser-of-the-World, God, have mercy on us. Ghost-Most-Holy, God, have mercy on us. O Sacred Three-foldhood, God-One-and-Only, *miserere nobis!* Holy Mary, pray for us. *Sancta Dei Genitrix, ora pro nobis. Sancta Virgo virginum, ora pro nobis . . .*" The thunder of the litany continued. Francis looked up at a painting of the Blessed Leibowitz, newly unveiled. The fresco was of heroic proportions. It portrayed the trial of the Beatus before the mob, but the face was not wryly smiling as it smiled in Fingo's work. It was, however, majestic, Francis thought, and in keeping with the rest of the basilica.

"Omnes sancti Martyres, orate pro nobis . . ."

When the litany was finished, again Monsignor Malfreddo Aguerra made his plea to the Pope, asking that the name of Isaac Edward Leibowitz be formally enrolled in the Calendar of Saints. Again the guiding Spirit was invoked, as the Pope chanted the *Veni, Creator Spiritus.*

And yet a third time Malfreddo Aguerra pleaded for the proclamation.

"Surgat ergo Petrus ipse. . . ."

At last it came. The twenty-first Leo intoned the decision of the Church, rendered under the guidance of the Holy Spirit, proclaiming the existing fact that an ancient and rather obscure technician named Leibowitz was truly a saint in Heaven, whose powerful intercession might, and of right ought to be, reverently implored. A feast day was named for a Mass in his honor.

"Holy Leibowitz, intercede for us," Brother Francis breathed with the others.

After a brief prayer, the choir burst into the *Te Deum.* After a Mass honoring the new saint, it was finished.

Escorted by two scarlet-liveried *sedarii* of the outer palace, the small party of pilgrims passed through a seemingly endless sequence of corridors and antechambers, halting occasionally before the ornate table of some new official who examined credentials and goose-quilled his signature on a *licet adire* for a *sedarius* to hand to the next official, whose title grew progressively longer and less pronounceable as the party proceeded. Brother Francis was shivering. Among his fellow pilgrims were two bishops, a man wearing ermine and gold, a clan chief of the forest people, converted but still wearing the panther skin tunic and panther headgear of his tribal totem, a leather-clad simpleton carrying a hooded peregrine falcon on one wrist—evidently as a gift to the Holy Father—and several women, all of whom seemed to be wives or concubines—as best Francis could judge by their actions—of the "converted" clan chief of the panther people; or perhaps they were ex-concubines put away by canon but not by tribal custom.

After climbing the *scala caelestis*, the pilgrims were welcomed by the somberly clad *cameralis gestor* and ushered into the small anteroom of the vast consistorial hall.

"The Holy Father will receive them here," the high-ranking lackey softly informed the *sedarius* who carried the credentials. He glanced over the pilgrims, rather disapprovingly, Francis thought. He whispered briefly to the *sedarius*. The *sedarius* reddened and whispered to the clan chief. The clan chief glowered and removed his fanged and snarling headdress, letting the panther head dangle over his shoulder. There was a brief conference about positions, while His Supreme Unctuousness, the leading lackey, in tones so soft as to seem reproving, stationed his visiting chess pieces about the room in accordance with some arcane protocol which only the *sedarii* seemed to understand.

The Pope was not long in arriving. The little man in the white cassock, surrounded by his retinue, strode briskly into the audience room. Brother Francis experienced a sudden dizzy spell. He remembered that Dom Arkos had threatened to flay him alive if he fainted during the audience, and he steeled himself against it.

The line of pilgrims knelt. The old man in white gently bade them arise. Brother Francis finally found the courage to focus his eyes. In the basilica, the Pope had been only a radiant spot of white in a sea of color. Gradually, here in the audience room, Brother Francis perceived at closer range that the Pope was *not*, like the fabled nomads, nine feet tall. To the monk's surprise, the frail old man, Father of Princes and Kings, Bridge-Builder of the World, and Vicar on Earth of Christ, appeared much less ferocious than Dom Arkos, *Abbas*.

The Pope moved slowly along the line of pilgrims, greeting each, embracing one of the bishops, conversing with each in his own dialect or through an interpreter, laughing at the expression of the monsignor to whom he transferred the task of carrying the falconer's bird, and addressing the clan

leader of the forest people with a peculiar hand gesture and
a grunted word of forest dialect which caused that panther-
clad chieftain to glow with a sudden grin of delight. The
Pope noticed the dangling panther headgear and paused to
replace it on the tribesman's head. The latter's chest bulged
with pride; he glared about the room, apparently to catch
the eye of His Supreme Unctuousness, the leading lackey,
but that official seemed to have vanished into the woodwork.

The Pope drew nearer to Brother Francis.

Ecce Petrus Pontifex . . . Behold Peter, the high priest. Leo
XXI, himself: "Whom alone, God did appoint Prince over all
countries and kingdoms, to root up, pull down, waste, destroy, plant, and build, that he might preserve a faithful
people—" And yet in the face of Leo, the monk saw a kindly
meekness which hinted that he was worthy of that title,
loftier than any bestowed upon princes and kings, whereby
he was called "the slave of the slaves of God."

Francis knelt quickly to kiss the Fisherman's ring. As he
arose, he found himself clutching the relic of the Saint behind him as if ashamed to display it. The Pontiff's amber
eyes compelled him gently. Leo spoke softly in the curial
manner: an affectation which he seemed to dislike as burden-
some, but which he practiced for custom's sake in speaking
to visitors less savage than the panther chief.

"Our heart was deeply grieved when we heard of your mis-
fortune, dear son. An account of your journey reached our
ears. At our own request you traveled here, but while on
your way, you were set upon by robbers. Is that not true?"

"Yes, Holy Father. But it is really of no importance. I
mean— It *was* important, except—" Francis stammered.

The white old man smiled gently. "We know that you
brought us a gift, and that it was stolen from you along the
way. Be not troubled for that. Your presence is gift enough
to us. Long have we cherished the hope of greeting in person
the discoverer of Emily Leibowitz' remains. We know, too,
of your labors at the abbey. For the Brothers of Saint Leibowitz, we have always felt a most fervent affection. Without your work, the world's amnesia might well be total. As
the Church, *Mysticum Christi Corpus,* is a Body, so has your
Order served as an organ of memory in that Body. We owe
much to your holy Patron and Founder. Future ages may
owe him even more. May we hear more of your journey,
dear son?"

Brother Francis produced the blueprint. "The highwayman

was kind enough to leave this in my keeping, Holy Father. He—he mistook it for a copy of the illumination which I was bringing as a gift."

"You did not correct his mistake?"

Brother Francis blushed. "I'm ashamed to admit, Holy Father—"

"This, then, is the original relic you found in the crypt?"

"Yes—"

The Pope's smile became wry. "So, then—the bandit thought your work was the treasure itself? Ah—even a robber can have a keen eye for art, yes? Monsignor Aguerra told us of the beauty of your commemoration. What a pity that it was stolen."

"It was nothing, Holy Father. I only regret that I wasted fifteen years."

"*Wasted?* How 'wasted'? If the robber had not been misled by the beauty of your commemoration, he might have taken *this*, might he not?"

Brother Francis admitted the possibility.

The twenty-first Leo took the ancient blueprint in his withered hands and carefully unrolled it. He studied its design for a time in silence, then: "Tell us, do you understand the symbols used by Leibowitz? The meaning of the, uh, thing represented?"

"No, Holy Father, my ignorance is complete."

The Pope leaned toward him to whisper: "So is ours." He chuckled, pressed his lips to the relic as if kissing an altar stone, then rerolled it and handed it to an attendant. "We thank you from the bottom of our heart for those fifteen years, beloved son," he added to Brother Francis. "Those years were spent to preserve this original. Never think of them as wasted. Offer them to God. Someday the meaning of the original may be discovered, and may prove important." The old man blinked—or was it a wink? Francis was almost convinced that the Pope had winked at him. "We'll have you to thank for that."

The wink, or the blink, seemed to bring the room into clearer focus for the monk. For the first time, he noticed a moth-hole in the Pope's cassock. The cassock itself was almost threadbare. The carpet in the audience room was worn through in spots. Plaster had fallen from the ceiling in several places. But dignity had overshadowed poverty. Only for a moment after the wink did Brother Francis notice hints of poverty at all. The distraction was transient.

"By you, we wish to send our warmest regards to all members of your community and to your abbot," Leo was saying. "To them, as to you, we wish to extend our apostolic benediction. We shall give you a letter to them announcing the benediction." He paused, then blinked, or winked, again. "Quite incidentally, the letter will be safeguarded. We shall affix to it the *Noli molestare,* excommunicating anyone who waylays the bearer."

Brother Francis murmured his thanks for such insurance against highwaymanship; he did not deem it fitting to add that the robber would be unable to read the warning or understand the penalty. "I shall do my best to deliver it, Holy Father."

Again, Leo leaned close to whisper: "And to you, we shall give a special token of our affection. Before you leave, see Monsignor Aguerra. We would prefer to give it to you by our own hand, but this is not the proper moment. The monsignor will present it for us. Do with it what you will."

"Thank you very much indeed, Holy Father."

"And now good-bye, beloved son."

The Pontiff moved on, speaking to each pilgrim in the line, and when it was over: the solemn benediction. The audience had ended.

Monsignor Aguerra touched Brother Francis' arm as the pilgrim group passed out the portals. He embraced the monk warmly. The postulator of the Saint's cause had aged so greatly that Francis recognized him only with difficulty at close range. But Francis, too, was gray at the temples, and had grown wrinkled about the eyes from squinting over the copy-table. The monsignor handed him a package and a letter as they descended the *scala caelestis.*

Francis glanced at the letter's address and nodded. His own name was written on the package, which bore a diplomatic seal. "For me, Messér?"

"Yes, a personal token from the Holy Father. Better not open it here. Now, can I do anything for you before you leave New Rome? I'd be glad to show you anything you've missed."

Brother Francis thought briefly. There had already been an exhaustive tour. "I *would* like to see the basilica just once again, Messér," he said at last.

"Why, of course. But is *that* all?"

Brother Francis paused again. They had fallen behind the

other departing pilgrims. "I would like to confess," he added softly.

"Nothing easier than that," said Aguerra, adding with a chuckle: "You're in the right town, you know. Here, you can get anything absolved that you're worried about. Is it something deadly enough to require the attention of the Pope?"

Francis reddened and shook his head.

"How about the Grand Penitentiary, then? He'll not only absolve you if you're repentant, he'll even hit you over the head with a rod in the bargain."

"I meant—I was asking *you*, Messér," the monk stammered.

"*Me?* Why me? I'm nobody fancy. Here you are in a whole town full of red hats, and you want to confess to Malfreddo Aguerra."

"Because—because you were our Patron's advocate," the monk explained.

"Oh, I see. Why of course I'll hear your confession. But I can't absolve you in the name of your Patron, you know. It'll have to be the Holy Trinity as usual. Will that do?"

Francis had little to confess, but his heart had long been troubled—at the prompting of Dom Arkos—by the fear that his discovery of the shelter might have hindered the case for the Saint. Leibowitz' postulator heard him, counseled him, and absolved him in the basilica, then led him around that ancient church. During the ceremony of canonization and the Mass that followed, Brother Francis had noticed only the majestic splendor of the building. Now the aged monsignor pointed to crumbling masonry, places in need of repair, and the shameful condition of some of the older frescoes. Again he caught a glimpse of a poverty which dignity veiled. The Church was not wealthy in this age.

At last, Francis was free to open the package. The package contained a purse. In the purse were two heklos of gold. He glanced at Malfreddo Aguerra. The monsignor smiled.

"You *did* say that the robber *won* the commemoration from you in a wrestling match, didn't you?" Aguerra asked.

"Yes, Messér."

"Well then, even if you were forced into it, you made the choice to wrestle him for it yourself, didn't you? You accepted his challenge?"

The monk nodded.

"Then I don't think you'd be condoning the wrong if you bought it back." He clapped the monk's shoulder and blessed him. Then it was time to go.

The small keeper of the flame of knowledge trudged back toward his abbey on foot. There were days and weeks on the trail, but his heart was singing as he approached the robber's outpost. *Do with it what you will,* Pope Leo had said of the gold. Not only that, the monk had now, in addition to the purse, an answer to the robber's scornful question. He thought of the books in the audience room, waiting there for a reawakening.

The robber, however, was not waiting at his outpost as Francis had hoped. There were recent footprints in the trail at that place, but the prints led cross-trail and there was no sign of the robber. The sun filtered through the trees to cover the ground with leafy shadows. The forest was not dense, but it offered shade. He sat down beside the trail to wait.

An owl hooted at midday from the relative darkness in the depths of some distant arroyo. Buzzards circled in a patch of blue beyond the treetops. It seemed peaceful in the forest that day. As he listened sleepily to the sparrows fluttering in nearby brush, he found himself not greatly concerned about whether the robber came today or tomorrow. So long was his journey, that he would not be unhappy to enjoy a day of rest while waiting. He sat watching the buzzards. Occasionally he glanced down the trail that led toward his distant home in the desert. The robber had chosen an excellent location for his lair. From this place, one could observe more than a mile of trail in either direction while remaining unobserved in the thatch of forest.

Something moved on the trail in the distance.

Brother Francis shielded his eyes and studied the distant movement. There was a sunny area down the road where a brush fire had cleared several acres of land around the trail that led southwest. The trail shimmered under a mirror of heat in the sunswept region. He could not see clearly because of the shiny reflections, but there was motion in the midst of the heat. There was a wriggling black iota. At times it seemed to wear a head. At times it was completely obscured in the heat glaze, but nevertheless he could determine that it was gradually approaching. Once, when the edge of a cloud brushed at the sun, the heat shimmer subsided for a few seconds; his tired and myopic eyes determined then that the wriggling iota was really a man, but at too great a distance for recognition. He shivered. Something about the iota was too familiar.

But no, it couldn't possibly be the same.

The monk crossed himself and began telling his rosary beads while his eyes remained intent on the distant thing in the heat shimmer.

While he had been waiting there for the robber, a debate had been in progress, higher on the side of the hill. The debate had been conducted in whispered monosyllables, and had lasted for nearly an hour. Now the debate was ended. Two-Hoods had conceded to One-Hood. Together, the Pope's children stole quietly from behind their brush table and crept down the side of the hill.

They advanced to within ten yards of Francis before a pebble rattled. The monk was murmuring the third Ave of the Fourth Glorious Mystery of the rosary when he happened to look around.

The arrow hit him squarely between the eyes.

"*Eat! Eat! Eat!*" the Pope's child cried.

On the trail to the southwest the old wanderer sat down on a log and closed his eyes to rest them against the sun. He fanned himself with a tattered basket hat and munched his spice-leaf quid. He had been wandering for a long time. The search seemed endless, but there was always the promise of finding what he sought across the next rise or beyond the bend in the trail. When he had finished fanning himself, he clapped the hat back on his head and scratched at his brushy beard while blinking around at the landscape. There was a patch of unburned forest on the hillside just ahead. It offered welcome shade, but still the wanderer sat there in the sunlight and watched the curious buzzards. They had congregated, and they were swooping rather low over the wooded patch. One bird made bold to descend among the trees, but it quickly flapped into view again, flew under power until it found a rising column of air, then went into gliding ascent. The dark host of scavengers seemed to be expending more than a usual amount of energy at flapping their wings. Usually they soared, conserving strength. Now they thrashed the air above the hillside as if impatient to land.

As long as the buzzards remained interested but reluctant, the wanderer remained the same. There were cougars in these hills. Beyond the peak were things even worse than cougars, and sometimes they prowled afar.

The wanderer waited. Finally the buzzards descended among the trees. The wanderer waited five minutes more. At last he arose and limped ahead toward the forested patch, dividing his weight between his game leg and his staff.

After a while he entered the forested area. The buzzards were busy at the remains of a man. The wanderer chased the birds away with his cudgel and inspected the human remnants. Significant portions were missing. There was an arrow through the skull, protruding at the back of the neck. The old man looked nervously around at the brush. There was no one in sight, but there were plenty of footprints in the vicinity of the trail. It was not safe to stay.

Safe or not, the job had to be done. The old wanderer found a place where the earth was soft enough for digging with hands and stick. While he dug, the angry buzzards circled low over the treetops. Sometimes darting earthward but then flapping their way skyward again. For an hour, then two, they fluttered anxiously over the wooded hillside.

One bird finally landed. It strutted indignantly about a mound of fresh earth with a rock marker at one end. Disappointed, it took wing again. The flock of dark scavengers abandoned the site and soared high on the rising currents of air while they hungrily watched the land.

There was a dead hog beyond the Valley of the Misborn. The buzzards observed it gaily and glided down for a feast. Later, in a far mountain pass, a cougar licked her chops and left her kill. The buzzards seemed thankful for the chance to finish her meal.

The buzzards laid their eggs in season and lovingly fed their young: a dead snake, and bits of a feral dog.

The younger generation waxed strong, soared high and far on black wings, waiting for the fruitful Earth to yield up her bountiful carrion. Sometimes dinner was only a toad. Once it was a messenger from New Rome.

Their flight carried them over the midwestern plains. They were delighted with the bounty of good things which the nomads left lying on the land during their ride-over toward the south.

The buzzards laid their eggs in season and lovingly fed their young. Earth had nourished them bountifully for centuries. She would nourish them for centuries more. . . .

Pickings were good for a while in the region of the Red River; but then out of the carnage, a city-state arose. For rising city-states, the buzzards had no fondness, although they approved of their eventual fall. They shied away from Texarkana and ranged far over the plain to the west. After the manner of all living things, they replenished the Earth many times with their kind.

Eventually it was the Year of Our Lord 3174.

There were rumors of war.

12 Marcus Apollo became certain of war's imminence the moment he overheard Hannegan's third wife tell a serving maid that her favorite courtier had returned with his skin intact from a mission to the tents of Mad Bear's clan. The fact that he had come back alive from the nomad encampment meant that a war was brewing. Purportedly, the emissary's mission had been to tell the Plains tribes that the civilized states had entered into the Agreement of the Holy Scourge concerning the disputed lands, and would hereafter wreak stern vengeance on the nomadic peoples and bandit groups for any further raiding activities. But no man carried such news to Mad Bear and came back alive. Therefore, Apollo concluded, the ultimatum had not been delivered, and Hannegan's emissary had gone out to the Plains with an ulterior purpose. And the purpose was all too clear.

Apollo picked his way politely through the small throng of guests, his sharp eyes searching out Brother Claret and trying to attract his glance. Apollo's tall figure in severe black cassock with a small flash of color at the waist to denote his rank stood out sharply in contrast to the kaleidoscope-whirl of color worn by others in the banquet hall, and he was not long in catching his clerk's eye and nodding him toward the table of refreshments which was now reduced to a litter of scraps, greasy cups, and a few roast squabs that looked overcooked. Apollo dragged at the dregs of the punch bowl with the ladle, observed a dead roach floating among the spices, and thoughtfully handed the first cup to Brother Claret as the clerk approached.

"Thank you, Messér," said Claret, not noticing the roach. "You wanted to see me?"

"As soon as the reception's over. In my quarters. Sarkal came back alive."

"Oh."

"I've never heard a more ominous 'oh.' I take it you understand the interesting implications?"

"Certainly, Messér. It means the Agreement was a fraud on Hannegan's part, and he intends to use it against—"

"Shhh. Later." Apollo's eyes signaled the approach of an audience, and the clerk turned to refill his cup from the punch bowl. His interest became suddenly absorbed there, and he did not look at the lean figure in watered-silk who strode toward them from the entrance. Apollo smiled formally and bowed to the man. Their hand-clasp was brief and noticeably chilly.

"Well, Thon Taddeo," said the priest, "your presence surprises me. I thought you shunned such festive gatherings. What could be so special about this one to attract such a distinguished scholar?" He lifted his brows in mock perplexity.

"You're the attraction, of course," said the newcomer, matching Apollo's sarcasm, "and my only reason for attending."

"I?" He feigned surprise, but the assertion was probably true. The wedding reception of a half-sister was not the sort of thing that would impel Thon Taddeo to bedeck himself in formal finery and leave the cloistered halls of the collegium.

"As a matter of fact, I've been looking for you all day. They told me you'd be here. Otherwise—" He looked around the banquet hall and snorted irritably.

The snort cut whatever thread of fascination was tying Brother Claret's gaze to the punch bowl, and he turned to bow to the thon. "Care for punch, Thon Taddeo?" he asked, offering a full cup.

The scholar accepted it with a nod and drained it. "I wanted to ask you a little more about the Leibowitzian documents we discussed," he said to Marcus Apollo. "I had a letter from a fellow named Kornhoer at the abbey. He assured me they have writings that date back to the last years of the European-American civilization."

If the fact that he himself had assured the scholar of the same thing several months ago was irritating to Apollo, his expression gave no hint of it. "Yes," he said. "They're quite authentic, I'm told."

"If so, it strikes me as very mysterious that nobody's heard—but never mind that. Kornhoer listed a number of documents and texts they claim to have and described them. If they exist at all, I've got to see them."

"Oh?"

"Yes. If it's a hoax, it should be found out, and if it isn't, the data might well be priceless."

The monsignor frowned. "I assure you there is no hoax," he said stiffly.

"The letter contained an invitation to visit the abbey and study the documents. They've evidently heard of me."

"Not necessarily," said Apollo, unable to resist the opportunity. "They aren't particular about who reads their books, as long as he washes his hands and doesn't deface their property."

The scholar glowered. The suggestion that there might exist literate persons who had never heard his name did not please him.

"But there, then!" Apollo went on affably. "You have no problem. Accept their invitation, go to the abbey, study their relics. They'll make you welcome."

The scholar huffed irritably at the suggestion. "And travel through the Plains at a time when Mad Bear's clan is—" Thon Taddeo broke off abruptly.

"You were saying?" Apollo prompted, his face showing no special alertness, although a vein in his temple began to throb as he stared expectantly at Thon Taddeo.

"Only that it's a long dangerous trip, and I can't spare six months' absence from the collegium. I wanted to discuss the possibility of sending a well-armed party of the Mayor's guardsmen to fetch the documents here for study."

Apollo choked. He felt a childish impulse to kick the scholar in the shins. "I'm afraid," he said politely, "that would be quite impossible. But in any case, the matter is outside my sphere, and I'm afraid I can't be of any help to you."

"Why not?" Thon Taddeo demanded. "Aren't you the Vatican's nuncio to the Court of Hannegan?"

"Precisely. I represent New Rome, not the monastic Orders. The government of an abbey is in the hands of its abbot."

"But with a little pressure from New Rome . . ."

The impulse to kick shins surged swiftly. "We'd better discuss it later," Monsignor Apollo said curtly. "This evening in my study, if you like." He half turned, and looked back inquiringly as if to say *Well?*

"I'll be there," the scholar said sharply, and marched away.

"Why didn't you tell him flatly *no*, then and there?" Claret fumed when they were alone in the embassy suite an hour later. "Transport priceless relics through bandit country in these times? It's unthinkable, Messér."

"Certainly."

"Then why—"

"Two reasons. First, Thon Taddeo is Hannegan's kinsman, and influential too. We have to be courteous to Caesar and his kin whether we like him or not. Second, he started to say something about the Mad Bear clan, and then broke off. I think he knows what's going to happen. I'm not going to engage in espionage, but if he volunteers any information, there's nothing to prevent our including it in the report you're about to deliver personally to New Rome."

"*I!*" The clerk looked shocked. "To New Rome—? But what—"

"Not so loud," said the nuncio, glancing at the door. "I'm going to have to send my estimate of this situation to His Holiness, and quickly. But it's the kind of thing that one doesn't dare put in writing. If Hannegan's people intercepted such a dispatch, you and I would probably be found floating face down in the Red River. If Hannegan's enemies get hold of it, Hannegan would probably feel justified in hanging us publicly as spies. Martyrdom is all very well, but we have a job to do first."

"And I'm to deliver the report orally at the Vatican?" Brother Claret muttered, apparently not relishing the prospect of crossing hostile country.

"It has to be that way. Thon Taddeo may, just possibly *may*, give us an excuse for your leaving abruptly for Saint Leibowitz abbey, or New Rome, or both. In case there are any suspicions around the Court. I'll try to steer it."

"And the substance of the report I'm to deliver, Messér?"

"That Hannegan's ambition to unite the continent under one dynasty isn't so wild a dream as we thought. That the Agreement of the Holy Scourge is probably a fraud by Hannegan, and that he means to use it to get both the empire of Denver and Laredan Nation into conflict with the Plains nomads. If Laredan forces are tied up in a running battle with Mad Bear, it wouldn't take much encouragement for the State of Chihuahua to attack Laredo from the south. After all, there's an old enmity there. Hannegan, of course, can then march victoriously to Rio Laredo. With Laredo under his thumb, he can look forward to tackling both Denver and the Mississippi Republic without worrying about a stab in the back from the south."

"Do you think Hannegan can do it, Messér?"

Marcus Apollo started to answer, then closed his mouth slowly. He walked to the window and stared out at the sun-lit city, a sprawling disorderly city built mostly of rubble from another age. A city without orderly patterns of streets. It had grown slowly over an ancient ruin, as perhaps some-day another city would grow over the ruin of this one.

"I don't know," he answered softly. "In these times, it's hard to condemn any man for wanting to unite this butchered continent. Even by such means as—but no, I don't mean that." He sighed heavily. "In any case, our interests are not the interests of politics. We must forewarn New Rome of what may be coming, because the Church will be affected by it, whatever happens. And forewarned, we may be able to keep out of the squabble."

"You really think so?"

"Of course not!" the priest said gently.

Thon Taddeo Pfardentrott arrived at Marcus Apollo's study as early in the day as could be construed as evening, and his manner had noticeably changed since the reception. He managed a cordial smile, and there was nervous eagerness in the way he spoke. This fellow, thought Marcus, is after something he wants rather badly, and he's even willing to be polite in order to get it. Perhaps the list of ancient writ-ings supplied by the monks at the Leibowitzian abbey had impressed the thon more than he wanted to admit. The nuncio had been prepared for a fencing match, but the scholar's evident excitement made him too easy a victim, and Apollo relaxed his readiness for verbal dueling.

"This afternoon there was a meeting of the faculty of the collegium," said Thon Taddeo as soon as they were seated. "We talked about Brother Kornhoer's letter, and the list of documents." He paused as if uncertain of an approach. The gray dusklight from the large arched window on his left made his face seem blanched and intense, and his wide gray eyes searched at the priest as if measuring him and making estimates.

"I take it there was skepticism?"

The gray eyes fell momentarily, and lifted quickly. "Shall I be polite?"

"Don't bother," Apollo chuckled.

"There was skepticism. 'Incredulity' is more nearly the word. My own feeling is that if such papers exist, they are probably forgeries dating back several centuries. I doubt if the present monks at the abbey are trying to perpetrate a hoax. Naturally, they would believe the documents valid."

"Kind of you to absolve them," Apollo said sourly.

"I offered to be polite. Shall I?"

"No. Go on."

The thon slid out of his chair and went to sit in the window. He gazed at the fading yellow patches of cloud in the west and pounded softly on the sill while he spoke. "The papers. No matter what we may believe of them, the idea that such documents may still exist intact—that there's even a slightest chance of their existing—is, well, so *arousing* a thought that we *must* investigate them immediately."

"Very well," said Apollo, a little amused. "They invited you. But tell me: what do you find so arousing about the documents?"

The scholar shot him a quick glance. "Are you acquainted with my work?"

The monsignor hesitated. He was acquainted with it, but admitting the acquaintance might force him to admit to an awareness that Thon Taddeo's name was being spoken in the same breath with names of natural philosophers dead a thousand years and more, while the thon was scarcely in his thirties. The priest was not eager to admit knowing that this young scientist showed promise of becoming one of those rare outcroppings of human genius that appear only a time or two every century to revolutionize an entire field of thought in one vast sweep. He coughed apologetically.

"I must admit that I haven't read a good deal of—"

"Never mind." Pfardentrott waved off the apology. "Most of it is highly abstract, and tedious to the layman. Theories of electrical essence. Planetary motion. Attracting bodies. Matters of that sort. Now Kornhoer's list mentions such names as

Laplace, Maxwell, and Einstein—do *they* mean anything to you?"

"Not much. History mentions them as natural philosophers, doesn't it? From before the collapse of the last civilization? And I think they're named in one of the pagan hagiologies, aren't they?"

The scholar nodded. "And that's all anyone knows about them, or what they did. Physicists, according to our not-so-reliable historians. Responsible for the rapid rise of the European-American culture, they say. Historians list nothing but trivia. I had nearly forgotten them. But Kornhoer's descriptions of the old documents they say they have are descriptions of papers that might well be taken from physical science texts of some kind. It's just impossible!"

"But you have to make certain?"

"We have to make certain. Now that it's come up, I wish I had never heard of it."

"Why?"

Thon Taddeo was peering at something in the street below. He beckoned to the priest. "Come here a moment. I'll show you why."

Apollo slipped from behind the desk and looked down at the muddy rutted street beyond the wall that encircled the palace and barracks and buildings of the collegium, cutting off the mayoral sanctuary from the seething plebeian city. The scholar was pointing at the shadowy figure of a peasant leading a donkey homeward at twilight. The man's feet were wrapped in sackcloth, and the mud had caked about them so that he seemed scarcely able to lift them. But he trudged ahead in one slogging step after another, resting half a second between footfalls. He seemed too weary to scrape off the mud.

"He doesn't ride the donkey," Thon Taddeo stated, "because this morning the donkey was loaded down with corn. It doesn't occur to him that the packs are empty now. What is good enough for the morning is also good enough for the afternoon."

"You know him?"

"He passes under my window too. Every morning and evening. Hadn't you noticed him?"

"A thousand like him."

"Look. Can you bring yourself to believe that that brute is the lineal descendant of men who supposedly invented machines that flew, who traveled to the moon, harnessed the forces of Nature, built machines that could talk and seemed to think? Can you believe there were such men?"

Apollo was silent.

"Look at him!" the scholar persisted. "No, but it's too dark now. You can't see the syphilis outbreak on his neck, the way the bridge of his nose is being eaten away. Paresis. But he was undoubtedly a moron to begin with. Illiterate, superstitious, murderous. He diseases his children. For a few coins he would kill them. He will sell them anyway, when they are old enough to be useful. Look at him, and tell me if you see the progeny of a once-mighty civilization? What *do* you see?"

"The image of Christ," grated the monsignor, surprised at his own sudden anger. "What did you expect me to see?"

The scholar huffed impatiently. "The incongruity. Men as you can observe them through any window, and men as historians would have us believe men once were. I can't accept it. How can a great and wise civilization have destroyed itself so completely?"

"Perhaps," said Apollo, "by being materially great and materially wise, and nothing else." He went to light a tallow lamp, for the twilight was rapidly fading into night. He struck steel and flint until the spark caught and he blew gently at it in the tinder.

"Perhaps," said Thon Taddeo, "but I doubt it."

"You reject all history, then, as myth?" A flame edged out from the spark.

"Not 'reject.' But it must be questioned. Who wrote your histories?"

"The monastic Orders, of course. During the darkest centuries, there was no one else to record them." He transferred flame to wick.

"There! You have it. And during the time of the antipopes, how many schismatic Orders were fabricating their own versions of things, and passing off their versions as the work of earlier men? You can't know, you can't *really* know. That there was on this continent a more advanced civilization than we have now—that can't be denied. You can look at the rubble and the rotted metal and know it. You can dig under a strip of blown sand and find their broken roadways. But where is there evidence of the kind of machines your historians tell us they had in those days? Where are the remains of self-moving carts, of flying machines?"

"Beaten into plowshares and hoes."

"*If* they existed."

"If you doubt it, why bother studying the Leibowitzian documents?"

"Because a doubt is not a denial. Doubt is a powerful tool, and it should be applied to history."

The nuncio smiled tightly. "And what do you want *me* to do about it, learned Thon?"

The scholar leaned forward earnestly. "Write to the abbot of this place. Assure him that the documents will be treated with utmost care, and will be returned after we have completely examined them for authenticity and studied their content."

"Whose assurance do you want me to give him—yours or mine?"

"Hannegan's, yours, *and* mine."

"I can give him only yours and Hannegan's. I have no troops of my own."

The scholar reddened.

"Tell me," the nuncio added hastily, "why—besides bandits—do you insist you must see them here, instead of going to the abbey?"

"The best reason you can give the abbot is that if the documents are authentic, *if* we have to examine them at the abbey, a confirmation wouldn't mean much to other secular scholars."

"You mean your colleagues might think the monks had tricked you into something?"

"Ummm, that might be inferred. But also important, if they're brought here, they can be examined by everyone in the collegium who's qualified to form an opinion. And any visiting thons from other principalities can have a look at them too. But we can't move the entire collegium to the southwest desert for six months."

"I see your point."

"Will you send the request to the abbey?"

"Yes."

Thon Taddeo appeared surprised.

"But it will be your request, not mine. And it's only fair to tell you that I don't think Dom Paulo, the abbot, will say yes."

The thon, however, appeared to be satisfied. When he had gone, the nuncio summoned his clerk.

"You'll be leaving for New Rome tomorrow," he told him.

"By way of Leibowitz Abbey?"

"Come back by way of it. The report to New Rome is urgent."

"Yes, Messér."

"At the abbey, tell Dom Paulo that Sheba expects Solomon to come to *her*. Bearing gifts. Then you better cover your ears. When he finishes exploding, hurry back so I can tell Thon Taddeo no."

13 Time seeps slowly on the desert and there is little change to mark its passage. Two seasons had passed since Dom Paulo had refused the request from across the Plains, but the matter had been settled only a few weeks ago. Or had it been settled at all? Texarkana was obviously unhappy with the results.

The abbot paced along the abbey walls at sundown, his jaw thrust ahead like a whiskery old crag against possible breakers out of the sea of events. His thinning hair fluttered in white pennants on the desert wind, and the wind wrapped his habit bandage-tight about his stooped body, making him look like an emaciated Ezekiel with a strangely round little paunch. He thrust his gnarled hands into his sleeves and glowered occasionally across the desert toward the village of Sanly Bowitts in the distance. The red sunlight threw his pacing shadow across the courtyard, and the monks who encountered it in crossing the grounds glanced up wonderingly at the old man. Their ruler had seemed moody of late, and given to strange forebodings. It was whispered that the time soon was coming when a new abbot would be appointed ruler over the Brothers of Saint Leibowitz. It was whispered that the old man was not well, not well at all. It was whispered that if the abbot heard the whispers, the whisperers should speedily climb over the wall. The abbot had heard, but it pleased him for once not to take note of it. He well knew that the whispers were true.

"Read it to me again," he said abruptly to the monk who stood motionless near at hand.

The monk's hood jogged slightly in the abbot's direction. "Which one, Domne?" he asked.

"You know which one."

"Yes, m'Lord." The monk fumbled in one sleeve. It seemed weighted down with half a bushel of documents and correspondence, but after a moment he found the right one. Affixed to the scroll was the label:

SUB IMMUNITATE APOSTOLICA HOC SUPPOSITUM EST.
QUISQUIS NUNTIUM MOLESTARE AUDEAT,
IPSO FACTO EXCOMMUNICETUR.
DET: R'dissimo Domno Paulo de Pecos, AOL, Abbati
(Monastery of the Leibowitzian Brethren,
Environs of Sanly Bowitts Village
Southwest Desert, Empire of Denver)
CUI SALUTEM DICIT: *Marcus Apollo*
Papatiae Apocrisarius Texarkanae

"All right, that's the one. So read it," the abbot said impatiently.

"*Accedite ad eum . . .*" The monk crossed himself and murmured the customary Blessing of Texts, said before reading or writing almost as punctiliously as the blessing at meals. For the preservation of literacy and learning throughout a black millennium had been the task of the Brothers of Leibowitz, and such small rituals helped keep that task in focus.

Having finished the blessing, he held the scroll high against the sunset so that it became a transparency. "'*Iterum oportet apponere tibi crucem ferendam, amice . . .*'"

His voice was faintly singsong as his eyes plucked the words out of a forest of superfluous pen-flourishings. The abbot leaned against the parapet to listen while he watched the buzzards circling over the mesa of Last Resort.

"'Again it is necessary to set before you a cross to be borne, old friend and shepherd of myopic bookworms,'" droned the voice of the reader, "'but perhaps the bearing of the cross will smack of triumph. It appears that Sheba is coming to Solomon after all, though probably to denounce him as a charlatan.

"'This is to notify you that Thon Taddeo Pfardentrott, D.N.Sc., Sage of Sages, Scholar of Scholars, Fair-Haired Son-out-of-Wedlock of a certain Prince, and God's Gift to an "Awakening Generation," has finally made up his mind to pay you a visit, having exhausted all hope of transporting your Memorabilia to this fair realm. He will be arriving about the Feast of the Assumption, if he manages to evade "bandit" groups along the way. He will bring his misgivings and a small party of armed cavalry, courtesy of Hannegan II, whose corpulent person is even now hovering over me as I write, grunting and scowling at these lines, which His Supremacy commanded me to write, and in which His Supremacy expects me to acclaim his cousin, the thon, in the hope that you'll honor him fittingly. But since His Supremacy's secretary is in bed with the gout, I shall be no less than candid here:

"'So first, let me caution you about this person, Thon Taddeo. Treat him with your customary charity, but trust him not. He is a brilliant scholar, but a secular scholar, and a political captive of the State. Here, Hannegan is the State. Furthermore, the thon is rather anti-clerical, I think—or perhaps solely anti-monastic. After his embarrassing birth, he was spirited away to a Benedictine monastery, and—but no, ask the courier about that . . .'"

The monk glanced up from his reading. The abbot was still watching the buzzards over Last Resort.

"You've heard about his childhood, Brother?" Dom Paulo asked.

The monk nodded.

"Read on."

The reading continued, but the abbot ceased to listen. He knew the letter nearly by heart, but still he felt that there was something Marcus Apollo had been trying to say between the lines that he, Dom Paulo, had not yet managed to understand. Marcus was trying to warn him—but of what? The tone of the letter was mildly flippant, but it seemed full of ominous incongruities which might have been designed to add up to some single dark congruity, if only he could add them right. What danger could there be in letting the secular scholar study at the abbey?

Thon Taddeo himself, according to the courier who had brought the letter, had been educated in the Benedictine monastery where he had been taken as a child to avoid embarassment to his father's wife. The thon's father was Hannegan's uncle, but his mother was a serving maid. The duchess, legitimate wife of the duke, had never protested the duke's philandering until this common servant girl bore him the son he had always wanted; then she cried unfair. She had borne him only daughters, and to be bested by a commoner aroused her wrath. She sent the child away, flogged and dismissed the servant, and renewed her grip on the duke. She herself meant to have a manchild out of him to re-establish her honor; she gave him three more girls. The duke waited patiently for fifteen years; when she died in miscarriage (of another girl), he promptly went to the Benedictines to reclaim the boy and make him his heir.

But the young Taddeo of Hannegan-Pfardentrott had become a bitter child. He had grown from infancy to adolescence within sight of the city and the palace where his first cousin was being prepared for the throne; if his family had entirely ignored him, however, he might have matured without coming to resent his status as an outcast. But both his father and the servant girl whose womb had borne him came to visit him with just enough frequency to keep him reminded that he was begotten of human flesh and not of stones, and thus to make him vaguely aware that he was deprived of love to which he was entitled. And then too, Prince Hannegan had come to the same monastery for one year of schooling, had lorded it over his bastard cousin, and had excelled him in all things but keenness of mind. The young Taddeo had hated the prince with a quiet fury, and had set out to outdistance him as far as possible in learning at least. The race had proved a sham, however; the prince left the monastic school the following year, as unlettered as he had come, nor was any further thought given to his education. Meanwhile, his exiled cousin continued the race alone and won high honors; but his victory was hollow, for Hannegan did not care. Thon Taddeo had come to despise the whole Court of Texarkana, but, with youthful inconsistency, he had returned willingly to that Court to be legitimized as the father's son at last, appearing to forgive everyone except the dead duchess who had exiled him and the monks who had cared for him in that exile.

Perhaps he thinks of our cloister as a place of durance vile, thought the abbot. There would be bitter memories, half-memories, and maybe a few imagined memories.

"'. . . seeds of controversy in the bed of the New Literacy,'" the reader continued. "'So take heed, and watch for the symptoms.

"'But, on the other hand, not only His Supremacy, but the dictates of charity and justice as well, insist that I recommend him to you as a well-meaning man, or at least as an unmalicious child, like most of these educated and gentlemanly pagans (and pagans they will make of themselves, in spite of all). He will behave if you are firm, but be careful, my friend. He has a mind like a loaded musket, and it can go off in any direction. I trust, however, that coping with him for a while will not be too taxing a problem for your ingenuity and hospitality.

"'*Quidam mihi calix nuper expletur, Paule. Precamini ergo Deum facere me fortiorem. Metuo ut hic pereat. Spero te et fratres saepius oraturos esse pro tremescente Marco Apolline. Valete in Christo, amici.*

"'*Texarkanae datum est Octavā Ss Petri et Pauli, Anno Domini termillesimo . . .*'"

"Let's see that seal again," said the abbot.

The monk handed him the scroll. Dom Paulo held it close to his face to peer at blurred lettering impressed at the bottom of the parchment by a badly inked wooden stamp:

> OKAYED BY HANNEGAN II, BY GRACE OF GOD MAYOR,
> RULER OF TEXARKANA, DEFENDER OF THE FAITH,
> AND VAQUERO SUPREME OF THE PLAINS.
> HIS MARK: X

"I wonder if His Supremacy had someone read the letter to him later?" worried the abbot.

"If so, m'Lord, would the letter have been sent?"

"I suppose not. But frivolity under Hannegan's nose just to spite the Mayor's illiteracy is not like Marcus Apollo, unless he was trying to tell me something between the lines—but couldn't quite think of a safe way to say it. That last part —about a certain chalice that he's afraid won't pass away. It's clear he's worried about something, but what? It isn't like Marcus; it isn't like him at all."

Several weeks had passed since the arrival of the letter; during those weeks Dom Paulo had slept badly, had suffered a recurrence of the old gastric trouble, had brooded overmuch on the past as if looking for something that might have been done differently in order to avert the future. What future? he demanded of himself. There seemed no logical reason to expect trouble. The controversy between monks and villagers had all but died. No signs of turmoil came from the herdsman tribes to the north and east. Imperial Denver was not pressing its attempt to levy taxes upon monastic congregations. There were no troops in the vicinity. The oasis was

still furnishing water. There seemed no current threat of
plague among animals or men. The corn was doing well
this year in the irrigated fields. There were signs of progress
in the world, and the village of Sanly Bowitts had achieved
the fantastic literary rate of eight per cent—for which the
villagers might, but did not, thank the monks of the Leibowitzian Order.

And yet he felt forebodings. Some nameless threat lurked
just around the corner of the world for the sun to rise again.
The feeling had been gnawing at him, as annoying as a swarm
of hungry insects that buzzed about one's face in the desert
sun. There was the sense of the imminent, the remorseless,
the mindless; it coiled like a heat-maddened rattler, ready
to strike at rolling tumbleweed.

It was a devil with which he was trying to come to grips,
the abbot decided, but the devil was quite evasive. The abbot's devil was rather small, as devils go: only knee-high, but
he weighed ten tons and had the strength of five hundred
oxen. He was not driven by maliciousness, as Dom Paulo
imagined him, not nearly as much as he was driven by frenzied compulsion, somewhat after the fashion of a rabid
dog. He bit through meat and bone and nail simply because
he had damned himself, and damnation created a damnably
insatiable appetite. And he was evil merely because he had
made a denial of Good, and the denial had become a part of
his essence, or a hole therein. Somewhere, Dom Paulo
thought, he's wading through a sea of men and leaving a
wake of the maimed.

What nonsense, old man! he chided himself. When you
tire of living, change itself seems evil, does it not? for then
any change at all disturbs the deathlike peace of the life-
weary. Oh there's the devil, all right, but let's not credit him
with more than his damnable due. Are you that life-weary,
old fossil?

But the foreboding lingered.

"Do you suppose the buzzards have eaten old Eleazar
yet?" asked a quiet voice at his elbow.

Dom Paulo glanced around with a start in the twilight.
The voice belonged to Father Gault, his prior and probable
successor. He stood fingering a rose and looking embarrassed
for having disturbed the old man's solitude.

"Eleazar? You mean Benjamin? Why, have you heard
something about him lately?"

"Well, no, Father Abbot." He laughed uneasily. "But

you seemed to be looking toward the mesa, and I thought you were wondering about the Old Jew." He glanced toward the anvil-shaped mountain, silhouetted against the gray patch of sky in the west. "There's a wisp of smoke up there, so I guess he's still alive."

"We shouldn't have to *guess*," Dom Paulo said abruptly. "I'm going to ride over there and pay him a visit."

"You sound like you're leaving tonight." Gault chuckled.

"In a day or two."

"Better be careful. They say he throws rocks at climbers."

"I haven't seen him for five years," the abbot confessed. "And I'm ashamed that I haven't. He's lonely. I'll go."

"If he's lonely, why does he insist on living like a hermit?"

"To escape loneliness—in a young world."

The young priest laughed. "That perhaps makes *his* kind of sense, Domne, but I don't quite see it."

"You will, when you're my age, or his."

"I don't expect to get that old. He lays claim to several thousand years."

The abbot smiled reminiscently. "And you know, I can't dispute him either. I met him when I was just a novice, fifty-odd years ago, and I'd swear he looked just as old then as he does now. He must be well over a hundred."

"Three thousand two hundred and nine, so he says. Sometimes even older. I think he believes it, too. An interesting madness."

"I'm not so sure he's mad, Father. Just devious in his sanity. What did you want to see me about?"

"Three small matters. First, how do we get the Poet out of the royal guest rooms—before Thon Taddeo arrives? He's due here in a few days, and the Poet's taken root."

"I'll handle the Poet-sirrah. What else?"

"Vespers. Will you be in the church?"

"Not until Compline. You take over. What else?"

"Controversy in the basement—over Brother Kornhoer's experiment."

"Who and how?"

"Well, the silly gist of it seems to be that Brother Armbruster has the attitude of *vespero mundi expectando*, while with Brother Kornhoer, it's the matins of the millennium. Kornhoer moves something to make room for a piece of equipment. Armbruster yells *Perdition!* Brother Kornhoer yells *Progress!* and they have at each other again. Then they come fuming to me to settle it. I scold them for losing their tempers. They get sheepish and fawn on each other for ten minutes. Six hours later, the floor shivers from Brother Armbruster's bellowing *Perdition!* down in the library. I can settle the blowups, but there seems to be a Basic Issue."

"A basic breach of conduct, I'd say. What do you want me to do about it? Exclude them from the table?"

"Not yet, but you might warn them."

"All right, I'll track it down. Is that all?"

"That's all, Domne." He started away, but paused. "Oh, by the way—do you think Brother Kornhoer's contraption is going to work?"

"I *hope* not!" the abbot snorted.

Father Gault appeared surprised. "But, then why let him—"

"Because I was curious at first. The work has caused so much commotion by now, though, that I'm sorry I let him start it."

"Then why not stop him?"

"Because I'm hoping that he will reduce himself to absurdity without any help from me. If the thing fails, it'll fail just in time for Thon Taddeo's arrival. That would be just the proper form of mortification for Brother Kornhoer —to remind him of his vocation, before he begins thinking that he was called to Religion mainly for the purpose of building a generator of electrical essences in the monastery basement."

"But, Father Abbot, you'll have to admit that it would be quite an achievement, if successful."

"I don't *have* to admit it," Dom Paulo told him curtly.

When Gault was gone, the abbot, after a brief debate with himself, decided to handle the problem of the Poet-sirrah! before the problem of perdition-versus-progress. The simplest solution to the problem of the Poet was for the Poet to get out of the royal suite, and preferably out of the abbey, out of the vicinity of the abbey, out of sight, hearing, and mind. But no one could expect a "simplest solution" to get rid of the Poet-sirrah!

The abbot left the wall and crossed the courtyard toward the guesthouse. He moved by feel, for the buildings were monoliths of shadow under the stars, and only a few windows glowed with candlelight. The windows of the royal suite were dark; but the Poet kept odd hours and might well be in.

Inside the building, he groped for the right door, found it, and knocked. There was no immediate answer, but only a faint bleating sound which might or might not have issued from within the suite. He knocked again, then tried the door. It opened.

Faint red light from a charcoal burner softened the darkness; the room reeked of stale food.

"Poet?"

Again the faint bleating, but closer now. He went to the burner, raked up an incandescent coal, and lit a splinter of kindling. He glanced around and shuddered at the litter of the room. It was empty. He transferred the flame to an oil lamp and went to explore the rest of the suite. It would have to be thoroughly scrubbed and fumigated (also, perhaps, exorcised) before Thon Taddeo moved in. He hoped to make the Poet-sirrah! do the scrubbing, but knew the chance was remote.

In the second room, Dom Paulo suddenly felt as if someone were watching him. He paused and looked slowly around.

A single eyeball peered at him from a vase of water on the shelf. The abbot nodded at it familiarly and went on.

In the third room, he met the goat. It was their first meeting.

The goat was standing atop a tall cabinet, munching turnip greens. It looked like a small breed of mountain goat, but it had a bald head that appeared bright blue by lamplight. Undoubtedly a freak by birth.

"Poet?" he inquired, softly, looking straight at the goat and touching his pectoral cross.

"In *here*," came a sleepy voice from the fourth room.

Dom Paulo sighed with relief. The goat went on munching greens. Now *that* had been a hideous thought, indeed.

The Poet lay sprawled across the bed with a bottle of wine within easy reach; he blinked irritably at the light with his one good eye. "I was asleep," he complained, adjusting his black eyepatch and reaching for the bottle.

"Then wake up. You're moving out of here immediately. Tonight. Dump your possessions in the hall to let the suite air out. Sleep in the stable boy's cell downstairs if you must. Then come back in the morning and scrub this place out."

The Poet looked like a bruised lily for a moment, then made a grab for something under the blankets. He brought out a fist and stared at it thoughtfully. "Who used these quarters last?" he asked.

"Monsignor Longi. Why?"

"I wondered who brought the bedbugs." The Poet opened his fist, pinched something out of his palm, cracked it between his nails, and flipped it away. "Thon Taddeo can have them. I don't want them. I've been eaten up alive ever since I moved in. I was planning on leaving, but now that you've offered me my old cell back, I'll be happy—"

"I didn't mean—"

"—to accept your kind hospitality a little longer. Only until my book is finished, of course."

"*What* book? But never mind. Just get your things out of here."

"Now?"

"Now."

"Good. I don't think I could stand these bugs another night." The Poet rolled out of bed, but paused for a drink.

"Give me the wine," the abbot ordered.

"Sure. Have some. It's a pleasant vintage."

"Thank you, since you stole it from our cellars. It happens to be sacramental wine. Did that occur to you?"

"It hasn't been consecrated."

"I'm surprised you thought of that." Dom Paulo took the bottle.

"I didn't steal it anyway. I—"

"Never mind the wine. Where did you steal the goat?"

"I didn't *steal* it," the Poet complained.

"It just—materialized?"

"It was a gift, Reverendissime."

"From whom?"

"A dear friend, Domnissime."

"*Whose* dear friend?"

"Mine, Sire."

"Now there's a paradox. Where, now, did you—"

"Benjamin, Sire."

A flicker of surprise crossed Dom Paulo's face. "You stole it from old Benjamin?"

The Poet winced at the word. "Please, not *stole*."

"Then what?"

"Benjamin insisted that I take it as a gift after I had composed a sonnet in his honor."

"The *truth!*"

The Poet-sirrah! swallowed sheepishly. "I won it from him at mumbly-peg."

"I see."

"It's true! The old wretch nearly cleaned me out, and then refused to allow me credit. I had to stake my glass eye against the goat. But I won everything back."

"Get the goat out of the abbey."

"But it's a marvelous species of goat. The milk is of an unearthly odor and contains essences. In fact it's responsible for the Old Jew's longevity."

"How much of it?"

"All fifty-four hundred and eight years of it."

"I thought he was only thirty-two hundred and—" Dom Paulo broke off disdainfully. "What were you doing up on Last Resort?"

"Playing mumbly-peg with old Benjamin."

"I mean—" The abbot steeled himself. "Never mind. Just get yourself moved out. And tomorrow get the goat back to Benjamin."

"But I won it fairly."

"We'll not discuss it. Take the goat to the stable, then. I'll have it returned to him myself."

"Why?"

"We have no use for a goat. Neither have you."

"Ho, ho," the Poet said archly.

"What did *that* mean, pray?"

"Thon Taddeo is coming. There'll be need of a goat before it's finished. You can be sure of that." He chuckled smugly to himself.

The abbot turned away in irritation. "Just get out," he added superfluously, and then went to wrestle with contention in the basement, where the Memorabilia now reposed.

14   The vaulted basement had been dug during the centuries of nomadic infiltration from the north, when the Bayring Horde had overrun most of the Plains and desert, looting and vandalizing all villages that lay in their path. The Memorabilia, the abbey's small patrimony of knowledge out of the past, had been walled up in underground vaults to protect the priceless writings from both nomads and *soi-disant* crusaders of the schismatic Orders, founded to fight the hordes, but turned to random pillaging and sectarian strife. Neither the nomads nor the Military Order of San Pancratz would have valued the abbey's books, but the nomads would have destroyed them for the joy of destruction and the military knights-friars would have burned many of them as "heretical" according to the theology of Vissarion, their Antipope.

Now a Dark Age seemed to be passing. For twelve centuries, a small flame of knowledge had been kept smoldering in the monasteries; only now were their minds ready to be kindled. Long ago, during the last age of reason, certain proud thinkers had claimed that valid knowledge was indestructible—that ideas were deathless and truth immortal. But that was true only in the subtlest sense, the abbot thought, and not superficially true at all. There was objective meaning in the world, to be sure: the nonmoral *logos* or design of the Creator; but such meanings were God's and not Man's, until they found an imperfect incarnation, a dark reflection, within the mind and speech and culture of a given human society, which might ascribe values to the meanings so that they became valid in a human sense within the culture. For Man was a culture-bearer as well as a soul-bearer, but his cultures were not immortal and they could die with a race or an age, and then human reflections of meaning and human portrayals of truth receded, and truth and meaning resided, unseen, only in the objective *logos* of Nature and the ineffable *Logos* of God. Truth could be crucified; but soon, perhaps, a resurrection.

The Memorabilia was full of ancient words, ancient formulae, ancient reflections of meaning, detached from minds that had died long ago, when a different sort of society had passed into oblivion. There was little of it that could still be understood. Certain papers seemed as meaningless as a Breviary would seem to a shaman of the nomad tribes. Others retained a certain ornamental beauty or an orderliness that hinted of meaning, as a rosary might suggest a necklace to a nomad. The earliest brothers of the Leibowitzian Order had tried to press a sort of Veronica's Veil to the face of a crucified civilization; it had come away marked with an image of the face of ancient grandeur, but the image was faintly printed, incomplete, and hard to understand. The monks had preserved the image, and now it

still survived for the world to inspect and try to interpret
if the world wanted to do so. The Memorabilia could not, of
itself, generate a revival of ancient science or high civilization, however, for cultures were begotten by the tribes of
Man, not by musty tomes; but the books could help, Dom
Paulo hoped—the books could point out directions and offer
hints to a newly evolving science. It had happened once
before, so the Venerable Boedullus had asserted in his *De
Vestigiis Antecessarum Civitatum.*

And this time, thought Dom Paulo, we'll keep them reminded of *who* kept the spark burning while the world slept.
He paused to look back; for a moment he had imagined
that he had heard a frightened bleat from the Poet's goat.

The clamor from the basement soon blanketed his hearing
as he descended the underground stairs toward the source
of the turmoil. Someone was hammering steel pins into
stone. Sweat mingled with the odor of old books. A feverish
bustle of unscholarly activity filled the library. Novices hurried past with tools. Novices stood in groups and studied
floor plans. Novices shifted desks and tables and heaved a
makeshift machinery, rocking it into place. Confusion by
lamplight. Brother Armbruster, the librarian and Rector of
the Memorabilia, stood watching it from a remote alcove
in the shelves, his arms tightly folded and his face grim.
Dom Paulo avoided his accusing gaze.

Brother Kornhoer approached his ruler with a lingering
grin of enthusiasm. "Well, Father Abbot, we'll soon have a
light such as no man alive has ever seen."

"This is not without a certain vanity, Brother," Paulo replied.

"Vanity, Domne? To put to good use what we've learned?"

"I had in mind our *haste* to put it to use in time to im-
press a certain visiting scholar. But never mind. Let's see
this engineer's wizardry."

They walked toward the makeshift machine. It reminded
the abbot of nothing useful, unless one considered engines
for torturing prisoners useful. An axle, serving as the shaft,
was connected by pulleys and belts to a waist-high turnstile.
Four wagon wheels were mounted on the axle a few inches
apart. Their thick iron tires were scored with grooves, and
the grooves supported countless birds'-nests of copper wire,
drawn from coinage at the local smithy in Sanly Bowitts.
The wheels were apparently free to spin in mid-air, Dom
Paulo noticed, for their tires touched no surface. However,

stationary blocks of iron faced the tires, like brakes, without quite touching them. The blocks too had been wound with innumerable turns of wire—"field coils" as Kornhoer called them. Dom Paulo solemnly shook his head.

"It'll be the greatest physical improvement at the abbey since we got the printing press a hundred years ago," Kornhoer ventured proudly.

"Will it work?" Dom Paulo wondered.

"I'll stake a month's extra chores on it, m'Lord."

You're staking more than that, thought the priest, but suppressed utterance. "Where does the light come out?" he asked, peering at the odd contraption again.

The monk laughed. "Oh, we have a special lamp for that. What you see here is only the 'dynamo.' It produces the electrical essence which the lamp will burn."

Ruefully, Dom Paulo contemplated the amount of space the dynamo was occupying. "This essence," he murmured, "—can't it be extracted from mutton fat, perhaps?"

"No, no— The electrical essence is, well— Do you want me to explain?"

"Better not. Natural science is not my bent. I'll leave it to you younger heads." He stepped back quickly to avoid being brained by a timber carried past by a pair of hurrying carpenters. "Tell me," he said, "if by studying writings from the Leibowitzian age you can learn how to construct this thing, why do you suppose none of our predecessors saw fit to construct it?"

The monk was silent for a moment. "It's not easy to explain," he said at last. "Actually, in the writings that survive, there's no direct information about the construction of a dynamo. Rather, you might say that the information is implicit in a whole collection of fragmentary writings. *Partially* implicit. And it has to be got out by deduction. But to get it, you also need some theories to work from—theoretical information our predecessors didn't have."

"But we do?"

"Well, yes—now that there have been a few men like—" his tone became deeply respectful and he paused before pronouncing the name "—like Thon Taddeo—"

"Was that a complete sentence?" the abbot asked rather sourly.

"Well, until recently, few philosophers have concerned themselves with new theories in physics. Actually, it was the work of, of Thon Taddeo—" the respectful tone again,

Dom Paulo noted, "—that gave us the necessary working axioms. His work of the Mobility of Electrical Essences, for example, and his Conservation Theorem—"

"He should be pleased, then, to see his work applied. But where is the lamp itself, may I ask? I hope it's no larger than the dynamo."

"This is it, Domne," said the monk, picking up a small object from the table. It seemed to be only a bracket for holding a pair of black rods and a thumbscrew for adjusting their spacing. "These are carbons," Kornhoer explained. "The ancients would have called it an 'arc lamp.' There was another kind, but we don't have the materials to make it."

"Amazing. Where does the light come from?"

"Here." The monk pointed to the gap between the carbons. "It must be a very tiny flame," said the abbot.

"Oh, but bright! Brighter, I expect, than a hundred candles."

"No!"

"You find that impressive?"

"I find it preposterous—" noticing Brother Kornhoer's sudden hurt expression, the abbot hastily added: "—to think how we've been limping along on beeswax and mutton fat."

"I have been wondering," the monk shyly confided, "if the ancients used them on their altars instead of candles."

"No," said the abbot. "Definitely, no. I can tell you that. Please dismiss that idea as quickly as possible, and don't even think of it again."

"Yes, Father Abbot."

"Now, where are you going to hang that thing?"

"Well—" Brother Kornhoer paused to stare speculatively around the gloomy basement. "I hadn't given it any thought. I suppose it should go over the desk where, Thon Taddeo—" (Why does he pause like that whenever he says it, Dom Paulo wondered irritably.) "—will be working."

"We'd better ask Brother Armbruster about that," the abbot decided, and then noticing the monk's sudden discomfort: "What's the matter? Have you and Brother Armbruster been—"

Kornhoer's face twisted apologetically. "Really, Father Abbot, I haven't lost my temper with him even once. Oh, we've had words, but—" He shrugged. "He doesn't want anything moved. He keeps mumbling about witchcraft and the like. It's not easy to reason with him. His eyes are half-

blind now from reading by dim light—and yet he says it's
Devil's work we're up to. I don't know what to say."

Dom Paulo frowned slightly as they crossed the room toward the alcove where Brother Armbruster still stood glowering upon the proceedings.

"Well, you've got your way now," the librarian said to
Kornhoer as they approached. "When'll you be putting in a
mechanical librarian, Brother?"

"We find hints, Brother, that once there were such things,"
the inventor growled. "In descriptions of the *Machina analytica*, you'll find references to—"

"Enough, enough," the abbot interposed; then to the librarian: "Thon Taddeo will need a place to work. What do
you suggest?"

Armbruster jerked one thumb toward the Natural Science
alcove. "Let him read at the lectern in there like anyone
else."

"What about setting up a study for him here on the open
floor, Father Abbot?" Kornhoer suggested in hasty counter-
proposal.

"Besides a desk, he'll need an abacus, a wall slate, and a
drawing board. We could partition it off with temporary
screens."

"I thought he was going to need our Leibowitzian references and earliest writings?" the librarian said suspiciously.

"He will."

"Then he'll have to walk back and forth a lot if you put
him in the middle. The rare volumes are chained, and the
chains won't reach that far."

"That's no problem," said the inventor. "Take off the chains.
They look silly anyway. The schismatic cults have all died
out or become regional. Nobody's heard of the Pancratzian
Military Order in a hundred years."

Armbruster reddened angrily. "Oh no you don't," he
snapped. "The chains stay on."

"But why?"

"It's not the book burners now. It's the villagers we have
to worry about. The chains stay on."

Kornhoer turned to the abbot and spread his hands. "See,
m'Lord?"

"He's right," said Dom Paulo. "There's too much agitation
in the village. The town council expropriated our school,
don't forget. Now they've got a village library, and they want

us to fill its shelves. Preferably with rare volumes, of course. Not only that, we had trouble with thieves last year. Brother Armbruster's right. The rare volumes stay chained."

"All right," Kornhoer sighed. "So he'll have to work in the alcove."

"Now, where do we hang your wondrous lamp?"

The monks glanced toward the cubicle. It was one of fourteen identical stalls, sectioned according to subject matter, which faced the central floor. Each alcove had its archway, and from an iron hook imbedded in the keystone of each arch hung a heavy crucifix.

"Well, if he's going to work in the alcove," said Kornhoer, "we'll just have to take the crucifix down and hang it there, temporarily. There's no other—"

"Heathen!" hissed the librarian. "Pagan! Desecrator!" Armbruster raised trembling hands heavenward. "God help me, lest I tear him apart with these hands! Where will he stop? Take him away, away!" He turned his back on them, his hands still trembling aloft.

Dom Paulo himself had winced slightly at the inventor's suggestion, but now he frowned sharply at the back of Brother Armbruster's habit. He had never expected him to feign a meekness that was alien to Armbruster's nature, but the aged monk's querulous disposition had grown definitely worse.

"Brother Armbruster, turn around, please."

The librarian turned.

"Now drop your hands, and speak more calmly when you—"

"But, Father Abbot, you heard what he—"

"Brother Armbruster, you will please get the shelf-ladder and remove that crucifix."

The color left the librarian's face. He stared speechless at Dom Paulo.

"This is *not* a church," said the abbot. "The placement of images is optional. For the present, you will please take down the crucifix. It's the only suitable place for the lamp, it seems. Later we may change it. Now I realize this whole thing has disturbed your library, and perhaps your digestion, but we hope it's in the interests of progress. If it isn't, then—"

"You'd make Our Lord move over to make room for progress!"

"Brother Armbruster!"

"Why don't you just hang the witch-light around His neck?"

The abbot's face went frigid. "I do not *force* your obedience, Brother. See me in my study after Compline."

The librarian wilted. "I'll get the ladder, Father Abbot," he whispered, and shuffled unsteadily away.

Dom Paulo glanced up at the Christ of the rood in the archway. Do You mind? he wondered.

There was a knot in his stomach. He knew the knot would exact its price of him later. He left the basement before anyone could notice his discomfort. It was not good to let the community see how such trivial unpleasantness could overcome him these days.

The installation was completed the following day, but Dom Paulo remained in his study during the test. Twice he had been forced to warn Brother Armbruster privately, and then to rebuke him publicly during Chapter. And yet he felt more sympathy for the librarian's stand than he did for Kornhoer's. He sat slumped at his desk and waited for the news from the basement, feeling small concern for the test's success or failure. He kept one hand tucked into the front of his habit. He patted his stomach as though trying to calm a hysterical child.

Internal cramping again. It seemed to come whenever unpleasantness threatened, and sometimes went away again when unpleasantness exploded into the open where he could wrestle with it. But now it was not going away.

He was being warned, and he knew it. Whether the warning came from an angel, from a demon, or from his own conscience, it told him to beware of himself and of some reality not yet faced.

What now? he wondered, permitting himself a silent belch and a silent *Beg pardon* toward the statue of Saint Leibowitz in the shrinelike niche in the corner of his study.

A fly was crawling along Saint Leibowitz' nose. The eyes of the saint seemed to be looking crosseyed at the fly, urging the abbot to brush it away. The abbot had grown fond of the twenty-sixth century wood carving; its face wore a curious smile of a sort that made it rather unusual as a sacramental image. The smile was turned down at one corner; the eyebrows were pulled low in a faintly dubious frown, although there were laugh-wrinkles at the corners of the eyes. Because of the hangman's rope over one shoulder, the saint's expression often seemed puzzling. Possibly it resulted from slight irregularities in the grain of the wood, such irregularities dictating to the carver's hand as that hand sought to bring out finer details than were possible with such wood. Dom Paulo was not certain whether the image had been growth-sculptured as a living tree before carving or not; sometimes the patient master-carvers of that period had begun with an oak or cedar sapling, and—by spending tedious years at pruning, barking, twisting, and tying living branches into desired positions—had tormented the growing wood into a striking dryad shape, arms folded or raised aloft, before cutting the mature tree for curing and carving. The resulting statue was unusually resistant to splitting or breaking, since most of the lines of the work followed the natural grain.

Dom Paulo often marveled that the wooden Leibowitz had also proved resistant to several centuries of his predecessors—marveled, because of the saint's most peculiar smile. That little grin will ruin you someday, he warned the image. . . . Surely, the saints must laugh in Heaven; the Psalmist says that God Himself shall chortle, but Abbot Malmeddy must have disapproved—God rest his soul. That solemn ass. How did you get by *him*, I wonder? You're not sanctimonious enough for some. That smile—Who do I know that grins that way? I like it, *but* . . . Someday, another grim dog will sit in this chair. *Cave canem.* He'll replace you with a plaster Leibowitz. Long-suffering. One who doesn't look crosseyed at flies. Then you'll be eaten by termites down in the storage room. To survive the Church's slow sifting of the arts, you have to have a surface that can please a righteous simpleton; and yet you need a depth beneath that surface to please a discerning sage. The sifting is slow, but it gets a turn of the sifter-handle now and then—when some new prelate inspects his episcopal chambers and mutters, "Some of this garbage has got to go." The sifter was usually full of dulcet pap. When the old pap was ground out, fresh pap was added. But what was *not* ground out was gold, and it lasted. If a church endured five centuries of priestly bad taste, occasional good taste had, by then, usually stripped away most of the transient tripe, had made it a place of majesty that overawed the would-be prettifiers.

The abbot fanned himself with a fan of buzzard feathers, but the breeze was not cooling. The air from the window was like an oven's breath off the scorched desert, adding to the discomfort caused him by whatever devil or ruthless angel was fiddling around with his belly. It was the kind of heat that hints of lurking danger from sun-crazed rattlers and brooding thunderstorms over the mountains, or rabid dogs and tempers made vicious by the scorch. It made the cramping worse.

"Please?" he murmured aloud to the saint, meaning a non-verbal prayer for cooler weather, sharper wits, and more insight into his vague sense of something wrong. Maybe it's that cheese that does it, he thought. Gummy stuff this season, and green. I *could* dispense myself—and take a more digestible diet.

But no, there we go again. Face it, Paulo: it's not the food for the belly that does it; it's the food for the brain. Something up there is not digesting.

"But what?"

The wooden saint gave him no ready answer. Pap. Sifting out chaff. Sometimes his mind worked in snatches. It was better to let it work that way when the cramps came and the world weighed heavily upon him. What did the world weigh? It weighs, but is not weighed. Sometimes its scales are crooked. It weighs life and labor in the balance against silver and gold. That'll *never* balance. But fast and ruthless, it keeps on weighing. It spills a lot of life that way, and sometimes a little gold. And blindfolded, a king comes riding across the desert, with a set of crooked scales, a pair of loaded dice. And upon the flags emblazoned—*Vexilla regis* . . .

"No!" the abbot grunted, suppressing the vision.

But of course! the saint's wooden smile seemed to insist.

Dom Paulo averted his eyes from the image with a slight shudder. Sometimes he felt that the saint was laughing *at* him. Do they laugh *at* us in Heaven? he wondered. Saint Maisie of York herself—remember her, old man—she died of a laughing fit. That's different. She died laughing at herself. No, that's not so different either. *Ulp!* The silent belch again. Tuesday's Saint Maisie's feast day, forsooth. Choir laughs reverently at the *Alleluia* of her Mass. "*Alleluia* ha ha! *Alleluia* ho ho!"

"*Sancta Maisie, interride pro me.*"

And the king was coming to weigh books in the basement with his pair of crooked scales. How "crooked," Paulo? And what makes you think the Memorabilia is completely free of pap? Even the gifted and Venerable Boedullus once remarked scornfully that about half of it should be called the Inscrutabilia. Treasured fragments of a dead civilization there were indeed—but how much of it has been reduced to gibberish, embellished with olive leaves and cherubims, by forty generations of us monastic ignoramuses, children of dark centuries, many, entrusted by adults with an incomprehensible message, to be memorized and delivered to other adults.

I made him travel all the way from Texarkana through dangerous country, thought Paulo. Now I'm just worrying that what we've got may prove worthless to him, that's all.

But no, that wasn't all. He glanced at the smiling saint again. And again: *Vexilla regis inferni prodeunt*. . . . Forth come the banners of the King of Hell, whispered a memory of that perverted line from an ancient *commedia*. It nagged like an unwanted tune in his thought.

The fist clenched tighter. He dropped the fan and breathed through his teeth. He avoided looking at the saint again. The ruthless angel ambushed him with a hot burst at his corporeal core. He leaned over the desk. That one had felt like a hot wire breaking. His hard breathing swept a clean spot in the film of desert dust on the desktop. The smell of the dust was choking. The room went pink, swarmed with black gnats. I don't dare belch, might shake something loose—but Holy Saint and Patron I've got to. Pain is. *Ergo sum*. Lord Christ God accept this token.

He belched, tasted salt, let his head fall onto the desk.

Does the chalice have to be now right this very minute Lord or can I wait awhile? But crucifixion is always now. Now ever since before Abraham even is always now. Before Pfardentrott even, now. Always for everybody anyhow is to get nailed on it and then to hang on it and if you drop off they beat you to death with a shovel so do it with dignity old man. If you can belch with dignity you may get to Heaven if you're sorry enough about messing up the rug. . . . He felt very apologetic.

He waited a long time. Some of the gnats died and the room lost its blush but went hàzy and gray.

Well, Paulo, are we going to hemorrhage now, or are we just going to fool around about it?

He probed the haze and found the face of the saint again. It was such a small grin—sad, understanding, and, something else. Laughing at the hangman? No, laughing *for* the hangman. Laughing at the *Stultus Maximus*, at Satan himself. It was the first time he had seen it clearly. In the *last* chalice, there could be a chuckle of triumph. *Haec commixtio* . . .

He was suddenly very sleepy; the saint's face grayed over, but the abbot continued to grin weakly in response.

Prior Gault found him slumped over the desk shortly before None. Blood showed between his teeth. The young priest quickly felt for a pulse. Dom Paulo awakened at once, straightened in his chair, and, as if still in a dream, he pontificated imperiously: "I tell you, it's all supremely ridiculous! It's absolutely idiotic! Nothing could be more *absurd.*"

"What's absurd, Domne?"

The abbot shook his head, blinked several times. "*What?*"

"I'll get Brother Andrew at once."

"Oh? *That's* absurd. Come back here. What did you want?"

"Nothing, Father Abbot. I'll be back as soon as I get Brother—"

"Oh, bother the medic! You didn't come in here for nothing. My door was closed. Close it again, sit down, say what you wanted."

"The test was successful. Brother Kornhoer's lamp, I mean."

"All right, let's hear about it. Sit down, start talking, tell me all*lll* about it." He straightened his habit and blotted his mouth with a bit of linen. He was still dizzy, but the fist in his belly had come unclenched. He could not have cared less about the prior's account of the test, but he tried his best to appear attentive. *Got to keep him here until I'm awake enough to think. Can't let him go for the medic—not yet; the news would get out: The old man is finished. Got to decide whether it's a safe time to be finished or not.*

15 Hongan Os was essentially a just and kindly man. When he saw a party of his warriors making sport of the Laredan captives, he paused to watch; but when they tied three Laredans by their ankles between horses and whipped the horses into frenzied flight, Hongan Os decided to intervene. He ordered that the warriors be flogged on the spot, for Hongan Os—Mad Bear—was known to be a merciful chieftain. He had never mistreated a horse.

"Killing captives is woman's work," he growled scornfully at the whipped culprits. "Cleanse yourselves lest you be squawmarked, and withdraw from camp until the New Moon, for you are banished twelve days." And, answering their moans of protest: "Suppose the horses had dragged one of them through camp? The grass-eater chieflings are our guests, and it is known that they are easily frightened by blood. Especially the blood of their own kind. Take heed."

"But *these* are grass-eaters from the South," a warrior objected, gesturing toward the mutilated captives. "Our guests are grass-eaters from the East. Is there not a pact between us real people and the East to make war upon the South?"

"If you speak of it again, your tongue shall be cut out and fed to the dogs!" Mad Bear warned. "Forget that you heard such things."

"Will the herb-men be among us for many days, O Son of the Mighty?"

"Who can know what the farmer-things plan?" Mad Bear asked crossly. "Their thought is not as our thought. They say that some of their numbers will depart from here to pass on across the Dry Lands—to a place of the grass-eater priests, a place of the dark-robed ones. The others will stay here to talk—but *that* is not for your ears. Now go, and be ashamed twelve days."

He turned his back that they might slink away without feeling his gaze pour upon them. Discipline was becoming lax of late. The clans were restless. It had become known among the people of the Plains that he, Hongan Os, had clasped arms across a treaty-fire with a messenger from Texarkana, and that a shaman had clipped hair and fingernails from each of them to make a good-faith doll as a defense against treachery by either party. It was known that an agreement had been made, and any agreement between people and grass-eaters was regarded by the tribes as a cause for shame. Mad Bear had felt the veiled scorn of the younger warriors, but there was no explaining to them until the right time came.

Mad Bear himself was willing to listen to good thought, even if it came from a dog. The thought of grass-eaters was seldom good, but he had been impressed by the messages of the grass-eater king in the east, who had expounded the value of secrecy and deplored the idle boast. If the Laredans learned that the tribes were being armed by Hannegan, the plan would surely fail. Mad Bear had brooded on this thought; it repelled him—for certainly it was more satisfying and more manly to tell an enemy what one intended to do to him before doing it; and yet, the more he brooded on it, the more he saw its wisdom. Either the grass-eater king was a craven coward, or else he was almost as wise as a man: Mad Bear had not decided which—but he judged the thought itself as wise. Secrecy was essential, even if it seemed womanly for a time. If Mad Bear's own people knew that the arms which came to them were gifts from Hannegan, and not really the spoils of border raids, then there would arise the possibility of Laredo's learning of the scheme from captives caught on raids. It was therefore necessary to let the tribes grumble about the shame of talking peace with the farmers of the east.

But the talk was not of peace. The talk was good, and it promised loot.

A few weeks ago, Mad Bear himself had led a "war party" to the east and had returned with a hundred head of horses, four dozen long rifles, several kegs of black powder, ample shot, and one prisoner. But not even the warriors who had accompanied him knew that the cache of arms had been planted there for him by Hannegan's men, or that the prisoner was in reality a Texarkanan cavalry officer who would in the future advise Mad Bear about probable Laredan tactics during the fighting to come. All grass-eater thought was shameless, but the officer's thought could probe that of the grass-eaters to the south. It could not probe that of Hongan Os.

Mad Bear was justifiably proud of himself as a bargainer. He had pledged nothing but to refrain from making war upon Texarkana and to stop stealing cattle from the eastern borders, but only as long as Hannegan furnished him with arms and supplies. The agreement to war against Laredo was an unspoken pledge of the fire, but it fitted Mad Bear's natural inclinations, and there was no need for a formal pact. Alliance with one of his enemies would permit him to deal with one foe at a time, and eventually he might regain the grazing lands that had been encroached upon and settled by the farmer-people during the previous century.

Night had fallen by the time the clans chief rode into camp, and a chill had come over the Plains. His guests from the east sat huddled in their blankets around the council fire with three of the old people while the usual ring of curious children gaped from surrounding shadows and peeped under tent skirts at the strangers. There were twelve strangers in all, but they separated themselves into two distinct parties which had traveled together but apparently cared little for each other's company. The leader of one party was obviously a madman. While Mad Bear did not object to insanity (indeed, it was prized by his shamans as the most intense of supernatural visitations), he had not known that the farmers likewise regarded madness as a virtue in a leader. But this one spent half of his time digging in the earth down by the dry riverbed and the other half jotting mysteriously in a small book. Obviously a witch, and probably not to be trusted.

Mad Bear stopped only long enough to don his ceremonial wolf robes and have a shaman paint the totem mark on his forehead before he joined the group at the fire.

"Be afraid!" an old warrior ceremonially wailed as the clans chief stepped into the firelight. "Be afraid, for the Mighty One walks among his children. Grovel, O clans, for his name is *Mad Bear*—a name well won, for as a youth he did overcome without weapons a bear run mad, with his naked hands did he strangle her, verily in the North-lands. . . ."

Hongan Os ignored the eulogies and accepted a cup of blood from the old woman who served the council fire. It was fresh from a butchered steer and still warm. He drained it before turning to nod at the Easterners who watched the brief wassail with apparent disquiet.

"Aaaah!" said the clans chief.

"Aaaah!" replied the three old people, together with one grass-eater who dared to chime in. The people stared at the grass-eater for a moment in disgust.

The insane one tried to cover his companion's blunder. "Tell me," said the madman when the chieftain was seated. "How is it that your people drink no water? Do your gods object?"

"Who knows what the gods drink?" rumbled Mad Bear. "It is said that water is for cattle and farmers, that milk is for children and blood for men. Should it be otherwise?"

The insane one was not insulted. He studied the chief for a moment with searching gray eyes, then nodded at one of his fellows. "That 'water for the cattle' explains it," he said. "The everlasting drought out here. A herdsman people would conserve what little water there is for the animals. I was wondering if they backed it by a religious taboo."

His companion grimaced and spoke in the Texarkanan tongue. "Water! Ye gods, why can't *we* drink water, Thon Taddeo? There's such a thing as too much conformity!" He spat dryly. "Blood! Blah! It sticks in the throat. Why can't we have one little sip of—"

"Not until we leave!"

"But, Thon—"

"No," snapped the scholar; then, noticing that the clans people were glowering at them, he spoke to Mad Bear in tongue of the Plains again. "My comrade here was speaking of the manliness and health of your people," he said. "Perhaps your diet is responsible."

"Ha!" barked the chief, but then called almost cheerfully to the old woman: "Give that outlander a cup of red."

Thon Taddeo's companion shuddered, but made no protest.

"I have, O Chief, a request to make of your greatness," said the scholar. "Tomorrow we shall continue our journey to the west. If some of your warriors could accompany our party, we would be honored."

"Why?"

Thon Taddeo paused. "Why—as guides . . ." He stopped, and suddenly smiled. "No, I'll be quite truthful. Some of your people disapprove of our presence here. While your hospitality has been—"

Hongan Os threw back his head and roared with laughter. "They are afraid of the lesser clans," he said to the old ones. "They fear being ambushed as soon as they leave my tents. They eat grass and are afraid of a fight."

The scholar flushed slightly.

"Fear nothing, outlander!" chortled the clans chief. "Real *men* shall accompany you."

Thon Taddeo inclined his head in mock gratitude.

"Tell us," said Mad Bear, "what is it you go to seek in the western Dry Land? New places for planting fields? I can tell you there are none. Except near a few water holes, nothing grows that even cattle will eat."

"We seek no new land," the visitor answered. "We are not all of us farmers, you know. We are going to look for—" He paused. In the nomad speech, there was no way to explain the purpose of the journey to the Abbey of St. Leibowitz "—for the skills of an ancient sorcery."

One of the old ones, a shaman, seemed to prick up his

ears. "An ancient sorcery in the west? I know of no magicians there. Unless you mean the dark-robed ones?"

"They are the ones."

"*Ha!* What magic do they have that's worth looking after? Their messengers can be captured so easily that it is no real sport—although they do endure torture well. What sorcery can you learn from them?"

"Well, for my part, I agree with you," said Thon Taddeo. "But it is said that writings, uh, *incantations* of great power are hoarded at one of their abodes. If it is true, then obviously the dark-robed ones don't know how to use them, but we hope to master them for ourselves."

"Will the dark-robes permit you to observe their secrets?"

Thon Taddeo smiled. "I think so. They don't dare hide them any longer. We could take them, if we had to."

"A brave saying," scoffed Mad Bear. "Evidently the farmers are braver among their own kind—although they are meek enough among *real* people."

The scholar, who had stomached his fill of the nomad's insults, chose to retire early.

The soldiers remained at the council fire to discuss with Hongan Os the war that was certain to come; but the war, after all, was none of Thon Taddeo's affair. The political aspirations of his ignorant cousin were far from his own interest in a revival of learning in a dark world, except when that monarch's patronage proved useful, as it already had upon several occasions.

16   The old hermit stood at the edge of the mesa and watched the approach of the dust speck across the desert. The hermit munched, muttered words and chuckled silently into the wind. His withered hide was burned the color of old leather by the sun, and his brushy beard was stained yellow about the chin. He wore a basket hat and a loincloth of rough homespun that resembled burlap—his only clothing except for sandals and a goat-skin water bag.

He watched the dust speck until it passed through the village of Sanly Bowitts and departed again by way of the road leading past the mesa.

"Ah!" snorted the hermit, his eyes beginning to burn. "*His* empire shall be multiplied, and there shall be no end of *his* peace: *he* shall sit upon *his* kingdom."

Suddenly he went down the arroyo like a cat with three legs, using his staff, bounding from stone to stone and sliding most of the way. The dust from his rapid descent plumed high on the wind and wandered away.

At the foot of the mesa he vanished into the mesquite and settled down to wait. Soon he heard the rider approaching at a lazy trot, and he began slinking toward the road to peer out through the brush. The pony appeared from around the bend, wrapped in a thin dust shroud. The hermit darted into the trail and threw up his arms.

"*Olla allay!*" he shouted; and as the rider halted, he darted forward to seize the reins and frown anxiously up at the man in the saddle.

His eyes blazed for a moment. "For a Child is born to us, and a Son is given us . . ." But then the anxious frown melted away into sadness. "It's not *Him!*" he grumbled irritably at the sky.

The rider had thrown back his hood and was laughing. The hermit blinked angrily at him for a moment. Recognition dawned.

"Oh," he grunted. "You! I thought you'd be dead by now. What are you doing out here?"

"I brought back your prodigal, Benjamin," said Dom Paulo. He tugged at a leash and the blue-headed goat trotted up from behind the pony. It bleated and strained at the rope upon seeing the hermit. "And . . . I thought I'd pay you a visit."

"The animal is the Poet's," the hermit grunted. "He won it *fairly* in a game of chance—although he *cheated* miserably. Take it back to him, and let me counsel you against meddling in worldly swindles that don't concern you. Good day." He turned toward the arroyo.

"Wait, Benjamin. Take your goat, or I'll give it to a peasant. I won't have it wandering around the abbey and bleating into the church."

"It's not a goat," the hermit said crossly. "It's the beast which your prophet saw, and it was made for a woman to ride. I suggest you curse it and drive it into the desert. You notice, however, that it divideth the hoof and cheweth the cud." He started away again.

The abbot's smile faded. "Benjamin, are you really going

back up that hill without even a 'hello' for an old friend?"

"Hello," the Old Jew called back, and marched indignantly on. After a few steps he stopped to glance over his shoulder. "You needn't look so hurt," he said. "It's been five years since you've troubled to come this way, 'old friend.' Hah!"

"So that's it!" muttered the abbot. He dismounted and hurried after the Old Jew. "Benjamin, Benjamin, I would have come—I have not been free."

The hermit stopped. "Well, Paulo, since you're here . . ."

Suddenly they laughed and embraced.

"It's good, you old grump," said the hermit.

"*I* a grump?"

"Well, *I'm* getting cranky too, I guess. The last century has been a trying one for me."

"I hear you've been throwing rocks at the novices who come hereabouts for their Lenten fast in the desert. Can this be true?" He eyed the hermit with mock reproof.

"Only pebbles."

"Miserable old pretzel!"

"Now, now, Paulo. One of them once mistook me for a distant relative of mine—name of Leibowitz. He thought I had been sent to deliver him a message—or some of your other scalawags thought so. I don't want it to happen again, so I throw pebbles at them sometimes. Hah! I'll not be mistaken for *that* kinsman again, for he stopped being any kin of mine."

The priest looked puzzled. "Mistook you for whom? Saint Leibowitz? Now, Benjamin! You're going too far."

Benjamin repeated it in a mocking singsong: "Mistook me for a distant relative of mine—name of Leibowitz, so I throw pebbles at them."

Dom Paulo looked thoroughly perplexed. "Saint Leibowitz has been dead a dozen centuries. How could—" He broke off and peered warily at the old hermit. "Now, Benjamin, let's don't start *that* tale wagging again. You haven't lived twelve cent—"

"Nonsense!" interrupted the Old Jew. "I didn't say it happened twelve centuries ago. It was only six centuries ago. Long after your Saint was dead; that's why it was so preposterous. Of course, your novices were more devout in those days, and more credulous. I think Francis was that one's name. Poor fellow. I buried him later. Told them in New

Rome where to dig for him. That's how you got his carcass back."

The abbot gaped at the old man as they walked through the mesquite toward the water hole, leading the horse and the goat. *Francis?* he wondered. Francis. That could be the Venerable Francis Gerard of Utah, perhaps?—to whom a pilgrim had once revealed the location of the old shelter in the village, so that story went—but that was before the village was there. And about six centuries ago, yes, and—now this old gaffer was claiming to have been that pilgrim? He sometimes wondered where Benjamin had picked up enough knowledge of the abbey's history to invent such tales. From the Poet, perhaps.

"That was during my earlier career, of course," the Old Jew went on, "and perhaps such a mistake was understandable."

"Earlier career?"

"Wanderer."

"How do you expect me to believe such nonsense?"

"Hmm-hnnn! The Poet believes me."

"Undoubtedly! The Poet certainly would never believe that the Venerable Francis met a saint. *That* would be superstition. The Poet would rather believe he met *you*—six centuries ago. A purely natural explanation, eh?"

Benjamin chuckled wryly. Paulo watched him lower a leaky bark cup into the well, empty it into his water skin, and lower it again for more. The water was cloudy and alive with creeping uncertainties as was the Old Jew's stream of memory. Or *was* his memory uncertain? Playing games with us all? wondered the priest. Except for his delusion of being older than Methuselah, old Benjamin Eleazar seemed sane enough, in his own wry way.

"Drink?" the hermit offered, extending the cup.

The abbot suppressed a shudder, but accepted the cup so as not to offend; he drained the murky liquid at a gulp.

"Not very particular, are you?" said Benjamin, watching him critically. "Wouldn't touch it myself." He patted the water skin. "For the animals."

The abbot gagged slightly.

"You've changed," said Benjamin, still watching him. "You've grown pale as cheese and wasted."

"I've been ill."

"You *look* ill. Come up to my shack, if the climb won't tire you out."

"I'll be all right. I had a little trouble the other day, and
our physician told me to rest. Fah! If an important guest
weren't coming soon, I'd pay no attention. But he's coming,
so I'm resting. It's quite tiresome."

Benjamin glanced back at him with a grin as they climbed
the arroyo. He waggled his grizzly head. "Riding ten miles
across the desert is resting?"

"For me it's rest. And, I've been wanting to see you,
Benjamin."

"What will the villagers say?" the Old Jew asked mockingly.
"They'll think we've become reconciled, and that will spoil
both our reputations."

"Our reputations never have amounted to much in the
market place, have they?"

"True," he admitted, but added cryptically: "for the present."

"Still waiting, Old Jew?"

"Certainly!" the hermit snapped.

The abbot found the climb tiring. Twice they stopped to
rest. By the time they reached the tableland, he had become
dizzy and was leaning on the spindly hermit for support.
A dull fire burned in his chest, warning against further
exertion, but there was none of the angry clenching that
had come before.

A flock of the blue-headed goat-mutants scattered at the
approach of a stranger and fled into straggly mesquite.
Oddly, the mesa seemed more verdant than the surrounding desert, although there was no visible supply of moisture.

"This way, Paulo. To my mansion."

The Old Jew's hovel proved to be a single room, window-
less and stone-walled, its rocks stacked loosely as a fence,
with wide chinks through which the wind could blow. The
roof was a flimsy patchwork of poles, most of them
crooked, covered by a heap of brush, thatch, and goatskins.
On a large flat rock, set on a short pillar beside the door,
was a sign painted in Hebrew:

פה מתקנין אוהלים

The size of the sign, and its apparent attempt to advertise,
led Abbot Paulo to grin and ask: "What does it say, Benjamin? Does it attract much trade up here?"

"Hah—what should it say? It says: Tents Mended Here."
The priest snorted his disbelief.

"All right, doubt me. But if you don't believe what's written there, you can't be expected to believe what's written on the *other* side of the sign."

"Facing the wall?"

"Obviously facing the wall."

The pillar was set close to the threshold, so that only a few inches of clearance existed between the flat rock and the wall of the hovel. Paulo stooped low and squinted into the narrow space. It took him a while to make it out, but sure enough there was something written on the back of the rock, in smaller letters:

שמע ישראל יהוה אלהינו יהוה אחד)

"Do you ever turn the rock around?"

"Turn it *around?* You think I'm *crazy?* In times like *these?*"

"What does it say back there?"

"Hmmm-*hnnnn!*" the hermit singsonged, refusing to answer. "But come on it, you who can't read from the backside."

"There's a wall slightly in the way."

"There always was, wasn't there?"

The priest sighed. "All right, Benjamin, I know what it was that you were commanded to write 'in the entry and on the door' of your house. But only *you* would think of turning it face down."

"Face *inward,*" corrected the hermit. "As long as there are tents to be mended in Israel—but let's not begin teasing each other until you've rested. I'll get you some milk, and you tell me about this visitor that's worrying you."

"There's wine in my bag if you'd like some," said the abbot, falling with relief onto a mound of skins. "But I'd rather not talk about Thon Taddeo."

"Oh? *That* one."

"You've heard of Thon Taddeo? Tell me, how is it you've always managed to know everything and everybody without stirring from this hill?"

"One hears, one sees," the hermit said cryptically.

"Tell me, what do you think of him?"

"I haven't see him. But I suppose he will be a pain. A birth-pain, perhaps, but a pain."

"Birth-pain? You really believe we're going to have a new Renaissance, as some say?"

"Hmmm-*hnnn.*"

"Stop smirking mysteriously, Old Jew, and tell me your opinion. You're bound to have one. You always do. Why is your confidence so hard to get? Aren't we friends?"

"On some grounds, on some grounds. But we have our differences, you and I."

"What have our differences got to do with Thon Taddeo and a Renaissance we'd both like to see? Thon Taddeo is a secular scholar, and rather remote from our differences."

Benjamin shrugged eloquently. "Difference, secular scholars," he echoed, tossing out the words like discarded apple pits. "*I* have been called a 'secular scholar' at various times by certain people, and sometimes I've been staked, stoned, and burned for it."

"Why, you never—" The priest stopped, frowning sharply. That madness again. Benjamin was peering at him suspiciously, and his smile had gone cold. *Now*, thought the abbot, he's looking at me as if I were one of *Them*—whatever formless "Them" it was that drove him here to solitude. Staked, stoned, and burned? Or did his "I" mean "We" as in "I, my people"?

"Benjamin—I am Paulo. Torquemada is dead. I was born seventy-odd years ago, and pretty soon I'll die. I have loved you, old man, and when you look at me, I wish you would see Paulo of Pecos and no other."

Benjamin wavered for a moment. His eyes became moist. "I sometimes—forget—"

"And sometimes you forget that Benjamin is only Benjamin, and not all of Israel."

"Never!" snapped the hermit, eyes blazing again. "For thirty-two centuries, I—" He stopped and closed his mouth tightly.

"Why?" the abbot whispered almost in awe. "Why do you take the burden of a people and its past upon yourself alone?"

The hermit's eyes flared a brief warning, but he swallowed a throaty sound and lowered his face into his hands. "You fish in dark waters."

"Forgive me."

"The burden—it was pressed upon me by others." He looked up slowly. "Should I refuse to take it?"

The priest sucked in his breath. For a time there was no sound in the shanty but the sound of the wind. There was a touch of divinity in this madness! Dom Paulo thought. The Jewish community was thinly scattered in these times. Benjamin had perhaps outlived his children, or somehow become an outcast. Such an old Israelite might wander for years without encountering others of his people. Perhaps in his loneliness he had acquired the silent conviction that he was *the last*, the one, the only. And, being the last, he ceased to be Benjamin, becoming Israel. And upon his heart had settled the history of five thousand years, no longer remote, but become as the history of his own lifetime. His "I" was the converse of the imperial "We."

But I, too, am a member of a oneness, thought Dom Paulo, a part of a congregation and a continuity. Mine, too, have been despised by the world. Yet for me the distinction between self and nation is clear. For you, old friend, it has somehow become obscure. A burden pressed upon you by others? And you accepted it? What must it weigh? What would it weigh for me? He set his shoulders under it and tried to heave, testing the bulk of it: I am a Christian monk and priest, and I am, therefore, accountable before God for the actions and deeds of every monk and priest who has breathed and walked the earth since Christ, as well as for the acts of my own.

He shuddered and began shaking his head.

No, no. It crushed the spine, this burden. It was too much for any man to bear, save Christ alone. To be cursed for a faith was burden enough. To bear the curses was possible, but then—to accept the illogic behind the curses, the illogic which called one to task not only for himself but also for every member of his race or faith, for their actions as well as one's own? To accept that too?—as Benjamin was trying to do?

No, no.

And yet, Dom Paulo's own Faith told him that the burden was there, had been there since Adam's time—and the burden imposed by a fiend crying in mockery, *"Man!"* at man. *"Man!"*—calling each to account for the deeds of all since the beginning; a burden impressed upon every generation before the opening of the womb, the burden of the guilt of original sin. Let the fool dispute it. The same fool with great delight accepted the *other* inheritance—the inheritance of ancestral glory, virtue, triumph, and dignity which rendered him "courageous and noble by reason of birthright," without protesting that he personally had done nothing to earn that inheritance beyond being born of the race of Man. The protest was reserved for the inherited burden which rendered him "guilty and outcast by reason of birthright," and against that verdict he strained to close his ears. The burden, indeed, was hard. His own Faith told him, too, that the burden had been lifted from him by the One whose image hung from a cross above the altars, although the burden's imprint still was there. The imprint was an easier yoke, compared to the full weight of the original curse. He could not bring himself to say it to the old man, since the old man already knew he believed it. Benjamin was looking for Another. And the last old Hebrew sat alone on a mountain and did penance for Israel and waited for a Messiah, and waited, and waited, and—

"God bless you for a brave fool. Even a wise fool."

"Hmmm-*hnnn!* Wise fool!" mimicked the hermit. "But you always did specialize in paradox and mystery, didn't you, Paulo? If a thing can't be in contradiction to itself, then it doesn't even interest you, does it? You have to find Threeness in Unity, life in death, wisdom in folly. Otherwise it might make too much common sense."

"To sense the responsibility is wisdom, Benjamin. To think you can carry it alone is folly."

"Not madness?"

"A little, perhaps. But a brave madness."

"Then I'll tell you a small secret. I've known all along that I can't carry it, ever since He called me forth again. But are we talking about the same thing?"

The priest shrugged. "You would call it the burden of being Chosen. I would call it the burden of Original Guilt. In either case, the implied responsibility is the same, although we might tell different versions of it, and disagree violently in words about what we mean *in* words by something that isn't really meant in words at all—since it's something that's meant in the dead silence of a heart."

Benjamin chuckled. "Well, I'm glad to hear you admit it, finally, even if all you say is that you've never really said anything."

"Stop cackling, you reprobate."

"But you've always used words so wordily in crafty defense of your Trinity, although He never needed such defense before you got Him from me as a Unity. Eh?"

The priest reddened but said nothing.

"*There!*" Benjamin yelped, bouncing up and down. "I made you want to argue for once! Ha! But never mind. I use quite a few words myself, but I'm never quite sure He and

I mean the same thing either. I suppose *you* can't be blamed; it must be more confusing with Three than with One."

"Blasphemous old cactus! I really wanted your opinion of Thon Taddeo and whatever's brewing."

"Why seek the opinion of a poor old anchorite?"

"Because, Benjamin Eleazar bar Joshua, if all these years of waiting for One-Who-Isn't-Coming haven't taught you wisdom, at least they've made you shrewd."

The Old Jew closed his eyes, lifted his face ceilingward, and smiled cunningly. "Insult me," he said in mocking tones, "rail at me, bait me, persecute me—but do you know what I'll say?"

"You'll say, 'Hmmm-*hnnn!*' "

"No! I'll say He's already here. I caught a glimpse of Him once."

"What? Who are you talking about? Thon Taddeo?"

"*No!* Moreover, I do not care to prophesy, unless you tell me what's really bothering you, Paulo."

"Well, it all started with Brother Kornhoer's lamp."

"Lamp? Oh, yes, the Poet mentioned it. *He* prophesied it wouldn't work."

"The Poet was wrong, as usual. So they tell me. I didn't watch the trial."

"It worked then? Splendid. And that started what?"

"Me wondering. How close are we to the brink of something? Or how close to a shore? Electrical essences in the basement. Do you realize how much things have changed in the past two centuries?"

Soon, the priest spoke at length of his fears, while the hermit, mender of tents, listened patiently until the sun had begun to leak through the chinks in the west wall to paint glowing shafts in the dusty air.

"Since the death of the last civilization, the Memorabilia has been our special province, Benjamin. And we've kept it. But now? I sense the predicament of the shoemaker who tries to sell shoes in a village of shoemakers."

The hermit smiled. "It could be done, if he manufactures a special and superior type of shoe."

"I'm afraid the secular scholars are already beginning to lay claim to such a method."

"Then go out of the shoemaking business, before you are ruined."

"A possibility," the abbot admitted. "It's unpleasant to

think of it however. For twelve centuries, we've been one little island in a very dark ocean. Keeping the Memorabilia has been a thankless task, but a hallowed one, we think. It's only our *worldly* job, but we've always been bookleggers and memorizers, and it's hard to think that the job's soon to be finished—soon to become unnecessary. I can't believe that somehow."

"So you try to best the other 'shoemakers' by building strange contraptions in your basement?"

"I must admit, it looks that way—"

"What will you do next to keep ahead of the seculars? Build a flying machine? Or revive the *Machina analytica*? Or perhaps step over their heads and resort to metaphysics?"

"You shame me, Old Jew. You know we are monks of Christ first, and such things are for others to do."

"I wasn't shaming you. I see nothing inconsistent in monks of Christ building a flying machine, although it would be more like them to build a praying machine."

"Wretch! I do my Order a disservice by sharing a confidence with you!"

Benjamin smirked. "I have no sympathy for you. The books you stored away may be hoary with age, but they were written by children of the world, and they'll be taken from you by children of the world, and you had no business meddling with them in the first place."

"Ah, *now* you care to prophesy!"

"Not at all. 'Soon the sun will set'—is *that* prophecy? No, it's merely an assertion of faith in the consistency of events. The children of the world are consistent too—so I say they will soak up everything you can offer, take your job away from you, and then denounce you as a decrepit wreck. Finally, they'll ignore you entirely. It's your own fault. The Book I gave you should have been enough for you. Now you'll just have to take the consequences for your meddling."

He had spoken flippantly, but his prediction seemed uncomfortably close to Dom Paulo's fears. The priest's countenance saddened.

"Pay me no mind," said the hermit. "I'll not venture to soothsay before I've seen this contraption of yours, or taken a look at this Thon Taddeo—who begins to interest me, by the way. Wait until I've examined the entrails of the new era in better detail, if you expect advice from me."

"Well, you won't see the lamp because you never come to the abbey."

"It's your abominable cooking I object to."

"And you won't see Thon Taddeo because he comes from the other direction. If you wait to examine the entrails of an era until after it's born, it's too late to prophesy its birth."

"Nonsense. Probing the womb of the future is bad for the child. I shall wait—and then I shall prophesy that it *was* born and that it *wasn't* what I'm waiting for."

"What a cheerful outlook! So what *are* you looking for?"

"Someone who shouted at me once."

"Shouted?"

" 'Come forth!' "

"What rot!"

"Hmmm-*hnnn!* To tell you the truth, I don't much expect Him to come, but I was told to wait, and—" he shrugged "—I wait." After a moment his twinkling eyes narrowed to slits, and he leaned forward with sudden eagerness. "Paulo, bring this Thon Taddeo past the foot of the mesa."

The abbot recoiled in mock horror. "Accoster of pilgrims! Molester of novices! I shall send you the Poet-sirrah!—and may he descend upon you and rest forever. Bring the thon past your lair! What an outrage."

Benjamin shrugged again. "Very well. Forget that I asked it. But let's hope this thon will be on our side, and not with the others this time."

"*Others*, Benjamin?"

"Manasses, Cyrus, Nebuchadnezzar, Pharaoh, Caesar, Hannegan the Second—need I go on? Samuel warned us against them, then gave us one. When they have a few wise men shackled nearby to counsel them, they become more dangerous than ever. That's all the advice I'll give you."

"Well, Benjamin, I've had enough of you now to last me another five years, so—"

"Insult me, rail at me, bait me—"

"Stop it. I'm leaving, old man. It's late."

"So? And how is the ecclesiastical belly fixed for the ride?"

"My stomach—?" Dom Paulo paused to explore, found himself more comfortable than at any time in recent weeks. "It's a mess, of course," he complained. "How else would it be after listening to you?"

"True—*El Shaddai* is merciful, but He is also just."

"Godspeed, old man. After Brother Kornhoer reinvents the flying machine, I'll send up some novices to drop rocks on you."

They embraced affectionately. The Old Jew led him to

the edge of the mesa. Benjamin stood wrapped in a prayer shawl, its fine fabric contrasting oddly with the rough burlap of his loincloth, while the abbot climbed down to the trail and rode back toward the abbey. Dom Paulo could still see him standing there at sundown, his spindly figure silhouetted against the twilight sky as he bowed and munched a prayer over the desert.

"*Memento, Domine, omnium famulorum tuorum,*" the abbot whispered in response, adding: "And may he finally win the Poet's eyeball at mumbly-peg. Amen."

17 "I can tell you definitely: There *will* be war," said the messenger from New Rome. "All Laredo's forces are committed to the Plains. Mad Bear has broken camp. There's a running cavalry battle, nomad style, all over the Plains. But the State of Chihuahua is threatening Laredo from the south. So Hannegan is getting ready to send Texarkana forces to the Rio Grande—to help 'defend' the frontier. With the Laredans' full approval, of course."

"King Goraldi is a doddering fool!" said Dom Paulo. "Wasn't he warned against Hannegan's treachery?"

The messenger smiled. "The Vatican diplomatic service always respects state secrets if we happen to learn them. Lest we be accused of espionage, we are always careful about—"

"Was he *warned?*" the abbot demanded again.

"Of course. Goraldi said the papal legate was lying to him; he accused the Church of fomenting dissension among the allies of the Holy Scourge, in an attempt to promote the Pope's temporal power. The idiot even told Hannegan about the legate's warning."

Dom Paulo winced and whistled. "So Hannegan did what?"

The messenger hesitated. "I suppose I can tell you: Monsignor Apollo is under arrest. Hannegan ordered his diplomatic files seized. There's talk in New Rome of placing the whole realm of Texarkana under interdict. Of course, Hannegan has already incurred *ipso facto* excommunication, but

that doesn't seem to bother many Texarkanans. As you surely
know, the population is about eighty per cent cultist anyhow, and the Catholicism of the ruling class has always
been a thin veneer."

"So now Marcus," the abbot murmured sadly. "And
what of Thon Taddeo?"

"I don't quite see how he expects to get across the Plains
without picking up a few musket-ball holes just now. It
seems clear why he hadn't wanted to make the trip. But I
know nothing about his progress, Father Abbot."

Dom Paulo's frown was pained. "If our refusal to send the
material to his university leads to his being killed—"

"Don't trouble your conscience about that, Father Abbot.
Hannegan looks out for his own. I don't know how, but I'm
sure the thon will get here."

"The world could ill afford to lose him, I hear. Well— But
tell me, why were you sent to report Hannegan's plans to
us? We're in the empire of Denver, and I can't see how this
region is affected."

"Ah, but I've told you only the beginning. Hannegan hopes
to unite the continent eventually. After Laredo's firmly
leashed, he will have broken the encirclement that's kept
him in check. Then the next move will be against Denver."

"But wouldn't that involve supply lines across nomad
country? It seems impossible."

"It's extremely difficult, and that's what makes the next
move certain. The Plains form a natural geographical barrier. If they were depopulated, Hannegan might regard his
western frontier as secure as it stands. But the nomads have
made it necessary for all states adjoining the Plains to tie
up permanent military forces around the nomad territory for
containment. The only way to subdue the Plains is to control both fertile strips, to the east and to the west."

"But even so," the abbot wondered, "the nomads—"

"Hannegan's plan for *them* is devilish. Mad Bear's warriors
can easily cope with Laredo's cavalry, but what they can't
cope with is a cattle plague. The Plains tribes don't know
it yet, but when Laredo set out to punish the nomads for
border raiding, the Laredans drove several hundred head of
diseased cattle ahead to mingle with the nomads' herds. It
was Hannegan's idea. The result will be famine, and then
it will be easy to set tribe against tribe. We don't, of course,
know all the details, but the goal is a nomad legion under a

puppet chieftain, armed by Texarkana, loyal to Hannegan, ready to sweep west to the mountains. If it comes to pass, this region will get the first breakers."

"But *why?* Surely Hannegan doesn't expect the barbarians to be dependable troops, or capable of holding an empire once they finish mutilating it!"

"No, m'Lord. But the nomad tribes will be disrupted, Denver will be shattered. Then Hannegan can pick up the pieces."

"To do what with them? It couldn't be a very rich empire."

"No, but secure on all flanks. He might then be in a better position to strike east or northeast. Of course, before it comes to that, his plans may collapse. But whether they collapse or not, this region may well be in danger of being overrun in the not-too-distant future. Steps should be taken to secure the abbey within the next few months. I have instructions to discuss with you the problem of keeping the Memorabilia safe."

Dom Paulo felt the blackness beginning to gather. After twelve centuries, a little hope had come into the world—and then came an illiterate prince to ride roughshod over it with a barbarian horde and . . .

His fist exploded onto the desktop. "We kept them outside our walls for a thousand years," he growled, "and we can keep them out for another thousand. This abbey was under siege three times during the Bayring influx, and once again during the Vissarionist schism. We'll keep the books safe. We've kept them that way for quite some time."

"But there is an added hazard these days, m'Lord."

"What may that be?"

"A bountiful supply of gunpowder and grapeshot."

The Feast of the Assumption had come and gone, but still there was no word of the party from Texarkana. Private votive masses for pilgrims and travelers were beginning to be offered by the abbey's priests. Dom Paulo had ceased taking even a light breakfast, and it was whispered that he was doing penance for having invited the scholar at all, in view of the present danger on the Plains.

The watchtowers remained constantly manned. The abbot himself frequently climbed the wall to peer eastward.

Shortly before Vespers on the Feast of Saint Bernard, a novice reported seeing a thin and distant dust trail, but darkness was coming on, and no one else had been able to make it out. Soon, Compline and the *Salve Regina* were sung, but still no one appeared at the gates.

"It might have been their advance scout," suggested Prior Gault.

"It might have been Brother Watchman's imagination," countered Dom Paulo.

"But if they've camped just ten miles or so down the way—"

"We'd see their fire from the tower. It's a clear night."

"Still, Domne, after the moon rises, we could send a rider—"

"Oh, no. That's a good way to get shot by mistake. If it's really them, they've probably kept their fingers on their triggers for the whole trip, especially at night. It can wait until dawn."

It was late the following morning when the expected party of horsemen appeared out of the east. From the top of the wall Dom Paulo blinked and squinted across the hot and dry terrain, trying to focus myopic eyes on the distance. Dust from the horses' hooves was drifting away to the north. The party had stopped for a parley.

"I seem to be seeing twenty or thirty of them," the abbot complained, rubbing his eyes in annoyance. "Are there really so many?"

"Approximately," said Gault.

"How will we ever take care of them all?"

"I don't think we'll be taking care of the ones with the wolfskins, m'Lord Abbot," the younger priest said stiffly.

"*Wolf*skins?"

"Nomads, m'Lord."

"Man the walls! Close the gates! Let down the shield! Break out the—"

"Wait, they're not *all* nomads, Domne."

"Oh?" Dom Paulo turned to peer again.

The parley was being ended. Men waved; the group split in two. The larger party galloped back toward the east. The remaining horsemen watched briefly, then reined around and trotted toward the abbey.

"Six or seven of them—some in uniform," the abbot murmured as they drew closer.

"The thon and his party, I'm sure."

"But with nomads? It's a good thing I didn't let you send a rider out last night. What were they doing with nomads?"

"It appeared that they came as guides," Father Gault said darkly.

"How neighborly of the lion to lie down with the lamb!"

The riders approached the gates. Dom Paulo swallowed dryness. "Well, we'd better go welcome them, Father," he sighed.

By the time the priests had descended from the wall, the travelers had reined up just outside the courtyard. A horse-man detached himself from the others, trotted forward, dis-mounted, and presented his papers.

"Dom Paulo of Pecos, Abbas?"

The abbot bowed. "*Tibi adsum.* Welcome in the name of Saint Leibowitz, Thon Taddeo. Welcome in the name of his abbey, in the name of forty generations who've waited for you to come. Be at home. We serve you." The words were heart-felt; the words had been saved for many years while awaiting this moment. Hearing a muttered monosyllable in reply, Dom Paulo looked up slowly.

For a moment his glance locked with the scholar's. He felt the warmth quickly fade. Those icy eyes—cold and search-ing gray. Skeptical, hungry, and proud. They studied him as one might study a lifeless curio.

That this moment might be as a bridge across a gulf of twelve centuries, Paulo had fervently prayed—prayed too that through him the last martyred scientist of that earlier age would clasp hands with tomorrow. There was indeed a gulf; that much was plain. The abbot felt suddenly that he belonged not to this age at all, that he had been left stranded somewhere on a sandbar in Time's river, and that there wasn't really ever a bridge at all.

"Come," he said gently. "Brother Visclair will attend to your horses."

When he had seen the guests installed in their lodgings and had retired to the privacy of his study, the smile on the face of the wooden saint reminded him unaccountably of the smirk of old Benjamin Eleazar, saying, "The children of this world are consistent too."

18 " 'Now even as in the time of Job,' " Brother Reader began from the refectory lectern:

"When the sons of God came to stand before the Lord, Satan also was present among them.

"And the Lord said to him: 'Whence comest thou, Satan?'

"And Satan answering said, as of old: 'I have gone round about the earth, and have walked through it.'

"And the Lord said to him: 'Hast thou considered that simple and upright prince, my servant *Name*, hating evil and loving peace?' "

"And Satan answering said: 'Doth *Name* fear God in vain? For hast Thou not blessed his land with great wealth and made him mighty among nations? But stretch forth Thy hand a little and decrease what he hath, and let his enemy be strengthened; then see if he blasphemeth Thee not to Thy face.'

"And the Lord said to Satan: 'Behold what he hath, and lessen it. See thou to it.'

"And Satan went forth from the presence of God and returned into the world.

"Now the Prince *Name* was not as Holy Job, for when his land was afflicted with trouble and his people less rich than before, when he saw his enemy become mightier, he grew fearful and ceased to trust in God, thinking unto himself: I must strike before the enemy overwhelmeth me without taking his sword in hand.

" 'And so it was in those days,' " said Brother Reader:

"that the princes of Earth had hardened their hearts against the Law of the Lord, and of their pride there was no end. And each of them thought within himself that it was better for all to be destroyed than for the will of other princes to prevail over his. For the mighty of the Earth did contend among themselves for supreme power over all; by stealth, treachery, and deceit they did seek to rule, and of war they feared greatly and did tremble; for the Lord God had suffered the wise men of those times to learn the means by which the world itself might be destroyed, and into their hands was given the sword of the Archangel wherewith Lucifer had been cast down, that men and princes might fear God and humble themselves before the Most High. But they were not humbled.

"And Satan spoke unto a certain prince, saying: 'Fear not to use the sword, for the wise men have deceived you in saying that the world would be destroyed thereby. Listen not to the counsel of weaklings, for they fear you exceedingly, and they serve your enemies by staying your hand against them. Strike, and know that you shall be king over all.'

"And the prince did heed the word of Satan, and he summoned all of the wise men of that realm and called upon them to give him counsel as to the ways in which the enemy might be destroyed without bringing down the wrath upon his own kingdom. But most of the wise men said, 'Lord, it is not possible, for your enemies also have the sword which we have given you, and the fieriness of it is as the flame of Hell and as the fury of the sun-star from whence it was kindled.'

"'Then thou shalt make me yet another which is yet seven times hotter than Hell itself,' commanded the prince, whose arrogance had come to surpass that of Pharaoh.

"And many of them said: 'Nay, Lord, ask not this thing of us; for even the smoke of such a fire, if we were to kindle it for thee, would cause many to perish.'

"Now the prince was angry because of their answer, and he suspected them of betraying him, and he sent his spies among them to tempt them and to challenge them; whereupon the wise men became afraid. Some among them changed their answers, that his wrath be not invoked against them. Three times he asked them, and three times they answered: 'Nay, Lord, even your own people will perish if you do this thing.' But one of the magi was like unto Judas Iscariot, and his testimony was crafty, and having betrayed his brothers, he lied to all the people, advising them not to fear the demon Fallout. The prince heeded this false wise man, whose name was Backeneth, and he caused spies to accuse many of the magi before the people. Being afraid, the less wise among the magi counseled the prince according to his pleasure, saying: 'The weapons may be used, only do not exceed such-and-such a limit, or all will surely perish.'

"And the prince smote the cities of his enemies with the new fire, and for three days and nights did his great catapults and metal birds rain wrath upon them. Over each city a sun appeared and was brighter than the sun of heaven, and immediately that city withered and melted as wax under the torch, and the people thereof did stop in the streets and their skins smoked and they became as fagots thrown on the coals. And when the fury of the sun had faded, the city was in flames; and a great thunder came out of the sky, like the great battering-ram *PIK-A-DON*, to crush it utterly. Poisonous fumes fell over all the land, and the land was aglow by night with the afterfire and the curse of the afterfire which caused a scurf on the skin and made the hair to fall and the blood to die in the veins.

"And a great stink went up from Earth even unto Heaven. Like unto Sodom and Gomorrah was the Earth and the ruins thereof, even in the land of that certain prince, for his enemies did not withhold their vengeance, sending fire in turn to engulf his cities as their own. The stink of the carnage was exceedingly offensive to the Lord, Who spoke unto the prince, *Name,* saying: 'WHAT BURNT OFFERING IS THIS THAT YOU HAVE PREPARED BEFORE ME? WHAT IS THIS SAVOR THAT ARISES FROM THE PLACE OF HOLOCAUST? HAVE YOU MADE ME A HOLOCAUST OF SHEEP OR GOATS, OR OFFERED A CALF UNTO GOD?'

"But the prince answered him not, and God said: 'YOU HAVE MADE ME A HOLOCAUST OF MY SONS.'

"And the Lord slew him together with Blackeneth, the betrayer, and there was pestilence in the Earth, and madness was upon mankind, who stoned the wise together with the powerful, those who remained.

"But there was in that time a man whose name was Leibowitz, who, in his youth like the holy Augustine, had loved the wisdom of the world more than the wisdom of God. But now seeing that great knowledge, while good, had not saved the world, he turned in penance to the Lord, crying:"

The abbot rapped sharply on the table and the monk who had been reading the ancient account was immediately silent.

"And that is your only account of it?" asked Thon Taddeo, smiling tightly at the abbot across the study.

"Oh, there are several versions. They differ in minor details. No one is certain which nation launched the first attack—not that it matters any more. The text Brother Reader was just reading was written a few decades after the death of Saint Leibowitz—probably one of the first accounts—after it became safe to write again. The author was a young monk who had not lived through the destruction himself; he got it second hand from Saint Leibowitz' followers, the original memorizers and bookleggers, and he had a liking for scriptural mimicry. I doubt if a single *completely* accurate account of the Flame Deluge exists anywhere. Once it started, it was apparently too immense for any one person to see the whole picture."

"In what land was this prince called Name, and this man Blackeneth?"

Abbot Paulo shook his head. "Not even the author of that account was certain. We've pieced enough together since that was written to know that even some of the *lesser* rulers of that time had got their hands on such weapons before the holocaust came. The situation he described prevailed in more than one nation. Name and Blackeneth were probably Legion."

"Of course I've heard similar legends. It's obvious that something rather hideous came to pass," the thon stated; and then abruptly: "But when may I begin to examine—what do you call it?"

"The Memorabilia."

"Of course." He sighed and smiled absently at the image of the saint in the corner. "Would tomorrow be too soon?"

"You may begin at once, if you like," said the abbot. "Feel free to come and go as you please."

The vaults were dimly filled with candlelight, and only a few dark-robed scholar-monks moved about in the stalls. Brother Armbruster pored gloomily over his records in a puddle of lamplight in his cubbyhole at the foot of the stone stairway, and one lamp burned in the Moral Theology alcove where a robed figure huddled over ancient manuscript. It was after Prime, when most of the community labored at their duties about the abbey, in kitchen, classroom, garden, stable, and office, leaving the library nearly empty until late afternoon and time for *lectio devina*. This morning, however, the vaults were comparatively crowded.

Three monks stood lounging in the shadows behind the new machine. They kept their hands tucked in their sleeves and watched a fourth monk who stood at the foot of the stairs. The fourth monk gazed patiently up toward a fifth monk who stood on the landing and watched the entrance to the stairway.

Brother Kornhoer had brooded over his apparatus like an anxious parent, but when he could no longer find wires to wiggle and adjustments to make and remake, he retired to the Natural Theology alcove to read and wait. To speak a summary of last-minute instructions to his crew would be permissible, but he chose to maintain the hush, and if any thought of the coming moment as a personal climax crossed his mind as he waited, the monastic inventor's expression gave no hint of it. Since the abbot himself had not bothered to watch a demonstration óf the machine, Brother Kornhoer betrayed no symptoms of expecting applause from any quarter, and he had even overcome his tendency to glance reproachfully at Dom Paulo.

A low hiss from the stairway alerted the basement again, although there had been several earlier false alarms. Clearly no one had informed the illustrious thon that a marvelous invention awaited his inspection in the basement. Clearly, if it had been mentioned to him at all, its importance had been minimized. Obviously, Father Abbot was seeing to it that they all cooled their heels. These were the wordless significances exchanged by glances among them as they waited.

This time the warning hiss had not been in vain. The monk who watched from the head of the stairs turned solemnly and bowed toward the fifth monk on the landing below.

"*In principio Deus,*" he said softly.

The fifth monk turned and bowed toward the fourth monk at the foot of the stairs. "*Caelum et terram creavit,*" he murmured in turn.

The fourth monk turned toward the three who lounged behind the machine. "*Vacuus autem erat mundus,*" he announced.

"*Cum tenebris in superficie profundorum,*" chorused the group.

"*Ortus est Dei Spiritus supra aquas,*" called Brother Kornhoer, returning his book to its shelf with a rattling of chains.

"*Gratias Creatori Spiritui,*" responded his entire team.

"*Dixitque Deus: 'FIAT LUX,'*" said the inventor in a tone of command.

The vigil on the stairs descended to take their posts. Four monks manned the treadmill. The fifth monk hovered over the dynamo. The sixth monk climbed the shelf-ladder and took his seat on the top rung, his head bumping the top of the archway. He pulled a mask of smoke-blackened oily parchment over his face to protect his eyes, then felt for the lamp fixture and its thumbscrew, while Brother Kornhoer watched him nervously from below.

"*Et lux ergo facta est,*" he said when he had found the screw.

"*Lucem esse bonam Deus vidit,*" the inventor called to the fifth monk.

The fifth monk bent over the dynamo with a candle for one last look at the brush contacts. "*Et secrevit lucem a tenebris,*" he said at last, continuing the lesson.

"*Lucem appellavit 'diem,'*" chorused the treadmill team, "*et tenebras 'noctes.'*" Whereupon they set their shoulders to the turnstile beams.

Axles creaked and groaned. The wagon-wheel dynamo began to spin, its low whir becoming a moan and then a whine as the monks strained and grunted at the drive-mill. The guardian of the dynamo watched anxiously as the spokes blurred with speed and became a film. "*Vespere occaso,*" he began, then paused to lick two fingers and touch them to the contacts. A spark snapped.

"*Lucifer!*" he yelped, leaping back, then finished lamely: "*ortus est et primo die.*"

"CONTACT!" said Brother Kornhoer, as Dom Paulo, Thon Taddeo and his clerk descended the stairs.

The monk on the ladder struck the arc. A sharp *spffft!*—and blinding light flooded the vaults with a brilliance that had not been seen in twelve centuries.

The group stopped on the stairs. Thon Taddeo gasped an oath in his native tongue. He retreated a step. The abbot, who had neither witnessed the testing of the device nor credited extravagant claims, blanched and stopped speech in mid-sentence. The clerk froze momentarily in panic and suddenly fled, screaming "Fire!"

The abbot made the sign of the cross. "I had not known!" he whispered.

The scholar, having survived the first shock of the flare, probed the basement with his gaze, noticing the drive-mill, the monks who strained at its beams. His eyes traveled along the wrapped wires, noticed the monk on the ladder, measured the meaning of the wagon-wheel dynamo and the monk who stood waiting, with downcast eyes, at the foot of the stairs.

"Incredible!" he breathed.

The monk at the foot of the stairs bowed in acknowledgment and depreciation. The blue-white glare cast knife-edge shadows in the room, and the candle flames became blurred wisps in the tide of light.

"Bright as a thousand torches," breathed the scholar. "It must be an ancient—but no! Unthinkable!"

He moved on down the stairs like a man in a trance. He stopped beside Brother Kornhoer and gazed at him curiously for a moment, then stepped onto the basement floor. Touching nothing, asking nothing, peering at everything, he wandered about the machinery, inspecting the dynamo, the wiring, the lamp itself.

"It just doesn't seem possible, but—"

The abbot recovered his senses and descended the stairs. "You're dispensed from silence!" he whispered at Brother Kornhoer. "Talk to him. I'm—a little dazed."

The monk brightened. "You like it, m'Lord Abbot?"

"Ghastly," wheezed Dom Paulo.

The inventor's countenance sagged.

"It's a shocking way to treat a guest! It frightened the thon's assistant out of his wits. I'm mortified!"

"Well, it *is* rather bright."

"Hellish! Go talk to him while I think of a way to apologize."

But the scholar had apparently made a judgment on the basis of his observations, for he stalked toward them swiftly. His face seemed strained, and his manner crisp.

"A lamp of electricity," he said. "How have you managed to keep it hidden for all these centuries! After all these years of trying to arrive at a theory of—" He choked slightly, and seemed to be fighting for self-control, as if he had been the victim of a monstrous practical joke. "*Why* have you hidden it? Is there some religious significance— And what—" Complete confusion stopped him. He shook his head and looking around as if for an escape.

"You misunderstand," the abbot said weakly, catching at Brother Kornhoer's arm. "For the love of God, Brother, *explain!*"

But there was no balm to soothe an affront to professional pride—then or in any other age.

19 After the unfortunate incident in the basement, the abbot sought by every conceivable means to make amends for that unhappy moment. Thon Taddeo gave no outward sign of rancor, and even offered his hosts an apology for his spontaneous judgment of the incident, after the inventor of the device had given the scholar a detailed account of its recent design and manufacture. But the apology succeeded only in convincing the abbot further that the blunder had been serious. It put the thon in the position of a mountaineer who has scaled an "unconquered" height only to find a rival's initials carved in the summit rock—and the rival hadn't told him in advance. It must have been shattering for him, Dom Paulo thought, because of the way it was handled.

If the thon had not insisted (with a firmness perhaps born of embarrassment) that its light was of a superior quality, sufficiently bright even for close scrutiny of brittle and age-worn documents which tended to be indecipherable by candlelight, Dom Paulo would have removed the lamp from the basement immediately. But Thon Taddeo had insisted that he liked it—only to discover, then, that it was necessary to keep at least four novices or postulants continuously employed at cranking the dynamo and adjusting the arc-gap; thereupon, he begged that the lamp be removed—but then it was Paulo's turn to become insistent that it remain in place.

So it was that the scholar began his researches at the abbey, continuously aware of the three novices who toiled at the drive-mill and the fourth novice who invited glare-blindness atop the ladder to keep the lamp burning and adjusted—a situation which caused the Poet to versify mercilessly concerning the demon Embarrassment and the outrages he perpetrated in the name of penitence or appeasement.

For several days the thon and his assistant studied the library itself, the files, the monastery's records apart from the Memorabilia—as if by determining the validity of the oyster, they might establish the possibility of the pearl. Brother Kornhoer discovered the thon's assistant on his knees in the entrance of the refectory, and for a moment he entertained the impression that the fellow was performing some special devotion before the image of Mary above the door, but a rattle of tools put an end to the illusion. The assistant laid a carpenter's level across the entranceway and measured the concave depression worn in the floor stones by centuries of monastic sandals.

"We're looking for ways of determining dates," he told Kornhoer when questioned. "This seemed like a good place to establish a standard for rate of wear, since the traffic's easy to estimate. Three meals per man per day since the stones were laid."

Kornhoer could not help being impressed by their thoroughness; the activity mystified him. "The abbey's architectural records are complete," he said. "They can tell you exactly when each building and wing was added. Why not save your time?"

The man glanced up innocently. "My master has a saying: 'Nayol is without speech, and therefore never lies.'"

"Nayol?"

"One of the Nature gods of the Red River people. He means it figuratively, of course. Objective evidence is the ultimate authority. Recorders may lie, but Nature is incapable of it." He noticed the monk's expression and added hastily: "No canard is implied. It is simply a doctrine of the thon's that everything must be cross-referenced to the objective."

"A fascinating notion," murmured Kornhoer, and bent down to examine the man's sketch of a cross-section of the floor's concavity. "Why, it's shaped like what Brother Majek calls a normal distribution curve. How strange."

"Not strange. The probability of a footstep deviating from the center-line would tend to follow the normal error function."

Kornhoer was enthralled. "I'll call Brother Majek," he said.

The abbot's interest in his guests' inspection of the premises was less esoteric. "*Why*," he demanded of Gault, "are they making detailed drawings of our fortifications?"

The prior looked surprised. "I hadn't heard of it. You mean Thon Taddeo—"

"No. The officers that came with him. They're going about it quite systematically."

"How did you find out?"

"The Poet told me."

"The Poet! Hah!"

"Unfortunately, he was telling the truth this time. He pickpocketed one of their sketches."

"You have it?"

"No, I made him return it. But I don't like it. It's ominous."

"I suppose the Poet asked a price for the information?"

"Oddly enough, he didn't. He took an instant dislike to the thon. He's gone around muttering to himself ever since they came."

"The Poet has always muttered."

"But not in a serious vein."

"Why do you suppose they're making the drawings?"

Paulo made a grim mouth. "Unless we find out otherwise, we'll assume their interest is recondite and professional. As a walled citadel, the abbey has been a success. It's never been taken by siege or assault, and perhaps their professional admiration is aroused."

Father Gault gazed speculatively across the desert toward the east. "Come to think of it, if an army meant to strike west across the plains, they'd probably have to establish a garrison somewhere in this region before marching on Denver." He thought for a few moments and began to look alarmed. "And here they'd have a fortress ready-made!"

"I'm afraid that's occurred to them."

"You think they were sent as spies?"

"No, no! I doubt if Hannegan himself has ever heard of us. But they are here, and they are officers, and they can't help looking around and getting ideas. And now very likely Hannegan is *going* to hear about us."

"What do you intend doing?"

"I don't know yet."

"Why not talk to Thon Taddeo about it?"

"The officers aren't his servants. They were only sent as an escort to protect him. What can he do?"

"He's Hannegan's kinsman, and he has influence."

The abbott nodded. "I'll try to think of a way to approach him on the matter. We'll watch what's going on for a while first, though."

In the days that followed, Thon Taddeo completed his study of the oyster and, apparently satisfied that it was not a disguised clam, focused his attention on the pearl. The task was not simple.

Quantities of facsimile copy were scrutinized. Chains rattled and clanked as the more precious books came down from their shelves. In the case of partially damaged or deteriorated originals, it seemed unwise to trust the facsimile-maker's interpretation and eyesight. The actual manuscripts dating back to Leibowitzian times which had been sealed in airtight casks and locked in special storage vaults for indefinitely long preservation were then brought out.

The thon's assistant assembled several pounds of notes. After the fifth day of it, Thon Taddeo's pace quickened, and his manner reflected the eagerness of a hungry hound catching scent of tasty game.

"Magnificent!" He vacillated between jubilation and amused incredulity. "Fragments from a twentieth century physicist! The equations are even consistent."

Kornhoer peered over his shoulder. "I've seen that," he said breathlessly. "I could never make heads or tails of it. Is the subject matter important?"

"I'm not sure yet. The mathematics is beautiful, *beautiful!* Look here—this expression—notice the extremely contracted form. This thing under the radical sign—it looks like the product of two derivatives, but it really represents a whole *set* of derivatives."

"How?"

"The indices permute into an expanded expression; otherwise, it couldn't possibly represent a line integral, as the author says it is. It's lovely. And see here—this simple-looking expression. The simplicity is deceptive. It obviously represents not one, but a whole system of equations, in a very contracted form. It took me a couple of days to realize that the author was thinking of the relationships—not just of quantities to quantities—but of whole systems to other systems. I don't yet know all the physical quantities involved, but the sophistication of the mathematics is just—just quietly superb! If it's a hoax, it's inspired! If it's authentic, we may be in unbelievable luck. In either case, it's magnificent. I must see the earliest possible copy of it."

Brother Librarian groaned as yet another lead-sealed cask was rolled out of storage for unsealing. Armbruster was not impressed by the fact that the secular scholar, in two days, had unraveled a bit of a puzzle that had been lying around, a complete enigma, for a dozen centuries. To the custodian of the Memorabilia, each unsealing represented another decrease in the probable lifetime of the contents of the cask, and he made no attempt to conceal his disapproval of the entire proceeding. To Brother Librarian, whose task in life was the preservation of books, the principal reason for the existence of books was that they might be preserved perpetually. Usage was secondary, and to be avoided if it threatened longevity.

Thon Taddeo's enthusiasm for his task waxed stronger as the days passed, and the abbot breathed easier as he watched the thon's earlier skepticism melt away with each new perusal of some fragmentary pre-Deluge science text. The scholar had not made any clear assertions about the intended scope of his investigation; perhaps, at first, his aim had been vague, but now he went about his work with the crisp precision of a man following a plan. Sensing the dawn of something, Dom Paulo decided to offer the cock a perch for crowing, in case the bird felt an impulse to announce a coming daybreak.

"The community has been curious about your labors," he told the scholar. "We'd like to hear about it, if you don't mind discussing it. Of course we've all heard of your theoretical work at your own collegium, but it's too technical for most of us to understand. Would it be possible for you to tell us something about it in—oh, general terms that non-specialists might understand? The community has been grumping at me because I hadn't invited you to lecture; but I thought you might prefer to get the feel of the place first. Of course if you'd rather not—"

The thon's gaze seemed to clamp calipers on the abbot's cranium and measure it six ways. He smiled doubtfully. "You'd like me to explain our work in the simplest possible language?"

"Something like that, if it's possible."

"That's just it." He laughed. "The untrained man reads a paper on natural science and thinks: 'Now why couldn't he explain it in simple language.' He can't seem to realize that what he tried to read was the simplest possible language—for that subject matter. In fact, a great deal of natural philosophy is simply a process of linguistic simplification—an effort to invent languages in which half a page of equations can express an idea which could not be stated in less than a thousand pages of so-called 'simple' language. Do I make myself clear?"

"I think so. Since you do make yourself clear, perhaps you could tell us about that aspect of it, then. Unless the suggestion is premature—as far as your work with the Memorabilia is concerned."

"Well, no. We now have a fairly clear idea of where we're going and what we have to work with here. It will still take considerable time to finish of course. The pieces have to be fitted together, and they don't all belong to the same puzzle. We can't yet predict what we *can* glean from it, but we're fairly sure of what we *can't*. I'm happy to say it looks hopeful. I have no objection to explaining the general scope, but—" He repeated the doubtful shrug.

"What bothers you?"

The thon seemed mildly embarrassed. "Only an uncer-

tainty about my audience. I would not wish to offend anyone's religious beliefs."

"But how could you? Isn't it a matter of natural philosophy? Of physical science?"

"Of course. But many people's ideas about the world have
become colored with religious—well, what I mean is—"

"But if your subject matter is the physical world, how could
you possibly offend? Especially this community. We've been
waiting for a long time to see the world start taking an
interest in itself again. At the risk of seeming boastful, I
might point out that we have a few rather clever amateurs in
natural science right here in the monastery. There's Brother
Majek, and there's Brother Kornhoer—"

"Kornhoer!" The thon glanced up warily at the arc lamp
and looked away blinking. "I can't understand it!"

"The *lamp?* But surely *you*—"

"No, no, not the lamp. The lamp's simple enough, once
you get over the shock of seeing it really work. It *should*
work. It would work on paper, assuming various undetermin-
ables and guessing at some unavailable data. But the clean
impetuous leap from the vague hypothesis to a working
model—". The thon coughed nervously. "It's Kornhoer himself
I don't understand. That gadget—" he waggled a forefinger
at the dynamo "—is a standing broad-jump across about
twenty years of preliminary experimentation, starting with an
understanding of the principles. Kornhoer just dispensed
with the preliminaries. You believe in miraculous interven-
tions? I don't, but there you have a *real* case of it.
Wagon wheels!" He laughed. "What could he do if he had a
machine shop? I can't understand what a man like that is
doing cooped up in a monastery."

"Perhaps Brother Kornhoer should explain *that* to you,"
said Dom Paulo, trying to keep an edge of stiffness out of his
tone.

"Yes, well—" Thon Taddeo's visual calipers began measuring the old priest again. "If you really feel that no one
would take offense at hearing non-traditional ideas, I would
be glad to discuss our work. But some of it may conflict
with established preju—uh—established opinion."

"Good! Then it should be fascinating."

A time was agreed upon, and Dom Paulo felt relief. The
esoteric gulf between Christian monk and secular investigator
of Nature would surely be narrowed by a free exchange of

ideas, he felt. Kornhoer had already narrowed it slightly, had he not? More communication, not less, was probably the best therapy for easing any tension. And the cloudy veil of doubt and mistrusting hesitancy would be parted, would it not? as soon as the thon saw that his hosts were not quite such unreasonable intellectual reactionaries as the scholar seemed to suspect. Paulo felt some shame for his earlier misgivings. Patience, Lord, with a well-meaning fool, he prayed.

"But you can't ignore the officers and their sketchbooks," Gault reminded him.

20 From the lectern in the refectory, the reader was intoning the announcements. Candlelight blanched the faces of the robed legions who stood motionless behind their stools and waited for the beginning of the evening meal. The reader's voice echoed hollowly in the high vaulted dining room whose ceiling was lost in brooding shadows above the pools of candle-glow that spotted the wooden tables.

"The Reverend Father Abbot has commanded me to announce," called the reader, "that the rule of abstinence for today is dispensed at tonight's meal. We shall have guests, as you may have heard. All religious may partake of tonight's banquet in honor of Thon Taddeo and his group; you may eat meat. Conversation—if you'll keep it quiet—will be permitted during the meal."

Suppressed vocal noises, not unlike strangled cheers, came from the ranks of the novices. The tables were set. Food had not yet made an appearance, but large dining trays replaced the usual mush bowls, kindling appetites with hints of a feast. The familiar milk mugs stayed in the pantry, their places taken for tonight by the best wine cups. Roses were scattered along the boards.

The abbot stopped in the corridor to wait for the reader to finish reading. He glanced at the table set for himself, Father Gault, the honored guest, and his party. Bad arithmetic again in the kitchen, he thought. Eight places had been set. Three officers, the thon and his assistant, and the two priests made seven—unless, in some unlikely case, Father Gault had asked Brother Kornhoer to sit with them. The reader concluded the announcements, and Dom Paulo entered the hall.

"*Flectamus genua,*" intoned the reader.

The robed legions genuflected with military precision as the abbot blessed his flock.

"*Levate.*"

The legions arose. Dom Paulo took his place at the special table and glanced back toward the entrance. Gault should be bringing the others. Previously their meals had been served in the guesthouse rather than the refectory, to avoid subjecting them to the austerity of the monks' own frugal fare.

When the guests came, he looked around for Brother Kornhoer, but the monk was not with them.

"Why the eighth place setting?" he murmured to Father Gault when they had taken their places.

Gault looked blank and shrugged.

The scholar filled the place on the abbot's right and the others fell in toward the foot of the table, leaving the place on his left empty. He turned to beckon Kornhoer to join them, but the reader began intoning the preface before he could catch the monk's eye.

"*Oremus,*" answered the abbot, and the legions bowed.

During the blessing, someone slipped quietly into the seat on the abbot's left. The abbot frowned but did not look up to identify the culprit during the prayer.

". . . *et Spiritus Sancti, Amen.*"

"*Sedete,*" called the reader, and the ranks began seating themselves.

The abbot glanced sharply at the figure on his left.

"Poet!"

The bruised lily bowed extravagantly and smiled. "Good evening, Sires, learned Thon, distinguished hosts," he orated. "What are we having tonight? Roast fish and honeycombs in honor of the temporal resurrection that's upon us? Or have you, m'Lord Abbot, finally cooked the goose of the mayor of the village?"

"I would like to cook—"

"Ha!" quoth the Poet, and turned affably toward the scholar. "Such culinary excellence one enjoys in this place, Thon Taddeo! You should join us more often. I suppose they are feeding you nothing but roast pheasant and unimaginative beef in the guesthouse. A shame! Here one fares better. I do hope Brother Chef has his usual gusto tonight, his inward flame, his enchanted touch. Ah . . ." The Poet rubbed his hands and smirked hungrily. "Perhaps we shall have his inspired Mock Pork with Maize à la Friar John, eh?"

"It sounds interesting," said the scholar. "What is it?"

"Greasy armadillo with parched corn, boiled in donkey milk. A regular Sunday special."

"Poet!" snapped the abbot; then to the thon: "I apologize for his presence. He wasn't invited."

The scholar surveyed the Poet with detached amusement. "M'Lord Hannegan, too, keeps several court fools," he told Paulo. "I'm familiar with the species. You needn't apologize for him."

The Poet sprang up from his stool and bowed deeply before the thon. "Allow me instead to apologize for the abbot, Sire!" he cried with feeling.

He held the bow for a moment. They waited for him to finish his foolishness. Instead, he shrugged suddenly, sat down, and speared a smoking fowl from the platter deposited before them by a postulant. He tore off a leg and bit into it with gusto. They watched him with puzzlement.

"I suppose you're right in not accepting my apology for him," he said to the thon at last.

The scholar reddened slightly.

"Before I throw you out, worm," said Gault, "let's probe the depths of this iniquity."

The Poet waggled his head and munched thoughtfully. "It's pretty deep, all right," he admitted.

Someday Gault is going to strangle himself on that foot of his, thought Dom Paulo.

But the younger priest was visibly annoyed, and sought to draw the incident out *ad absurdum* in order to find grounds for quashing the fool. "Apologize at length for your host, Poet," he commanded. "And explain yourself as you go."

"Drop it, Father, drop it," Paulo said hastily.

The Poet smiled graciously at the abbot. "That's all right, m'Lord," he said. "I don't mind apologizing for you in the least. You apologize for me, I apologize for you, and isn't that a fitting maneuver in charity and good will? Nobody need apologize for himself—which is always so humiliating. Using my system, however, everyone gets apologized for, and nobody has to do his own apologizing."

Only the officers seemed to find the Poet's remarks amusing. Apparently the expectation of humor was enough to produce the illusion of humor, and the comedian could elicit laughter with gesture and expression, regardless of what he said. Thon Taddeo wore a dry smirk, but it was the kind of look a man might give a clumsy performance by a trained animal.

"And so," the Poet was continuing, "if you would but allow me to serve as your humble helper, m'Lord, you would never have to eat your own crow. As your Apologetic Advocate, for example, I might be delegated by you to offer contrition to important guests for the existence of bedbugs. And to bedbugs for the abrupt change of fare."

The abbot glowered and resisted an impulse to grind the Poet's bare toe with the heel of his sandal. He kicked the fellow's ankle, but the fool persisted.

"I would assume all the blame for you, of course," he said, noisily chewing white meat. "It's a fine system, one which I was prepared to make available to you too, Most Eminent Scholar. I'm sure you would have found it convenient. I have been given to understand that systems of logic and methodology must be devised and perfected before science advances. And my system of negotiable and transferable apologetics would have been of particular value to you, Thon Taddeo."

"Would have?"

"Yes. It's a pity. Somebody stole my blue-headed goat."

"Blue-headed goat?"

"He had a head as bald as Hannegan's, Your Brilliance, and blue as the tip of Brother Armbruster's nose. I meant to make you a present of the animal, but some dastard filched him before you came."

The abbot clenched his teeth and held his heel poised over the Poet's toe. Thon Taddeo was frowning slightly, but he seemed determined to untangle the Poet's obscure skein of meaning.

"Do we need a blue-headed goat?" he asked his clerk.

"I can see no pressing urgency about it, sir," said the clerk.

"But the need is obvious!" said the Poet. "They say you are writing equations that will one day remake the world. They say a new light is dawning. If there's to be light, then somebody will have to be blamed for the darkness that's past."

"Ah, thence the goat." Thon Taddeo glanced at the abbot. "A sickly jest. Is it the best he can do?"

"You'll notice he's unemployed. But let us talk of something sensib—"

"No, no, no, *no!*" objected the Poet. "You mistake my meaning, Your Brilliance. The goat is to be enshrined and honored, not blamed! Crown him with the crown Saint Leibowitz sent you, and thank him for the light that's rising. Then blame Leibowitz, and drive *him* into the desert. That way *you* won't have to wear the second crown. The one with thorns. Responsibility, it's called."

The Poet's hostility had broken out into the open, and he was no longer trying to seem humorous. The thon gazed at him icily. The abbot's heel wavered again over the Poet's toe, and again had reluctant mercy on it.

"And when," said the Poet, "your patron's army comes to seize this abbey, the goat can be placed in the courtyard and taught to bleat 'There's been nobody here but me, nobody here but me' whenever a stranger comes by."

One of the officers started up from his stool with an angry grunt, his hand reaching reflexively for his saber. He broke the hilt clear of the scabbard, and six inches of steel glistened a warning at the Poet. The thon seized his wrist and tried to force the blade back in the sheath, but it was like tugging at the arm of a marble statue.

"Ah! A swordsman as well as a draftsman!" taunted the Poet, apparently unafraid of dying. "Your sketches of the abbey's defenses show such promise of artistic—"

The officer barked an oath and the blade leaped clean of the scabbard. His comrades seized him, however, before he could lunge. An astonished rumble came from the congregation as the startled monks came to their feet. The Poet was still smiling blandly.

"—artistic growth," he continued. "I predict that one day your drawing of the underwall tunnels will be hung in a museum of fine—"

A dull *chunk!* came from under the table. The Poet paused in mid-bite, lowered the wishbone from his mouth, and turned slowly white. He munched, swallowed, and continued to lose color. He gazed abstractly upward.

"You're grinding it off," he muttered out of the side of his mouth.

"Through talking?" the abbot asked, and continued to grind.

"I think I have a bone in my throat," the Poet admitted.

"You wish to be excused?"

"I am afraid I must."

"A pity. We shall miss you." Paulo gave the toe one last grind for good measure. "You may go then."

The Poet exhaled gustily, blotted his mouth, and arose. He drained his wine cup and inverted it in the center of the tray. Something in his manner compelled them to watch him. He pulled down his eyelid with one thumb, bent his head over his cupped palm and pressed. The eyeball popped out into his palm, bringing a choking sound from the Texarkanans who were apparently unaware of the Poet's artificial orb.

"Watch him carefully," said the Poet to the glass eye, and then deposited it on the upturned base of his wine cup where it stared balefully at Thon Taddeo. "Good evening, m'Lords," he said cheerfully to the group, and marched away.

The angry officer muttered a curse and struggled to free himself from the grasp of his comrades.

"Take him back to his quarters and sit on him till he cools off," the thon told them. "And better see that he doesn't get a chance at that lunatic."

"I'm mortified," he said to the abbot, when the livid guardsman was hauled away. "They aren't my servants, and I can't give them orders. But I can promise you he will grovel for this. And if he refuses to apologize and leave immediately, he'll have to match that hasty sword against mine before noon tomorrow."

"No bloodshed!" begged the priest. "It was nothing. Let's all forget it." His hands were trembling, his countenance gray.

"He will make apology and go," Thon Taddeo insisted, "or I shall offer to kill him. Don't worry, he doesn't dare fight me because if he won, Hannegan would have him impaled on the public stake while they forced his wife to—but never mind that. He'll grovel and go. Just the same, I'm deeply ashamed that such a thing could have come about."

"I should have had the Poet thrown out as soon as he showed up. He provoked the whole thing, and I failed to stop it. The provocation was clear."

"Provocation? By the fanciful lie of a vagrant fool? Josard reacted as if the Poet's charges were true."

"Then you don't know that they *are* preparing a comprehensive report on the military value of our abbey as a fortress?"

The scholar's jaw fell. He stared from one priest to the other in apparent unbelief.

"Can this be true?" he asked after a long silence.

The abbot nodded.

"And you've permitted us to stay."

"We keep no secrets. Your companions are welcome to make such a study if they wish. I would not presume to ask *why* they want the information. The Poet's assumption, of course, was merest fantasy."

"Of course," the thon said weakly, not looking at his host.

"Surely your prince has no aggressive ambitions in this region, as the Poet hinted."

"Surely not."

"And even if he did, I'm sure he would have the wisdom —or at least the wise counselors to lead him—to understand that our abbey's value as a storehouse of ancient wisdom is many times greater than its value as a citadel."

The thon caught the note of pleading, the undercurrent of supplication for help, in the priest's voice, and he seemed to brood on it, picking lightly at his food and saying nothing for a time.

"We'll speak of this matter again before I return to the collegium," he promised quietly.

A pall had fallen on the banquet, but it began to lift during the group singing in the courtyard after the meal, and it vanished entirely when the time came for the scholar's lecture in the Great Hall. Embarrassment seemed at an end, and the group had resumed a surface cordiality.

Dom Paulo led the thon to the lectern; Gault and the don's clerk followed, joining them on the platform. Applause rang out heartily following the abbot's introduction of the thon; the hush that followed suggested the silence of a courtroom awaiting a verdict. The scholar was no gifted orator, but the verdict proved satisfying to the monastic throng.

"I have been amazed at what we've found here," he told them. "A few weeks ago I would not have believed, *did not* believe, that records such as you have in your Memorabilia could still be surviving from the fall of the last mighty civilization. It is still hard to believe, but evidence forces us to adopt the hypothesis that the documents are authentic. Their survival here is incredible enough; but even more fantastic, *to me,* is the fact that they have gone unnoticed during *this* century, until now. Lately there have been men capable of appreciating their potential value—and not only myself. What Thon Kaschler might have done with them while he was alive!—even seventy years ago."

The sea of monks' faces was alight with smiles upon hearing so favorable a reaction to the Memorabilia from one so gifted as the thon. Paulo wondered why they failed to sense the faint undercurrent of resentment—or was it suspicion?—in the speaker's tone. "Had I known of these sources ten years ago," he was saying, "much of my work in optics would have been unnecessary." *Ahha!* thought the abbot, *so that's it.* Or at least part of it. He's finding out that some of his discoveries are only rediscoveries, and it leaves a bitter taste. But surely he must know that never during his lifetime can he be more than a recoverer of lost works; however brilliant, he can only do what others before him had done. And so it would be, inevitably, until the world became as highly developed as it had been before the Flame Deluge.

Nevertheless, it was apparent that Thon Taddeo was impressed.

"My time here is limited," he went on. "From what I have seen, I suspect that it will take twenty specialists several decades to finish milking the Memorabilia for understandable information. Physical science normally proceeds by inductive reasoning tested by experiment; but here the task is deductive. From a few broken bits of general principles, we must attempt to grasp particulars. In some cases, it may prove impossible. For example—" He paused for a moment to produce a packet of notes and thumbed through them briefly. "Here is a quotation which I found buried downstairs. It's from a four-page fragment of a book which may have been an advanced physics text. A few of you may have seen it."

" '—and if the space terms predominate in the expression for the interval between event-points, the interval is said to be space-like, since it is then possible to select a co-ordinate system—belonging to an observer with an admissible velocity—in which the events appear simultaneous, and therefore separated only spatially. If, however, the interval is timelike, the events cannot be simultaneous in any co-ordinate system, but there exists a co-ordinate system in which the space terms will vanish entirely, so that the separation between events will be purely temporal, *id est,* occurring at the same place, but at different times. Now upon examining the extremals of the real interval—' "

He looked up with a whimsical smile. "Has anyone here looked at that reference lately?"

The sea of faces remained blank.

"Anyone ever remember seeing it?"

Kornhoer and two others cautiously lifted their hands.

"Anyone know what it means?"

The hands quickly went down.

The thon chuckled. "It's followed by a page and a half of mathematics which I won't try to read, but it treats some of our fundamental concepts as if they weren't basic at all, but evanescent appearances that change according to one's point of view. It ends with the word *'therefore'* but the rest of the page is burned, and the conclusion with it. The reasoning is impeccable, however, and the mathematics quite elegant, so that I can write the conclusion myself. It seems the conclusion of a madman. It began with assumptions, however, which appeared equally mad. Is it a hoax? If it isn't, what is its place in the whole scheme of the science of the ancients? What precedes it as prerequisite to understanding? What follows, and how can it be tested? Questions I can't answer. This is only *one* example of the many enigmas posed by these papers you've kept so long. Reasoning which touches experiential reality *nowhere* is the business of angel-ologists and theologians, not of physical scientists. And yet such papers as these describe systems which touch *our* experience nowhere. Were they within the experimental reach of the ancients? Certain references tend to indicate it. One paper refers to elemental transmutation—which we just recently established as theoretically impossible—and then it says 'experiment proves.' But *how?*

"It may take generations to evaluate and understand some of these things. It is unfortunate that they must remain here in this inaccessible place, for it will take a concentrated effort by numerous scholars to make meaning of them. I am sure you realize that your present facilities are inadequate —not to mention 'inaccessible' to the rest of the world."

Seated on the platform behind the speaker, the abbot began to glower, waiting for the worst. Thon Taddeo chose, however, to offer no proposals. But his remarks continued to make clear his feeling that such relics belonged in more competent hands than those of the monks of the Albertian Order of Saint Leibowitz, and that the situation as it prevailed was absurd. Perhaps sensing the growing uneasiness in the room, he soon turned to the subject of his immediate studies, which involved a more thorough investigation into the nature of light than had been made previously. Several of the abbey's treasures were proving to be of much help, and he hoped to devise soon an experimental means for testing his theories. After some discussion of the phenomenon of refraction, he paused, then said apologetically: "I hope none of this offends anybody's religious beliefs," and looked around quizzically. Seeing that their faces remained curious and bland, he continued for a time, then invited questions from the congregation.

"Do you mind a question from the platform?" asked the abbot.

"Not at all," said the scholar, looking a bit doubtful, as if thinking *et tu, Brute*.

"I was wondering what there is about the refrangible property of light that you thought might be offensive to religion?"

"Well—" The thon paused uncomfortably. "Monsignor Apollo, whom you know, grew quite heated on the subject. He said that light could not possibly have been refrangible before the Flood, because the rainbow was supposedly—"

The room burst into roaring laughter, drowning the rest of the remark. By the time the abbot had waved them to silence, Thon Taddeo was beet red, and Dom Paulo had some difficulty in maintaining his own solemn visage.

"Monsignor Apollo is a good man, a good priest, but all men are apt to be incredible asses at times, especially outside their domains. I'm sorry I asked the question."

"The answer relieves me," said the scholar. "I seek no quarrels."

There were no further questions and the thon proceeded to his second topic: the growth and the present activities of his collegium. The picture as he painted it seemed encouraging. The collegium was flooded with applicants who wanted to study at the institute. The collegium was assuming an educational function as well as an investigative one. Interest in natural philosophy and science was on the increase among the literate laity. The institute was being liberally endowed. Symptoms of revival and renaissance.

"I might mention a few of the current researches and investigations being conducted by our people," he went on. "Following Bret's work on the behavior of gases, Thon Viche

Mortoin is investigating the possibilities for the artificial production of ice. Thon Friider Halb is seeking a practical means for transmitting messages by electrical variations along a wire—" The list was long, and the monks appeared impressed. Studies in many fields—medicine, astronomy, geology, mathematics, mechanics—were being undertaken. A few seemed impractical and ill-considered, but most seemed to promise rich rewards in knowledge and practical application. From Jejene's search for the Universal Nostrum to Bodalk's reckless assault on orthodox geometries, the collegium's activities exhibited a healthy hankering to pry open Nature's private files, locked since mankind had burned its institutional memories and condemned itself to cultural amnesia more than a millennium ago.

"In addition to these studies, Thon Maho Mahh is heading a project which seeks further information about the origin of the human species. Since this is primarily an archaeological task, he asked me to search your library for any suggestive material on the subject, after I complete my own study here. However, perhaps I'd better not dwell on this at any length, since it's tending to cause controversy with the theologians. But if there are any questions—"

A young monk who was studying for the priesthood stood up and was recognized by the thon.

"Sir, I was wondering if you were acquainted with the suggestions of Saint Augustine on the subject?"

"I am not."

"A fourth century bishop and philosopher. He suggested that in the beginning, God created all things in their germinal causes, including the physiology of man, and that the germinal causes inseminate, as it were, the formless matter—which then gradually *evolved* into the more complex shapes, and eventually Man. Has this hypothesis been considered?"

The thon's smile was condescending, although he did not openly brand the proposal childish. "I'm afraid it has not, but I shall look it up," he said, in a tone that indicated he would not.

"Thank you," said the monk, and sat down meekly.

"Perhaps the most daring research of all, however," continued the sage, "is being conducted by my friend Thon Esser Shon. It is an attempt to synthesize living matter. Thon Esser hopes to create living protoplasm, using only six basic ingredients. This work could lead to—yes? You have a question?"

A monk in the third row had risen and was bowing toward the speaker. The abbot leaned forward to peer at him and recognized, with horror, that it was Brother Armbruster, the librarian.

"If you would do an old man the kindness," croaked the monk, dragging out his words in a plodding monotone. "This Thon Esser Shon—who limits himself to only six basic ingredients—is very interesting. I was wondering—are they permitting him to use both hands?"

"Why, I—" The thon paused and frowned.

"And may I also inquire," Armbruster's dry voice dragged on, "whether this remarkable feat is to be performed from the sitting, standing, or prone position? Or perhaps on horseback while playing two trumpets?"

The novices snickered audibly. The abbot came quickly to his feet.

"Brother Armbruster, you have been warned. You are excommunicated from the common table until you make satisfaction. You may wait in the Lady Chapel."

The librarian bowed again and stole quietly out of the hall, his carriage humble, but his eyes triumphant. The abbot murmured apologetically to the scholar, but the thon's glance was suddenly chilly.

"In conclusion," he said, "a brief outline of what the world can expect, in my opinion, from the intellectual revolution that's just beginning." Eyes burning, he looked around at them, and his voice changed from casual to fervent rhythms. "Ignorance has been our king. Since the death of empire, he sits unchallenged on the throne of Man. His dynasty is age-old. His right to rule is now considered legitimate. Past sages have affirmed it. They did nothing to unseat him.

"Tomorrow, a new prince shall rule. Men of understanding, men of science shall stand behind his throne, and the universe will come to know his might. His name is Truth. His empire shall encompass the Earth. And the mastery of Man over the Earth shall be renewed. A century from now, men will fly through the air in mechanical birds. Metal carriages will race along roads of man-made stone. There will be buildings of thirty stories, ships that go under the sea, machines to perform all works.

"And how will this come to pass?" He paused and lowered his voice. "In the same way all change comes to pass, I fear. And I am sorry it is so. It will come to pass by violence and upheaval, by flame and by fury, for no change comes calmly over the world."

He glanced around, for a soft murmur arose from the community.

"It will *be* so. We do not *will* it so.

"But *why?*

"Ignorance is king. Many would not profit by his abdication. Many enrich themselves by means of his dark monarchy. They are his Court, and in his name they defraud and govern, enrich themselves and perpetuate their power. Even literacy they fear, for the written word is another channel of communication that might cause their enemies to become united. Their weapons are keen-honed, and they use them with skill. They will press the battle upon the world when their interests are threatened, and the violence which follows will last until the structure of society as it now exists is leveled to rubble, and a new society emerges. I am sorry. But that is how I see it."

The words brought a new pall over the room. Dom Paulo's hopes sank, for the prophecy gave form to the scholar's probable outlook. Thon Taddeo knew the military ambitions of his monarch. He had a choice: to approve of them, to disapprove of them, or to regard them as impersonal phenomena beyond his control like a flood, famine, or whirlwind.

Evidently, then, he accepted them as inevitable—to avoid having to make a moral judgment. *Let there be blood, iron and weeping. . . .*

How could such a man thus evade his own conscience and disavow his responsibility—and so easily! the abbot stormed to himself.

But then the words came back to him. *For in those days, the Lord God had suffered the wise men to know the means by which the world itself might be destroyed. . . .*

He also suffered them to know how it might be saved, and, as always, let them choose for themselves. And perhaps they had chosen as Thon Taddeo chooses. To wash their hands before the multitude. Look you to it. Lest they themselves be crucified.

And they had been crucified anyhow. Without dignity. Always for anybody anyhow is to get nailed on it and hang on it and if you drop off they beat you . . .

There was sudden silence. The scholar had stopped talking.

The abbot blinked around the hall. Half the community

was staring toward the entrance. At first his eyes could make out nothing.

"What is it?" he whispered to Gault.

"An old man with a beard and shawl," hissed Gault. "It looks like— No, he wouldn't—"

Dom Paulo arose and moved to the front of the dais to stare at the faintly defined shape in the shadows. Then he called out to it softly.

"Benjamin?"

The figure stirred. It drew its shawl tighter about spindly shoulders and hobbled slowly into the light. It stopped again, muttering to itself as it looked around the room; then its eyes found the scholar at the lectern.

Leaning on a crooked staff, the old apparition hobbled slowly toward the lectern, never taking its eyes from the man who stood behind it. Thon Taddeo looked humorously perplexed at first, but when no one stirred or spoke, he seemed to lose color as the decrepit vision came near him. The face of the bearded antiquity blazed with hopeful ferocity of some compelling passion that burned more furiously in him than the life principle long since due to depart.

He came close to the lectern, paused. His eyes twitched over the startled speaker. His mouth quivered. He smiled. He reached out one trembling hand toward the scholar. The thon drew back with a snort of revulsion.

The hermit was agile. He vaulted to the dais, dodged the lectern, and seized the scholar's arm.

"What madness—"

Benjamin kneaded the arm while he stared hopefully into the scholar's eyes.

His face clouded. The glow died. He dropped the arm. A great keening sigh came from the dry old lungs as hope vanished. The eternally knowing smirk of the Old Jew of the Mountain returned to his face. He turned to the community, spread his hands, shrugged eloquently.

"It's still not Him," he told them sourly, then hobbled away.

Afterwards, there was little formality.

21 It was during the tenth week of Thon Taddeo's visit that the messenger brought the black news. The head of the ruling dynasty of Laredo had demanded that Texarkanan troops be evacuated forthwith from the realm. The King died of poison that night, and a state of war was proclaimed between the states of Laredo and Texarkana. The war would be short-lived. It could with assurance be assumed that the war had ended the day after it had begun, and that Hannegan now controlled all lands and peoples from the Red River to the Rio Grande.

That much had been expected, but not the accompanying news.

Hannegan II, by Grace of God Mayor, Viceroy of Texarkana, Defender of the Faith, and Vaquero Supreme of the Plains, had, after finding Monsignor Marcus Apollo to be guilty of "treason" and espionage, caused the papal nuncio to be hanged, and then, while still alive to be cut down, drawn, quartered, and flayed, as an example to anyone else who might try to undermine the Mayor's state. In pieces, the priest's carcass had been thrown to the dogs.

The messenger hardly needed to add that Texarkana was under absolute interdict by a papal decree which contained certain vague but ominous allusions to *Regnans in Excelsis,* a sixteenth century bull ordering a monarch deposed. There was no news of Hannegan's countermeasures, as yet.

On the Plains, the Laredan forces would now have to fight their way back home through the nomad tribes, only to lay down their arms at their own borders, for their nation and their kin were hostage.

"A tragic affair!" said Thon Taddeo, with an apparent degree of sincerity. "Because of my nationality, I offer to leave at once."

"Why?" Dom Paulo asked. "You don't approve of Hannegan's actions, do you?"

The scholar hesitated, then shook his head. He looked around to make certain no one overheard them. "Personally, I condemn them. But in public—" He shrugged. "There is

178

the collegium to think of. If it were only a question of my *own* neck, well—"

"I understand."

"May I venture an opinion in confidence?"

"Of course."

"Then someone ought to warn New Rome against making idle threats. Hannegan's not above crucifying several dozen Marcus Apollos."

"Then some new martyrs will attain Heaven; New Rome doesn't make idle threats."

The thon sighed. "I supposed that you'd look at it that way, but I renew my offer to leave."

"Nonsense. Whatever your nationality, your common humanity makes you welcome."

But a rift had appeared. The scholar kept his own company afterward, seldom conversing with the monks. His relationship with Brother Kornhoer became noticeably formal, although the inventor spent an hour or two each day in servicing and inspecting the dynamo and the lamp, and keeping himself informed concerning the progress of the thon's work, which was now proceeding with unusual haste. The officers seldom ventured outside the guesthouse.

There were hints of an exodus from the region. Disturbing rumors kept coming from the Plains. In the village of Sanly Bowitts, people began discovering reasons to depart suddenly on pilgrimages or to visit in other lands. Even the beggars and vagrants were getting out of town. As always, the merchants and artisans were faced with the unpleasant choice of abandoning their property to burglars and looters or staying with it to see it looted.

A citizens' committee headed by the mayor of the village visited the abbey to request sanctuary for the townspeople in the event of invasion. "My final offer," said the abbot, after several hours of argument, "is this: we will take in all the women, children, invalids, and aged, without question. But as for men capable of bearing arms, we'll consider each case individually, and we may turn some of them away."

"*Why?*" the mayor demanded.

"That should be obvious, even to you!" Dom Paulo said sharply. "We may come under attack ourselves, but unless we're directly attacked, we're going to stay out of it. I'll not let this place be used by anybody as a garrison from which to launch a counterattack if the only attack is on the village itself. So in case of males able to bear arms, we'll have to insist on a pledge—to defend the abbey under *our* orders. And we'll decide in individual cases whether a pledge is trustworthy or not."

"It's unfair!" howled a committeeman. "You'll discriminate—"

"Only against those who can't be trusted. What's the matter? Were you hoping to hide a reserve force here? Well, it won't be allowed. You're *not* going to plant any part of a town militia out here. That's final."

Under the circumstances, the committee could not refuse any help offered. There was no further argument. Dom Paulo meant to take in anyone, when the time came, but for the present he meant to forestall plans by the village to involve the abbey in military planning. Later there would be officers from Denver with similar requests; they would be less interested in saving life than in saving their political regime. He intended to give them a similar answer. The abbey had been built as a fortress of faith and knowledge, and he meant to preserve it as such.

The desert began to crawl with wanderers out of the east. Traders, trappers, and herdsmen, in moving west, brought news from the Plains. The cattle plague was sweeping like wildfire among the herds of the nomads; famine seemed imminent. Laredo's forces had suffered a mutinous cleavage since the fall of the Laredan dynasty. Part of them were returning to their homeland as ordered, while the others set out under a grim vow to march on Texarkana and not stop until they took the head of Hannegan II or died in trying. Weakened by the split, the Laredans were being wiped out gradually by the hit-and-run assaults from Mad Bear's warriors who were thirsty for vengeance against those who had brought the plague. It was rumored that Hannegan had generously offered to make Mad Bear's people his protected dependents, if they would swear fealty to "civilized" law, accept his officers into their councils, and embrace the Christian Faith. "Submit or starve" was the choice which fate and Hannegan offered the herdsman peoples. Many would choose to starve before giving allegiance to an agrarian-merchant state. Hongan Os was said to be roaring his defiance southward, eastward, and heavenward; he accomplished the latter by burning one shaman a day to punish the tribal gods for betraying him. He threatened to become a Christian if Christian gods would help slaughter his enemies.

It was during the brief visit of a party of shepherds that the Poet vanished from the abbey. Thon Taddeo was the first to notice the Poet's absence from the guesthouse and to inquire about the versifying vagrant.

Dom Paulo's face wrinkled in surprise. "Are you certain he's moved out?" he asked. "He often spends a few days in the village, or goes over to the mesa for an argument with Benjamin."

"His belongings are missing," said the thon. "Everything's gone from his room."

The abbot made a wry mouth. "When the Poet leaves, that's a bad sign. By the way, if he's really missing, then I would advise you to take an immediate inventory of your *own* belongings."

The thon looked thoughtful. "So that's where my boots—"

"No doubt."

"I set them out to be polished. They weren't returned. That was the same day he tried to batter down my door."

"Batter down—who, the *Poet?*"

Thon Taddeo chuckled. "I'm afraid I've been having a little sport with him. I have his glass eye. You remember the night he left it on the refectory table?"

"Yes."

"I picked it up."

The thon opened his pouch, groped in it for a moment, then laid the Poet's eyeball on the abbot's desk. "He knew I had it, but I kept denying it. But we've had sport with him ever since, even to creating rumors that it was really the long-lost eyeball of the Bayring idol and ought to be returned to the museum. He became quite frantic after a time. Of course I had meant to return it before we go home. Do you suppose he'll return after we leave?"

"I doubt it," said the abbot, shuddering slightly as he glanced at the orb. "But I'll keep it for him, if you like. Although it's just as probable that he'd turn up in Texarkana looking for it there. He claims it's a potent talisman."

"How so?"

Dom Paulo smiled. "He says he can see much better when he's wearing it."

"What nonsense!" The thon paused; ever ready, apparently, to give any sort of outlandish premise at least a moment's consideration, he added: "Isn't it nonsense—unless filling the empty socket somehow affects the muscles of *both* sockets. Is that what he claims?"

"He just swears he can't see as well without it. He claims he has to have it for the perception of 'true meanings'—although it gives him blinding headaches when he wears it. But one never knows whether the Poet is speaking fact, fancy, or allegory. If fancy is clever enough, I doubt that the Poet would admit a difference between fancy and fact."

The thon smiled quizzically. "Outside my door the other day, he yelled that *I* needed it more than he did. That seems to suggest that he thinks of it as being, in itself, a potent fetish—good for anyone. I wonder why."

"He said *you* needed it? Oh ho!"

"What amuses you?"

"I'm sorry. He probably meant it as an insult. I'd better not try to explain the Poet's insult; it might make me seem a party to them."

"Not at all. I'm curious."

The abbot glanced at the image of Saint Leibowitz in the corner of the room. "The Poet used the eyeball as a running joke," he explained. "When he wanted to make a decision, or to think something over, or to debate a point, he'd put the glass eye in the socket. He'd take it out again when he saw something that displeased him, when he was pretending to overlook something, or when he wanted to play stupid. When he wore it, his manner changed. The brothers began calling it 'the Poet's conscience,' and he went along with the joke. He gave little lectures and demonstrations on the advantages of a removable conscience. He'd pretend some frantic compulsion possessed him—something trivial, usually—like a compulsion aimed at a bottle of wine.

"Wearing his eye, he'd stroke the wine bottle, lick his lips, pant and moan, then jerk his hand away. Finally it would possess him again. He'd grab the bottle, pour about a thimbleful in a cup and gloat over it for a second. But then conscience would fight back, and he'd throw the cup across the room. Soon he'd be leering at the wine bottle again, and start to moan and slobber, but fighting the compulsion anyhow—" the abbot chuckled in spite of himself "—hideous to watch. Finally, when he became exhausted, he'd pluck out his glass eye. Once the eye was out, he'd suddenly relax. The compulsion stopped being compulsive. Cool and arrogant then, he'd pick up the bottle, look around and laugh. 'I'm going to do it anyhow,' he'd say. Then, while everyone was expecting him to drink it, he'd put on a beatific smile and pour the whole bottle over his own head. The advantage of a removable conscience, you see."

"So he thinks I need it more than he does."

Dom Paulo shrugged. "He's only the Poet-sirrah!"

The scholar puffed a breath of amusement. He prodded at the vitreous spheroid and rolled it across the table with his thumb. Suddenly he laughed. "I rather like that. I think I know who does need it more than the Poet. Perhaps I'll keep it after all." He picked it up, tossed it, caught it, and glanced doubtfully at the abbot.

Paulo merely shrugged again.

Thon Taddeo dropped the eye back in his pouch. "He can have it if he ever comes to claim it. But by the way, I meant to tell you: my work is nearly finished here. We'll be leaving in a very few days."

"Aren't you worried about the fighting on the Plains?"

Thon Taddeo frowned at the wall. "We're to camp at a butte, about a week's ride to the east from here. A group of, uh— Our escort will meet us there."

"I do hope," said the abbot, relishing the polite bit of savagery, "that your escort-group hasn't reversed its political allegiance since you made the arrangements. It's getting harder to tell foes from allies these days."

The thon reddened. "Especially if they come from Texarkana, you mean?"

"I didn't say that."

"Let's be frank with each other, Father. I can't fight the prince who makes my work possible—no matter what I think of his policies or his politics. I appear to support him, superficially, or at least to overlook him—for the sake of the collegium. If he extends his lands, the collegium may incidentally profit. If the collegium prospers, mankind will profit from our work."

"The ones who survive, perhaps."

"True—but that's always true in any event."

"No, no— Twelve centuries ago, not even the survivors profited. Must we start down that road again?"

Thon Taddeo shrugged. "What can I do about it?" he asked crossly. "Hannegan is prince, not I."

"But you promise to begin restoring Man's control over Nature. But who will govern the use of the power to control natural forces? Who will use it? To what end? How will you hold him in check? Such decisions can still be made,

But if you and your group don't make them now, others will soon make them for you. Mankind will profit, you say. By whose sufferance? The sufferance of a prince who signs his letters X? Or do you really believe that your collegium can stay aloof from his ambitions when he begins to find out that you're valuable to him?"

Dom Paulo had not expected to convince him. But it was with a heavy heart that the abbot noticed the plodding patience with which the thon heard him through; it was the patience of a man listening to an argument which he had long ago refuted to his own satisfaction.

"What you really suggest," said the scholar, "is that we wait a little while. That we dissolve the collegium, or move it to the desert, and somehow—with no gold and silver of our own—revive an experimental and theoretical science in some slow hard way, and tell nobody. That we save it all up for the day when Man is good and pure and holy and wise."

"That is not what I meant—"

"That is not what you meant to *say*, but it is what your *saying* means. Keep science cloistered, don't try to apply it, don't try to do anything about it until men are holy. Well, it won't work. You've been doing it here in this abbey for generations."

"We haven't withheld anything."

"You haven't withheld it; but you sat on it so quietly, nobody knew it was here, and you did nothing with it."

Brief anger flared in the old priest's eyes. "It's time you met our founder, I think," he growled, pointing to the wood-carving in the corner. "He was a scientist like yourself before the world went mad and he ran for sanctuary. He founded this Order to save what could be saved of the records of the last civilization. 'Saved' from what, and for what? Look where he's standing—see the kindling? the books? That's how little the world wanted your science then, and for centuries afterward. So he died for our sake. When they drenched him with fuel oil, legend says he asked them for a cup of it. They thought he mistook it for water, so they laughed and gave him a cup. He blessed it and—some say the oil changed to wine when he blessed it—and then: '*Hic est enim calix Sanguinis Mei*,' and he drank it before they hung him and set him on fire. Shall I read you a list of our martyrs? Shall I name all the battles we have fought to keep these records intact? All the monks blinded in the copyroom? for your sake? Yet you say we did nothing with it, withheld it by silence."

"Not intentionally," the scholar said, "but in effect you did—and for the very motives you imply should be mine. If you try to save wisdom until the world is wise, Father, the world will never have it."

"I can see the misunderstanding is basic!" the abbot said gruffly. "To serve God first, or to serve Hannegan first— that's your choice."

"I have little choice, then," answered the thon. "Would you have me work for the Church?" The scorn in his voice was unmistakable.

22 It was Thursday within the Octave of All Saints. In preparation for departure, the thon and his party sorted their notes and records in the basement. He had attracted a small monastic audience, and a spirit of friendliness prevailed as the time to leave drew near. Overhead, the arc lamp still sputtered and glared, filling the ancient library with blue-white harshness while the team of novices pumped wearily at the hand-powered dynamo. The inexperience of the novice who sat atop the ladder to keep the arc gap adjusted caused the light to flicker erratically; he had replaced the previous skilled operator who was at present confined to the infirmary with wet dressings over his eyes.

Thon Taddeo had been answering questions about his work with less reticence than usual, no longer worried, apparently, about such controversial subjects as the refrangible property of light, or the ambitions of Thon Esser Shon.

"Now unless this hypothesis is meaningless," he was saying, "it must be possible to confirm it in some way by observation. I set up the hypothesis with the help of some new —or rather, some very old—mathematical forms suggested by our study of your Memorabilia. The hypothesis seems to offer a simpler explanation of optical phenomena, but frankly, I could think of no way to test it at first. That's where your Brother Kornhoer proved a help." He nodded toward the inventor with a smile and displayed a sketch of a proposed testing device.

"What is it?" someone asked after a brief interval of mystification.

"Well—this is a pile of glass plates. A beam of sunlight striking the pile at this angle will be partially reflected and partially transmitted. The reflected part will be polarized. Now we adjust the pile to reflect the beam through this thing, which is Brother Kornhoer's idea, and let the light fall on this second pile of glass plates. The second pile is set at just the right angle to reflect almost all of the polarized beam, and transmit nearly none of it. Looking through the glass, we'd scarcely see the light. All this has been tried. But now if my hypothesis is correct, closing this switch on Brother Kornhoer's field coil here should cause a sudden brightening of the transmitted light. If it doesn't—" he shrugged "—then we throw out the hypothesis."

"You might throw out the coil instead," Brother Kornhoer suggested modestly. "I'm not sure it'll produce a strong enough field."

"I am. You have an instinct for these things. I find it much easier to develop an abstract theory than to construct a practical way to test it. But you have a remarkable gift for seeing everything in terms of screws, wires, and lenses, while I'm still thinking abstract symbols."

"But the abstractions would never occur to me in the first place, Thon Taddeo."

"We would make a good team, Brother. I wish you would join us at the collegium, at least for a while. Do you think your abbot would grant you leave?"

"I would not presume to guess," the inventor murmured, suddenly uncomfortable.

Thon Taddeo turned to the others. "I've heard mention of 'brothers on leave.' Isn't it true that some members of your community are employed elsewhere temporarily?"

"Only a very few, Thon Taddeo," said a young priest. "Formerly, the Order supplied clerks, scribes, and secretaries to the secular clergy, and to both royal and ecclesiastical courts. But that was during the times of most severe hardship and poverty here at the abbey. Brothers working on leave have kept the rest of us from starving at times. But that's no longer necessary, and it's seldom done. Of course, we have a few brothers studying in New Rome now, but—"

"That's *it!*" said the thon with sudden enthusiasm. "A scholarship at the collegium for you, Brother. I was talking to your abbot, and—"

"Yes?" asked the young priest.

"Well, while we disagree on a few things, I can understand his point of view. I was thinking that an exchange of scholarships might improve relations. There would be a stipend, of course, and I'm sure your abbot could put that to good use."

Brother Kornhoer inclined his head but said nothing.

"Come now!" The scholar laughed. "You don't seem pleased by the invitation, Brother."

"I am flattered, of course. But such matters are not for me to decide."

"Well, I understand that, of course. But I wouldn't dream of asking your abbot if the idea displeased you."

Brother Kornhoer hesitated. "My vocation is to Religion," he said at last, "that is—to a life of prayer. We think of our work as a kind of prayer too. But that—" he gestured toward his dynamo "—for me seems more like play. However, if Dom Paulo were to send me—"

"You'd reluctantly go," the scholar finished sourly. "I'm sure I could get the collegium to send your abbot at least a hundred gold hannegans a year while you were with us, too. I—" He paused to look around at their expressions. "Pardon me, did I say something wrong?"

Halfway down the stairs, the abbot paused to survey the group in the basement. Several blank faces were turned toward him. After a few seconds Thon Taddeo noticed the abbot's presence and nodded pleasantly.

"We were just speaking of you, Father," he said. "If you heard, perhaps I should explain—"

Dom Paulo shook his head. "That's not necessary."

"But I *would* like to discuss—"

"Can it wait? I'm in a hurry this minute."

"Certainly," said the scholar.

"I'll be back shortly." He climbed the stairs again. Father Gault was waiting for him in the courtyard.

"Have they heard about it yet, Domne?" the prior asked grimly.

"I didn't ask, but I'm sure they haven't," Dom Paulo answered. "They're just making silly conversation down there. Something about taking Brother K back to Texarkana with them."

"Then they *haven't* heard, that's certain."

"Yes. Now where is he?"

"In the guesthouse, Domne. The medic's with him. He's delirious."

"How many of the brothers know he's here?"

"About four. We were singing None when he came in the gate."

"Tell those four not to mention it to anyone. Then join our guests in the basement. Just be pleasant, and *don't* let them know."

"But shouldn't they be told before they leave, Domne?"

"Of course. But let them get ready first. You know it won't stop them from going back. So to minimize embarrassment, let's wait until the last minute to tell them. Now, do you have it with you?"

"No, I left it with his papers in the guesthouse."

"I'll go see him. Now, warn the brothers, and join our guests."

"Yes, Domne."

The abbot hiked toward the guesthouse. As he entered, Brother Pharmacist was just leaving the fugitive's room.

"Will he live, Brother?"

"I cannot know, Domne. Mistreatment, starvation, exposure, fever—if God wills it—" He shrugged.

"May I speak to him?"

"I'm sure it won't matter. But he doesn't make sense."

The abbot entered the room and softly closed the door behind him.

"Brother Claret?"

"Not again," gasped the man on the bed. "For the love of God, not again—I've told you all I know. I betrayed him. Now just let me—be."

Dom Paulo looked down with pity on the secretary to the late Marcus Apollo. He glanced at the scribe's hands. There were only festering sores where the fingernails had been.

The abbot shuddered and turned to the small table near the bed. Out of a small collection of papers and personal effects, he quickly found the crudely printed document which the fugitive had brought with him from the east:

HANNEGAN THE MAYOR, by Grace of God: Sovereign of Texarkana, Emperor of Laredo, Defender of the Faith, Doctor of Laws, Clans Chief of the Nomads, and Vaquero Supreme of the Plains, to ALL BISHOPS, PRIESTS, AND PRELATES of the Church throughout Our Rightful Realm, Greetings & TAKE HEED, for it is the LAW, viz & to wit:

(1) Whereas a certain foreign prince, one Benedict XXII, Bishop of New Rome, presuming to assert an authority which is not rightly his over the clergy of this nation, has dared to attempt, first, to place the Texarkanan Church under a sentence of interdict, and, later, to suspend this sentence, thereby creating great confusion and spiritual neglect among all the faithful, We, the only legitimate ruler over the Church in this realm, acting in concord with a council of bishops and clergy, hereby declare to Our loyal people that the aforesaid prince and bishop, Benedict XXII, is a heretic, simoniac, murderer, sodomite, and atheist, unworthy of any recognition by Holy Church in lands of Our kingdom, empire, or protectorate. Who serves him serves not Us.

(2) Be it known, therefore, that both the decree of interdict and the decree suspending it are hereby QUASHED, ANNULLED, DECLARED VOID AND OF NO CONSEQUENCE, for they were of no original validity. . . .

Dom Paulo glanced at the rest of it only briefly. There was no need to read further. The mayoral *TAKE HEED* ordered the licensing of the Texarkanan clergy, made the administration of the Sacraments by unlicensed persons a crime under the law, and made an oath of supreme allegiance to the Mayorality a condition for licensing and recognition. It was signed not only with the Mayor's mark, but also by several "bishops" whose names were unfamiliar to the abbot.

He tossed the document back on the table and sat down beside the bed. The fugitive's eyes were open, but he only stared at the ceiling and panted.

"Brother Claret?" he asked gently. "Brother . . ."

In the basement, the scholar's eyes had come alight with the brash exuberance of one specialist invading the field of another specialist for the sake of straightening out the whole region of confusion. "As a matter of fact, *yes!*" he said in response to a novice's question. "I *did* locate one source here that should, I think, be of interest to Thon Maho. Of course, I'm no historian, but—"

"Thon Maho? Is he the one who's, uh, trying to correct Genesis?" Father Gault asked wryly.

"Yes, that's—" the scholar broke off with a startled glance at Gault.

"That's all right," the priest said with a chuckle. "Many

of us feel that Genesis is more or less allegorical. What have you found?"

"We located one pre-Diluvian fragment that suggests a *very* revolutionary concept, as I see it. If I interpret the fragment correctly, Man was not created until shortly before the fall of the last civilization."

"Wh-a-at? Then where did civilization come from?"

"Not from humanity. It was developed by a preceding race which became extinct during the Diluvium Ignis."

"But Holy Scripture goes back thousands of years before the Diluvium!"

Thon Taddeo remained meaningfully silent.

"You are proposing," said Gault, suddenly dismayed, "that *we* are not the descendants of Adam? not related to historical humanity?"

"Wait! I only offer the conjecture that the pre-Deluge race, which called itself Man, succeeded in creating life. Shortly before the fall of their civilization, they successfully created the ancestors of present humanity—'after their own image'—as a servant species."

"But even if you totally reject Revelation, that's a completely unnecessary complication under plain common sense!" Gault complained.

The abbot had come quietly down the stairs. He paused on the lower landing and listened incredulously.

"It might seem so," Thon Taddeo argued, "until you consider how many things it would account for. You know the legends of the Simplification. They all become more meaningful, it seems to me, if one looks at the Simplification as a rebellion by a created servant species against the original creator species, as the fragmentary reference suggests. It would also explain why present-day humanity seems so inferior to the ancients, why our ancestors lapsed into barbarism when their masters were extinct, why—"

"God have mercy on this house!" cried Dom Paulo, striding toward the alcove. "Spare us, Lord—we know not what we did."

"I should have known," the scholar muttered to the world at large.

The old priest advanced like a nemesis on his guest. "So we are but creatures of creatures, then, Sir Philosopher? Made by lesser gods than God, and therefore understandably less than perfect—through no fault of ours, of course."

"It is only conjecture but it would account for much," the thon said stiffly, unwilling to retreat.

"And absolve of much, would it not? Man's rebellion against his makers was, no doubt, merely justifiable tyrannicide against the infinitely wicked sons of Adam, then."

"I didn't say—"

"*Show me*, Sir Philosopher, this amazing reference!"

Thon Taddeo hastily shuffled through his notes. The light kept flickering as the novices at the drive-mill strained to listen. The scholar's small audience had been in a state of shock until the abbot's stormy entrance shattered the numb dismay of the listeners. Monks whispered among themselves; someone dared to laugh.

"Here it is," Thon Taddeo announced, passing several note pages to Dom Paulo.

The abbot gave him a brief glare and began reading. The silence was awkward. "You found this over in the 'Unclassified' section, I believe?" he asked after a few seconds.

"Yes, but—"

The abbot went on reading.

"Well, I suppose I should finish packing," muttered the scholar, and resumed his sorting of papers. Monks shifted restlessly, as if wishing to slink quietly away. Kornhoer brooded alone.

Satisfied after a few minutes of reading, Dom Paulo handed the notes abruptly to his prior. "*Lege!*" he commanded gruffly.

"But what—?"

"A fragment of a play, or a dialogue, it seems. I've seen it before. It's something about some people creating some artificial people as slaves. And the slaves revolt against their makers. If Thon Taddeo had read the Venerable Boedullus' *De Inanibus*, he would have found that one classified as 'probable fable or allegory.' But perhaps the thon would care little for the evaluations of the Venerable Boedullus, when he can make his own."

"But what sort of—"

"*Lege!*"

Gault moved aside with the notes. Paulo turned toward the scholar again and spoke politely, informatively, emphatically: " 'To the image of God He created them: male and female He created them.' "

"My remarks were only conjecture," said Thon Taddeo. "Freedom to speculate is necessary—"

" 'And the Lord God took Man, and put him into the paradise of pleasure, to dress it, and to keep it. And—' "

"—to the advancement of science. If you would have us hampered by blind adherence, unreasoned dogma, then you would prefer—"

" 'God commanded him, saying: Of every tree of paradise thou shalt eat; but of the tree of knowledge of good and evil, thou shalt—' "

"—to leave the world in the same black ignorance and superstition that you say your Order has struggled—"

" '—not eat. For in what day soever thou shalt eat of it, thou shalt die the death.' "

"—against. Nor could we ever overcome famine, disease, or misbirth, or make the world one bit better than it has been for—"

" 'And the serpent said to the woman: God doth know that in what day soever you shall eat thereof, your eyes shall be opened, and you shall be as Gods, knowing good and evil.' "

"—twelve centuries, if every direction of speculation is to be closed off and every new thought denounced—"

"It never *was* any better, it never *will* be any better. It will only be richer or poorer, sadder but not wiser, until the very last day."

The scholar shrugged helplessly. "You see? I knew you would be offended, but you told me— Oh, what's the use? You have your account of it."

"The 'account' that I was quoting, Sir Philosopher, was not an account of the manner of creation, but an account of the manner of the temptation that led to the Fall. Did that escape you? 'And the serpent said to the woman—' "

"Yes, yes, but the freedom to speculate is essential—"

"No one has tried to deprive you of that. Nor is anyone offended. But to abuse the intellect for reasons of pride, vanity, or escape from responsibility, is the fruit of that same tree."

"You question the honor of my motives?" asked the thon, darkening.

"At times I question my own. I accuse you of nothing. But ask yourself this: Why do you take delight in leaping to such a wild conjecture from so fragile a springboard? Why do you wish to discredit the past, even to dehumanizing the last civilization? So that you need not learn from their mistakes?

Or can it be that you can't bear being only a 'rediscoverer,'
and must feel that you are a 'creator' as well?"

The thon hissed an oath. "These records should be placed
in the hands of competent people," he said angrily. "What
irony this is!"

The light sputtered and went out. The failure was not mechanical. The novices at the drive-mill had stopped work.

"Bring candles," called the abbot.

Candles were brought.

"Come down," Dom Paulo said to the novice atop the
ladder. "And bring that thing with you. Brother Kornhoer?
Brother Korn—"

"He stepped into the storeroom a moment ago, Domne."

"Well, call him." Dom Paulo turned to the scholar again,
handing him the document which had been found among
Brother Claret's effects. "Read, if you can make it out by
candlelight, Sir Philosopher!"

"A mayoral edict?"

"Read it and rejoice in your cherished freedom."

Brother Kornhoer slipped into the room again. He was
carrying the heavy crucifix which had been displaced from
the head of the archway to make room for the novel lamp.
He handed the cross to Dom Paulo.

"How did you know I wanted this?"

"I just decided it was about time, Domne." He shrugged.

The old man climbed the ladder and replaced the rood on
its iron hook. The corpus glittered with gold by candlelight.
The abbot turned and called down to his monks.

"Who reads in this alcove henceforth, let him read *ad
Lumina Christi!*"

When he descended the ladder, Thon Taddeo was already
cramming the last of his papers into a large case for later
sorting. He glanced warily at the priest but said nothing.

"You read the edict?"

The scholar nodded.

"If, by some unlikely chance, you would like political
asylum here—"

The scholar shook his head.

"Then may I ask you to clarify your remark about placing
our records in competent hands?"

Thon Taddeo lowered his gaze. "It was said in the heat of
the moment, Father. I retract it."

"But you haven't stopped meaning it. You've meant it all
along."

The thon did not deny it.

"Then it would be futile to repeat my plea for your intercession on our behalf—when your officers tell your cousin what a fine military garrison this abbey would make. But for his own sake, tell him that when our altars or the Memorabilia have been threatened, our predecessors did not hesitate to resist with the sword." He paused. "Will you be leaving today or tomorrow?"

"Today I think would be better," Thon Taddeo said softly.

"I'll order provisions made ready." The abbot turned to go, but paused to add gently: "But when you get back, deliver a message to your colleagues."

"Of course. Have you written it?"

"No. Just say that anyone who wishes to study here will be welcome, in spite of the poor lighting. Thon Maho, especially. Or Thon Esser Shon with his six ingredients. Men must fumble awhile with error to separate it from truth, I think—as long as they don't seize the error hungrily because it has a pleasanter taste. Tell them too, my son, that when the time comes, as it will surely come, that not only priests but philosophers are in need of sanctuary—tell them our walls are thick out here."

He nodded a dismissal to the novices, then, and trudged up the stairs to be alone in his study. For the Fury was twisting his insides again, and he knew that torture was coming.

Nunc dimittis servum tuum, Domine. . . . Quia viderunt oculi mei salutare. . . .

Maybe it will twist clean loose this time, he thought almost hopefully. He wanted to summon Father Gault to hear his confession, but decided that it would be better to wait until the guests had gone. He stared at the edict again.

A knock at the door soon interrupted his agony.

"Can you come back later?"

"I'm afraid I won't be here later," answered a muffled voice from the corridor.

"Oh, Thon Taddeo—come in, then." Dom Paulo straightened; he took a firm grip on pain, not trying to dismiss it but only to control it as he would an unruly servant.

The scholar entered and placed a folder of papers on the abbot's desk. "I thought it only proper to leave you these," he said.

"What do we have here?"

"The sketches of your fortifications. The ones the officers made. I suggest you burn them immediately."

"Why have you done this?" Dom Paulo breathed. "After our words downstairs—"

"Don't misunderstand," Thon Taddeo interrupted. "I would have returned them in any event—as a matter of honor, not to let them take advantage of your hospitality for—but never mind. If I had returned the sketches any sooner, the officers would have had plenty of time and opportunity to draw up another set."

The abbot arose slowly and reached for the scholar's hand.

Thon Taddeo hesitated. "I promise no effort on your behalf—"

"I know."

"—because I think what you have here should be open to the world."

"It is, it was, it always will be."

They shook hands gingerly, but Dom Paulo knew that it was no token of any truce but only of mutual respect between foes. Perhaps it would never be more.

But why must it all be acted again?

The answer was near at hand; there was still the serpent whispering: For God doth know that in what day soever you shall eat thereof, your eyes shall be opened: and you shall be as Gods. The old father of lies was clever at telling half-truths: How shall you "know" good and evil, until you shall have sampled a little? Taste and be as Gods. But neither infinite power nor infinite wisdom could bestow godhood upon men. For that there would have to be infinite love as well.

Dom Paulo summoned the younger priest. It was very nearly time to go. And soon it would be a new year.

That was the year of the unprecedented torrent of rain on the desert, causing seed long dry to burst into bloom.

That was the year that a vestige of civilization came to the nomads of the Plains, and even the people of Laredo began to murmur that it was possibly all for the best. Rome did not agree.

In that year a temporary agreement was formalized and broken between the states of Denver and Texarkana. It was the year that the Old Jew returned to his former vocation of Physician and Wanderer, the year that the monks of the Albertian Order of Leibowitz buried an abbot and bowed to a new one. There were bright hopes for tomorrow.

It was the year a king came riding out of the east, to subdue the land and own it. It was a year of Man.

23 It was unpleasantly hot beside the sunny trail that skirted the wooded hillside, and the heat had aggravated the Poet's thirst. After a long time he dizzily lifted his head from the ground and tried to look around. The melee had ended; things were fairly quiet now, except for the cavalry officer. The buzzards were even gliding down to land.

There were several dead refugees, one dead horse, and the dying cavalry officer who was pinned under the horse. At intervals, the cavalryman awoke and faintly screamed. Now he screamed for Mother, and again he screamed for a priest. At times he awoke to scream for his horse. His screaming disquieted the buzzards and further disgruntled the Poet, who was feeling peevish anyhow. He was a very dispirited Poet. He had never expected the world to act in a courteous, seemly, or even sensible manner, and the world had seldom done so; often he had taken heart in the consistency of its rudeness and stupidity. But never before had the world shot the Poet in the abdomen with a musket. This he found not heartening at all.

Even worse, he had not now the stupidity of the world to blame but only his own. The Poet himself had blundered. He had been minding his own business and bothering no one when he noticed the party of refugees galloping toward the hill from the east with a cavalry troop in close pursuit. To avoid the affray, he had hidden himself behind some scrub that grew from the lip of the embankment flanking the trail, a vantage point from which he could have seen the whole spectacle without being seen. It was not the Poet's fight. He cared nothing whatever for the political and religious tastes of either the refugees or the cavalry troop. If slaughter had been fated, fate could have found no less disinterested a witness than the Poet. Whence, then, the blind impulse?

The impulse had sent him leaping from the embankment to tackle the cavalry officer in the saddle and stab the fellow three times with his own belt-knife before the two of them toppled to the ground. He could not understand why he had done it. Nothing had been accomplished. The officer's men had shot him down before he ever climbed to his feet. The slaughter of refugees had continued. They had all ridden away then in pursuit of other fugitives, leaving the dead behind.

He could hear his abdomen growl. The futility, alas, of trying to digest a rifle ball. He had done the useless deed, he decided finally, because of the part with the dull saber. If the officer had merely hacked the woman out of the saddle with one clean stroke, and ridden on, the Poet would have overlooked the deed. But to keep hacking and hacking that way—

He refused to think about it again. He thought of water.

"O God—O God—" the officer kept complaining.

"Next time, sharpen your cutlery," the Poet wheezed.

But there would be no next time.

The Poet could not remember ever fearing death, but he had often suspected Providence of plotting the worst for him as to the manner of his dying when the time came to go. He had expected to rot away. Slowly and not very fragrantly. Some poetic insight had warned him that he would surely die a blubbering leprous lump, cravenly penitential but impenitent. Never had he anticipated anything so blunt and final as a bullet in the stomach, and with not even an audience at hand to hear his dying quips. The last thing they had heard him say when they shot him was: *"Oof!"*—his testament for posterity. *Ooof!*—a memorabile for you, Domnissime.

"Father? Father?" the officer moaned.

After a while the Poet mustered his strength and lifted his head again, blinked dirt out of his eye, and studied the officer for a few seconds. He was certain the officer was the same one he had tackled, even though the fellow by now had turned a chalky shade of green. His bleating for a priest that way began to annoy the Poet. At least three clergymen lay dead among the refugees, and yet the officer was not now being so particular about specifying his denominational persuasions. Maybe I'll do, the Poet thought.

He began dragging himself slowly toward the cavalryman. The officer saw him coming and groped for a pistol. The Poet paused; he had not expected to be recognized. He prepared to roll for cover. The pistol was wavering in his direction. He watched it waver for a moment, then decided to continue his advance. The officer pulled the trigger. The shot went wild by yards, worse luck.

The officer was trying to reload when the Poet took the gun away from him. He seemed delirious, and kept trying to cross himself.

"Go ahead," the Poet grunted, finding the knife.

"Bless me, Father, for I have sinned—"

"*Ego te absolvo,* son," said the Poet, and plunged the knife into his throat.

Afterward, he found the officer's canteen and drank a little. The water was hot from the sun, but it seemed delicious. He lay with his head pillowed on the officer's horse and waited for the shadow of the hill to creep over the road. Jesus, how it hurt! That last bit isn't going to be as easy to explain, he thought; and me without my eyeball too. If there's really anything to explain. He looked at the dead cavalryman.

"Hot as hell down there, isn't it?" he whispered hoarsely.

The cavalryman was not being informative. The Poet took another drink from the canteen, then another. Suddenly there was a very painful bowel movement. He was quite unhappy about it for a moment or two.

The buzzards strutted, preened, and quarreled over dinner; it was not yet properly cured. They waited a few days for the wolves. There was plenty for all. Finally they ate the Poet.

As always the wild black scavengers of the skies laid their eggs in season and lovingly fed their young. They soared high over prairies and mountains and plains, searching for the fulfillment of that share of life's destiny which was theirs according to the plan of Nature. Their philosophers demonstrated by unaided reason alone that the Supreme *Cathartes aura regnans* had created the world especially for buzzards. They worshipped him with hearty appetites for many centuries.

Then, after the generations of the darkness came the generations of the light. And they called it the Year of Our Lord 3781—a year of His peace, they prayed.

Fiat Voluntas Tua

24 There were spaceships again in that century, and the ships were manned by fuzzy impossibilities that walked on two legs and sprouted tufts of hair in unlikely anatomical regions. They were a garrulous kind. They belonged to a race quite capable of admiring its own image in a mirror, and equally capable of cutting its own throat before the altar of some tribal god, such as the deity of Daily Shaving. It was a species which often considered itself to be, basically, a race of divinely inspired toolmakers; any intelligent entity from Arcturus would instantly have perceived them to be, basically, a race of impassioned after-dinner speechmakers.

It was inevitable, it was manifest destiny, they felt (and not for the first time) that such a race go forth to conquer stars. To conquer them several times, if need be, and certainly to make speeches about the conquest. But, too, it was inevitable that the race succumb again to the old maladies on new worlds, even as on Earth before, in the litany of life and in the special liturgy of Man: Versicles by Adam, Rejoinders by the Crucified.

We are the centuries.

We are the chin-choppers and the golly-woppers, and soon we shall discuss the amputation of your head.

We are your singing garbage men, Sir and Madam, and we march in cadence behind you, chanting rhymes that some think odd.

Hut two threep foal
Left!
Left!
He-had-a-good-wife-but-he
Left!
Left!
Left!
    Right!
Left!

Wir, as they say in the old country, *marschieren weiter wenn alles in Scherben fällt.*

We have your eoliths and your mesoliths and your neoliths. We have your Babylons and your Pompeiis, your Caesars and your chromium-plated (vital-ingredient-impregnated) artifacts.

We have your bloody hatchets and your Hiroshimas. We march in spite of Hell, we do—

Atrophy, Entropy, and *Proteus vulgaris,*

telling bawdy jokes about a farm girl name of Eve
and a traveling salesman called Lucifer.

We bury your dead and their reputations.
We bury you. We are the centuries.

Be born then, gasp wind, screech at the surgeon's slap, seek manhood, taste a little of godhood, feel pain, give birth, struggle a little while, succumb:

(Dying, leave quietly by the rear exit, please.)

Generation, regeneration, again, again, as in a ritual, with blood-stained vestments and nail-torn hands, children of Merlin, chasing a gleam. Children, too, of Eve, forever building Edens—and kicking them apart in berserk fury because somehow it isn't the same. (AGH! AGH! AGH!—an idiot screams his mindless anguish amid the rubble. But quickly! let it be inundated by the choir, chanting Alleluias at ninety decibels.)

Hear then, the last Canticle of the Brethren of the Order of Leibowitz, as sung by the century that swallowed its name:

℣: Lucifer is fallen.

℟: *Kyrie eleison.*

℣: Lucifer is fallen.

℟: *Christe eleison.*

℣: Lucifer is fallen.

℟: *Kyrie eleison, eleison imas!*

LUCIFER IS FALLEN; the code words, flashed electrically across the continent, were whispered in conference rooms, were circulated in the form of crisp memoranda stamped *SUPREME SECRETISSIMO*), were prudently withheld from the press. The words rose in a threatening tide behind a dike of official secrecy. There were several holes in the dike, but the holes were fearlessly plugged by bureaucratic Dutch boys whose forefingers became exceedingly swollen while they dodged verbal spitballs fired by the press.

FIRST REPORTER: What is Your Lordship's comment on Sir Rische Thon Berker's statement that the radiation count on the Northwest Coast is ten times the normal level?

DEFENSE MINISTER: I have not read the statement.

FIRST REPORTER: Assuming it to be true, what could be responsible for such an increase?

DEFENSE MINISTER: The question calls for conjecture. Perhaps Sir Rische discovered a rich uranium deposit. No, strike that out. I have no comment.

SECOND REPORTER: Does Your Lordship regard Sir Rische as a competent and responsible scientist?

DEFENSE MINISTER: He has never been employed by my department.

SECOND REPORTER: That is not a responsive answer.

DEFENSE MINISTER: It is quite responsive. Since he has never been employed by my department, I have no way of knowing his competence or responsibility. I am not a scientist.

LADY REPORTER: Is it true that a nuclear explosion occurred recently somewhere across the Pacific?

DEFENSE MINISTER: As Madam well knows, the testing of atomic weapons of any kind is a high crime and an act of war under present international law. We are not at war. Does that answer your question?

LADY REPORTER: No, Your Lordship, it does not. I did not ask if a test had occurred. I asked whether an explosion had occurred.

DEFENSE MINISTER: We set off no such explosion. If they set one off, does Madam suppose that this government would be informed of it by them?

(*Polite laughter.*)

LADY REPORTER: That does *not* answer my—

FIRST REPORTER: Your Lordship, Delegate Jerulian has

charged the Asian Coalition with the assembly of hydrogen weapons in deep space, and he says our Executive Council knows it and does nothing about it. Is that true?

DEFENSE MINISTER: I believe it is true that the Opposition's Tribune made some such ridiculous charge, yes.

FIRST REPORTER: Why is the charge ridiculous? Because they are *not* making space-to-earth missiles in space? Or because we *are* doing something about it?

DEFENSE MINISTER: Ridiculous either way. I should like to point out, however, that the manufacture of nuclear weapons has been prohibited by treaty ever since they were redeveloped. Prohibited everywhere—in space or on Earth.

SECOND REPORTER: But there's no treaty to proscribe the orbiting of fissionable materials, is there?

DEFENSE MINISTER: Of course not. The space-to-space vehicles are all nuclear powered. They have to be fueled.

SECOND REPORTER: And there's no treaty to prohibit orbiting of other materials from which nuclear weapons might be manufactured?

DEFENSE MINISTER (*irritably*): To my knowledge, the existence of matter outside our atmosphere has not been outlawed by any treaty or act of parliament. It is my understanding that space is chock-full of things like the moon and the asteroids, which are *not* made of green cheese.

LADY REPORTER: Is Your Lordship suggesting that nuclear weapons could be manufactured without raw materials from Earth?

DEFENSE MINISTER: I was not suggesting that, no. Of course it's theoretically possible. I was saying that no treaty or law prohibits the orbiting of any special raw materials—only nuclear weapons.

LADY REPORTER: If there was a recent test shot in the Orient, which do you think more probable: a subterranean explosion that broke surface, or a space-to-earth missile with a defective warhead?

DEFENSE MINISTER: Madam, your question is so conjectural that you force me to say: "No comment."

LADY REPORTER: I was only echoing Sir Rische and Delegate Jerulian.

DEFENSE MINISTER: They are free to indulge in wild speculation. I am not.

SECOND REPORTER: At the risk of seeming wry— What is Your Lordship's opinion of the weather?

DEFENSE MINISTER: Rather warm in Texarkana, isn't it? I

understand they're having some bad dust storms in the Southwest. We may catch some of it hereabouts.

LADY REPORTER: Are you in favor of Motherhood, Lord Ragelle?

DEFENSE MINISTER: I am sternly opposed to it, Madam. It exerts a malign influence on youth, particularly upon young recruits. The military services would have superior soldiers if our fighting men had not been corrupted by Motherhood.

LADY REPORTER: May we quote you on that?

DEFENSE MINISTER: Certainly, Madam—but only in my obituary, not sooner.

LADY REPORTER: Thank you. I'll prepare it in advance.

Like other abbots before him, the Dom Jethrah Zerchi was by nature not an especially contemplative man, although as spiritual ruler of his community he was vowed to foster the development of certain aspects of the contemplative life in this flock, and, as a monk, to attempt the cultivation of a contemplative disposition in himself. Dom Zerchi was not very good at either of these. His nature impelled him toward action even in thought; his mind refused to sit still and contemplate. There was a quality of restlessness about him which had driven him to the leadership of the flock; it made him a bolder ruler, occasionally even a more successful ruler, than some of his predecessors, but that same restlessness could easily become a liability, or even a vice.

Zerchi was vaguely aware, most of the time, of his own inclination toward hasty or impulsive action when confronted by unslayable dragons. Just now, however, the awareness was not vague but acute. It operated in unfortunate retrospect. The dragon had already bitten St. George.

The dragon was an Abominable Autoscribe, and its malignant enormity, electronic by disposition, filled several cubical units of hollow wall space and a third of the volume of the abbot's desk. As usual, the contraption was on the blink. It miscapitalized, mispunctuated, and interchanged various words. Only a moment ago, it had committed electrical *lèse majesté* on the person of the sovereign abbot, who, after calling a computer repairman and waiting three days for him to appear, had decided to repair the stenographic abomination himself. The floor of his study was littered with typed scraps of trial dictation. Typical among these was one which bore the information:

tEsting tesTing testiNg? TESting tesTing? damNatioN?
whY the craZY capITALs# now Is the tiMe foR alL gooD
memoriZERS to Gum to tHe aCHe of the bookLEGgerS?
Drat; caN yOu do beTTer in LAtin# noW traNsLaTe;
nECCesse Est epistULam sacri coLLegio mIttendAm esse
statim dictem? What's wronG WITH tHe blasTED THing#

Zerchi sat on the floor in the midst of the litter and tried
to massage the involuntary tremor out of his forearm, which
had been recently electrified while exploring the Autoscribe's intestinal regions. The muscular twitching reminded
him of the galvanic response of a severed frog's leg. Since
he had prudently remembered to disconnect the machine
before tampering with it, he could only suppose that the
fiend who invented the thing had provided it with facilities
for electrocuting customers even without power. While
tweaking and tugging at connections in a search for loose
wires, he had been assaulted by a high voltage filter capaci-
tor which had taken advantage of an opportunity to dis-
charge itself to ground through the person of the Reverend
Father Abbot when Reverend Father's elbow brushed against
the chassis. But Zerchi had no way of knowing whether he
had fallen victim to a law of Nature for filter capacitors or to
a cunningly devised booby trap aimed at discouraging cus-
tomer-tampering. Anyway, he had fallen. His posture on the
floor had come about involuntarily. His only claim to competence at the repair of polylinguistic transcription devices
lay in his proud record of once having extracted a dead
mouse from the information storage circuitry, thereby correcting a mysterious tendency on the part of the machine
to write double syllables (doudoubleble sylsylabablesles).
Having discovered no dead mice this time, he could feel for
loose wires and hope Heaven had granted him charismata
as an electronic healer. But it was apparently not so.

"Brother Patrick!" he called toward the outer office, and
climbed wearily to his feet.

"Hey, Brother Pat!" he shouted again.

Presently the door opened and his secretary waddled in,
glanced at the open wall cabinets with their stupefying
maze of computer circuitry, scanned the cluttered floor, then
warily studied his spiritual ruler's expression. "Shall I call
the repair service again, Father Abbot?"

"Why bother?" Zerchi grunted. "You've called them
three times. They've made three promises. We've waited

three days. I need a stenographer. Now! Preferably a Christian. *That* thing—" he waved irritably toward the Abominable Autoscribe—"is a damned infidel or worse. Get rid of it. I want it out of here."

"The APLAC?"

"The APLAC. Sell it to an atheist. No, that wouldn't be kind. Sell it as junk. I'm through with it. Why, for Heaven's sake, did Abbot Boumous—may his soul be blessed—ever buy the silly contraption?"

"Well, Domne, they say your predecessor was fond of gadgets, and it *is* convenient to be able to write letters in languages you yourself can't speak."

"It is? You mean it *would* be. That contraption—listen, Brother, they claim it thinks. I didn't believe it at first. Thought, implying rational principle, implying soul. Can the principle of a 'thinking machine'—man-made—be a rational soul? Bah! It seemed a thoroughly pagan notion at first. But do you know what?"

"Father?"

"Nothing could be that perverse without premeditation! It *must* think! It knows good and evil, I tell you, and it chose the latter. Stop that snickering, will you? It's not funny. The notion isn't even pagan. Man made the contraption, but he didn't make its principle. They speak of the vegetative principle as a soul, don't they? A vegetable soul? And the animal soul? Then the rational human soul, and that's all they list in the way of incarnate vivifying principles, angels being disembodied. But how do we know the list is comprehensive? Vegetative, animative, rational—and then what else? *That's* what else, right there. That thing. And it *fell*. Get it out of here— But first I've *got* to get a radiogram off to Rome."

"Shall I get my pad, Reverend Father?"

"Do you speak Alleghenian?"

"No, I don't."

"Neither do I, and Cardinal Hoffstraff doesn't speak Southwest."

"Why not Latin, then?"

"Which Latin? The Vulgate or Modern? I don't trust my own Anglo-Latin, and if I did, *he'd* probably not trust his." He frowned at the bulk of the robotic stenographer.

Brother Patrick frowned with him, then stepped over to the cabinets and began peering into the maze of subminiature circuit components.

"No mouse," the abbot assured him.

"What are all these little knobs?"

"*Don't touch!*" Abbot Zerchi yelped as his secretary curiously fingered one of several dozen sub-chassis dial settings. These sub-chassis controls were mounted in neat square array in a box, the cover of which the abbot had removed, bore the irresistible warning: FACTORY ADJUSTMENTS ONLY.

"You didn't move it, did you?" he demanded, going to Patrick's side.

"I might have wiggled it a little, but I think it's back where it was."

Zerchi showed him the warning on the box's cover. "Oh," said Pat, and both of them stared.

"It's the punctuation, mostly, isn't it, Reverend Father?"

"That and stray capitals, and a few confused words."

They contemplated the squiggles, quiggles, quids, thingumbobs, and doohickii in mystified silence.

"Did you ever hear of the Venerable Francis of Utah?" the abbot asked at last.

"I don't recall the name, Domne. Why?"

"I was just hoping he's in a position to pray for us right now, although I don't believe he was ever canonized. Here, let's try turning this whatsis up a bit."

"Brother Joshua used to be some kind of an engineer. I forget what. But he was in space. They have to know a lot about computers."

"I've already called him. He's afraid to touch it. Here, maybe it needs—"

Patrick edged away. "If you would excuse me, m'Lord, I—"

Zerchi glanced up at his wincing scribe. "Oh, ye of little faith!" he said, correcting another FACTORY ADJUSTMENT.

"I thought I heard someone outside."

"Before the cock crows thrice—besides, you touched the first knob, didn't you?"

Patrick wilted. "But the cover was off, and . . ."

"*Hinc igitur effuge.* Out, out, before I decide it was your fault."

Alone again, Zerchi inserted the wall plug, sat at his desk, and, after muttering a brief prayer to Saint Leibowitz (who in recent centuries had come into wider popularity as the patron saint of electricians than he had ever won as the founder of the Albertian Order of Saint Leibowitz), flipped the switch. He listened for spitting and hissing noises, but none came. He heard only the faint clicking of delay relays and the familiar purr of timing motors as they came up to full speed. He sniffed. No smoke or ozone to be detected. Finally, he opened his eyes. Even the indicator lights of the desktop control panel were burning as usual. FACTORY ADJUSTMENTS ONLY, indeed!

Somewhat reassured, he switched the format selector to RADIOGRAM, turned the process selector to DICTATE-RECORD, the translator unit to SOUTHWEST IN and ALLEGHENIAN OUT, made certain the transcription switch was on OFF, keyed his microphone button and began dictating:

"Priority Urgent: To His Most Reverend Eminence, Sir Eric Cardinal Hoffstraff, Vicar Apostolic Designate, Provisional Vicariate Extraterrestris, Sacred Congregation of Propaganda, Vatican, New Rome. . . .

"Most Eminent Lord: In view of the recent renewal of world tensions, hints of a new international crisis, and even reports of a clandestine nuclear armaments race, we should be greatly honored if Your Eminence deems it prudent to counsel us concerning the present status of certain plans held in abeyance. I have reference to matters outlined in the *Motu proprio* of Pope Celestine the Eighth, of happy memory, given on the Feast of the Divine Overshadowing of the Holy Virgin, *Anno Domini* 3735, and beginning with the words—" he paused to look through the papers on his desk—"'*Ab hac planeta nativitatis aliquos filios Ecclesiae usque ad planetas solium alienorum iam abisse et numquam redituros esse intelligimus.*' Refer also to the confirming document of Anno Domini 3749, *Quo peregrinatur grex, pastor secum*, authorizing the purchase of an island, uh—certain vehicles. Lastly refer to *Casu belli nunc remoto*, of the late Pope Paul, Anno Domini 3756, and the correspondence which followed between the Holy Father and my predecessor, culminating with an order transferring to us the task of holding the plan *Quo peregrinatur* in a state of, uh—suspended animation, but only so long as Your Eminence approves. Our state of readiness with respect to *Quo peregrinatur* has been maintained, and should it become desirable to execute the plan, we would need perhaps six weeks' notice. . . .'"

While the abbot dictated, the Abominable Autoscribe did no more than record his voice and translate it into a phoneme code on tape. After he had finished speaking, he switched the process selector to ANALYZE and pressed a button marked TEXT PROCESSING. The ready-lamp winked off. The machine began processing.

Meanwhile, Zerchi studied the documents before him.

A chime sounded. The ready-lamp winked on. The machine was silent. With only one nervous glance at the FACTORY ADJUSTMENT ONLY box, the abbot closed his eyes and pressed the WRITE button.

Clatterty-chat-clatter-spatter-pip   popperty-kak-fub-clotter, the automatic writer chattered away at what he hoped would be the text of the radiogram. He listened hopefully to the rhythm of the keys. That first *clattery-chat-clatter-spatter-pip* had sounded quite authoritative. He tried to hear the rhythms of Alleghenian speech in the sound of the typing, and after a time he decided that there was indeed a certain Allegheny lilt mixed into the rattle of the keys. He opened his eyes. Across the room, the robotic stenographer was briskly at work. He left his desk and went to watch it work. With utmost neatness, the Abominable Autoscribe was writing the Alleghenian equivalent of:

RADIOGRAM—PRIORITY URGENT

TO: His Most Reverend Eminence, Sir Eric Cardinal Hoffstraff, Vicar Apostolic Designate, Provisional Vicariate Extraterrestris Sacred Congregation of Propaganda, Vatican, New Rome

FROM: Rev. Jethrah Zerchi, AOL, Abbas Abbey of Saint Leibowitz Sanly Bowitts, Sou W Territory

SUBJECT: Quo Peregrinatur Grex

Most Eminent Lord:

In view of the recent renewal of world tensions, hints of a new world crisis, and even reports of a clandestine nuclear armaments race, we should . . .

"Hey, Brother Pat!"

He turned off the machine in disgust. Holy Leibowitz! Did

we labor for *this?* He could not see that it was any improvement over a carefully trimmed goose-quill and a pot of mulberry ink.

"*Hey, Pat!*"

There was no immediate response from the outer office, but after a few seconds a monk with a red beard opened the door, and, after glancing at the open cabinets, the littered floor, and the abbot's expression, he had the gall to smile.

"What's the matter, Magister meus? Don't you like our modern technology?"

"Not particularly, no!" Zerchi snapped. "Hey, *Pat!*"

"He's out, m'Lord."

"Brother Joshua, can't you fix this thing? Really."

"Really?—No, I can't."

"I've got to send a radiogram."

"That's too bad, Father Abbot. Can't do that either. They just took our crystal and padlocked the shack."

"They?"

"Zone Defense Interior. All private transmitters have been ordered off the air."

Zerchi wandered to his chair and sank into it. "A defense alert. Why?"

Joshua shrugged. "There's talk about an ultimatum. That's all I know, except what I hear from the radiation counters."

"Still rising?"

"Still rising."

"Call Spokane."

By midafternoon the dusty wind had come. The wind came over the mesa and over the small city of Sanly Bowitts. It washed over the surrounding countryside, noisily through the tall corn in the irrigated fields, tearing streamers of blowing sand from the sterile ridges. It moaned about the stone walls of the ancient abbey and about the aluminum and glass walls of the modern additions to the abbey. It besmirched the reddening sun with the dirt of the land, and sent dust devils scurrying across the pavement of the six-lane highway that separated the ancient abbey from its modern additions.

On the side road which at one point flanked the highway and led from the monastery by way of a residential suburb into the city, an old beggar clad in burlap paused to listen to the wind. The wind brought the throb of practice rocketry explosively from the south. Ground-to-space interceptor missiles were being fired toward target orbits from a launching range far across the desert. The old man gazed at the faint red disk of the sun while he leaned on his staff and muttered to himself or to the sun, "Omens, omens—"

A group of children were playing in the weed-filled yard of a hovel just across the side road, their games proceeding under the mute but all-seeing auspices of a gnarled black woman who smoked a weed-filled pipe on the porch and offered an occasional word of solace or remonstrance to one or another tearful player who came as plaintiff before the grandmotherly court of her hovel porch.

One of the children soon noticed the old tramp who stood across the roadway, and presently a shout went up: "Lookit, lookit! It's old Lazar! Auntie say, he be old Lazar, same one 'ut the Lor' Hesus raise up! Lookit! Lazar! Lazar!"

The children thronged to the broken fence. The old tramp regarded them grumpily for a moment, then wandered on along the road. A pebble skipped across the ground at his feet.

"Hey, Lazar . . . !"

"Auntie say, what the Lor' Hesus raise up, it stay up! Lookit him! Ya! Still huntin' for the Lor' 'ut raise him. Auntie say—"

Another rock skipped after the old man, but he did not look back. The old woman nodded sleepily. The children returned to their games. The dust storm thickened.

Across the highway from the ancient abbey, atop one of the new aluminum and glass buildings, a monk on the roof was sampling the wind. He sampled it with a suction device which ate the dusty air and blew the filtered wind to the intake of an air compresser on the floor below. The monk was no longer a youth, but not yet middle-aged. His short red beard seemed electrically charged, for it gathered pendant webs and streamers of dust; he scratched it irritably from time to time, and once he thrust his chin into the end of the suction hose; the result caused him to mutter explosively, then to cross himself.

The compressor's motor coughed and died. The monk switched off the suction device, disconnected the blower hose and pulled the device across the roof to the elevator and into the cage. Drifts of dust had settled in the corners. He closed the gate and pressed the Down button.

In the laboratory on the uppermost floor, he glanced at the compressor's gauge—it registered MAX NORM—he closed the door, removed his habit, shook the dust out of it, hung it on a peg, and went over it with the suction device. Then, going to the deep sheet-steel sink at the end of the laboratory work-bench, he turned on the cold water and let it rise to the 200 Jug mark. Thrusting his head into the water, he washed the mud from his beard and hair. The effect was pleasantly icy. Dripping and sputtering, he glanced at the door. The likelihood of visitors just now seemed small. He removed his underwear, climbed into the tank, and settled back with a shivery sigh.

Abruptly the door opened. Sister Helene came in with a tray of newly uncrated glassware. Startled, the monk leaped to his feet in the tub.

"Brother Joshua!" the sister shrieked. Half a dozen beakers shattered on the floor.

The monk sat down with a splash that sprayed the room. Sister Helene clucked, sputtered, squeaked, dumped the tray on the workbench, and fled. Joshua vaulted out of the sink and donned his habit without bothering to dry himself or put on his underwear. When he got to the door, Sister Helene was already out of the corridor—probably out of the building and halfway to the sister's chapel just down the side lane. Mortified, he hastened to complete his labors.

He emptied the suction device's contents and collected a sample of the dust in a phial. He took the phial to the work-bench, plugged in a pair of headphones, and held the phial at a measured distance from the detector element of a radiation counter while he consulted his watch and listened.

The compressor had a built-in counter. He pressed a stud marked: RESET. The whirling decimal register flipped back to zero and began counting again. He stopped it after one min-ute and wrote the count on the back of his hand. It was mostly plain air, filtered and compressed; but there was a whiff of something else.

He closed the lab for the afternoon. He went down to the office on the subjacent floor, wrote the count on a wall chart, eyed its perplexing upswing, then sat at his desk and flipped the viewphone switch. He dialed by feel, while gazing at the telltale wallchart. The screen flashed, the phone beeped, and the viewer fluttered into focus on the back of an empty desk chair. After a few seconds a man slid into the chair and peered into the viewer. "Abbot Zerchi here," the abbot grunted. "Oh, Brother Joshua. I was about to call you. Have you been taking a bath?"

"Yes, m'Lord Abbot."

"You might at least blush!"

"I am."

"Well, it doesn't show up on the viewer. Listen. On *this* side of the highway, there's a sign just outside our gates. You've noticed it, of course? It says, 'Women Beware. Enter Not Lest'—and so forth. You've noticed it?"

"Surely, m'Lord."

"Take your baths on *this* side of the sign."

"Certainly."

"Mortify yourself for offending Sister's modesty. I'm aware that you haven't got any. Listen, I suppose you can't even bring yourself to pass the reservoir without jumping in, baby-spanking bald, for a swim."

"Who told you that, m'Lord? I mean—I've only waded—"

"Ye-e-s-s? Well, never mind. Why did you call me?"

"You wanted me to call Spokane."

"Oh, yes. Did you?"

"Yes." The monk gnawed at a bit of dry skin at the corner of his wind-cracked lips and paused uneasily. "I talked to Father Leone. They've noticed it too."

"The increased radiation count?"

"That's not all." He hesitated again. He did not like saying it. To communicate a fact seemed always to lend it fuller existence.

"Well?"

"It's connected with that seismic disturbance a few days ago. It's carried by the upper winds from that direction. All things considered, it looks like fallout from a low altitude burst in the megaton range."

"Heu!" Zerchi sighed and covered his eyes with a hand. "*Luciferum ruisse mihi dicis?*"

"Yes, Domne, I'm afraid it was a weapon."

"Not possibly an industrial accident?"

"No."

"But if there were a war on, we'd know. An illicit test? but not that either. If they wanted to test one, they could test it on the far side of the moon, or better, Mars, and not be caught."

Joshua nodded.

"So what does that leave?" the abbot went on. "A display? A threat? A warning shot fired over the bow?"

"That's all I could think of."

"So that explains the defense alert. Still, there's nothing

in the news except rumors and refusals to comment. And with dead silence from Asia."

"But the shot *must* have been reported from some of the observation satellites. Unless—I don't like to suggest this, but—unless somebody has discovered a way to shoot a space-to-earth missile past the satellites, without detection until it's on the target."

"Is that possible?"

"There's been some talk about it, Father Abbot."

"The government knows. The government *must* know. Several of them know. And yet we hear nothing. We are being protected from hysteria. Isn't that what they call it? Maniacs! The world's been in a *habitual* state of crisis for fifty years. *Fifty?* What am I saying? It's been in a habitual state of crisis since the beginning—but for half a century now, almost unbearable. And *why*, for the love of God? What is the fundamental irritant, the essence of the tension? Political philosophies? Economics? Population pressure? Disparity of culture and creed? Ask a dozen experts, get a dozen answers. Now Lucifer again. Is the species congenitally insane, Brother? If we're born mad, where's the hope of Heaven? Through Faith alone? Or isn't there any? God forgive me, I don't mean that. Listen, Joshua—"

"m'Lord?"

"As soon as you close up shop, come back over here. . . . That radiogram—I had to send Brother Pat into town to get it translated and sent by regular wire. I want you around when the answer comes. Do you know what it's about?"

Brother Joshua shook his head.

"*Quo peregrinatur grex.*"

The monk slowly lost color. "To go into effect, Domne?"

"I'm just trying to learn the status of the plan. Don't mention it to anybody. Of course, you'll be affected. See me here when you're through."

"Certainly."

"*Chris'tecum.*"

"*Cum spiri'tuo.*"

The circuit opened, the screen faded. The room was warm, but Joshua shivered. He gazed out the window into a premature twilight murky with dust. He could see no farther than the storm fence next to the highway where a passing procession of truck headlights made traveling halos in the dust haze. After a while he became aware of someone standing

near the gate where the driveway opened on to the turnpike
approach. The figure was dimly visible in silhouette whenever the headlights' aurorae flashed by in review. Joshua
shivered again.

The silhouette was unmistakably that of Mrs. Grales.
No one else would have been recognizable in such poor
visibility, but the shape of the hooded bundle on her left
shoulder, and the way her head tilted toward the right, made
her outline uniquely that of Old Ma'am Grales. The monk
pulled curtains across the window and turned on the light.
He was not repelled by the old woman's deformity; the
world had grown blasé about such genetic mishaps and
pranks of the genes. His own left hand still bore a tiny scar
where a sixth finger had been removed during his infancy.
But the heritage of the *Diluvium Ignis* was something he preferred to forget for the moment, and Mrs. Grales was one of
its more conspicuous heirs.

He fingered a globe of the world on his desk. He spun it so
that the Pacific Ocean and East Asia drifted past. Where? Precisely where? He twirled the globe faster, slapping it lightly
again and again so that the world spun like a gaming
wheel, faster and yet faster until the continents and oceans
became a blur. Place your bets, Sir and Madam: Where? He
braked the globe abruptly with his thumb. Bank: India pays
off. Please collect, Madam. The divination was wild. He
spun the globe again until the axial mountings rattled;
"days" flitted by as briefest instants— In a reverse sense, he
noticed suddenly. If Mother Gaia pirouetted in the same
sense, the sun and other passing scenery would rise in the
west and set in the east. Reversing time thereby? Said the
namesake of my namesake: *Move not, O Sun, toward Gab-
aon, nor thou, O Moon, toward the valley*—a neat trick, forsooth, and useful in these times too. *Back up, O Sun, et tu,
Luna, recedite in orbitas reversas.* . . . He kept spinning the
globe in reverse, as if hoping the simulacrum of Earth possessed the Chronos for unwinding time. A third of a million
turns might unwind enough days to carry it back to the
Diluvium Ignis. Better to use a motor and spin it back to the
beginning of Man. He stopped it again with his thumb;
once more the divination was wild.

Still he lingered in the office and dreaded going "home"
again. "Home" was only across the highway, in the haunted
halls of those ancient buildings whose walls still contained

stones which had been the rubbled concrete of a civilization that had died eighteen centuries ago. Crossing the highway to the old abbey was like crossing an eon. Here in the new aluminum and glass buildings, he was a technician at a workbench where events were only phenomena to be observed with regard for their *How*, not questioning their *Why*. On *this* side of the road, the falling of Lucifer was only an inference derived by cold arithmetic from the chatter of radiation counters, from the sudden swing of a seismograph pen. But in the old abbey, he ceased to be a technician; over there he was a monk of Christ, a booklegger and memorizer in the community of Leibowitz. Over there, the question would be: "Why, Lord, why?" But the question had already come, and the abbot had said: "See me."

Joshua reached for his bindlestiff and went to obey the summons of his ruler. To avoid meeting Mrs. Grales, he used the pedestrian underpass; it was no time for pleasant conversations with the bicephalous old tomato woman.

25 The dike of secrecy had broken. Several dauntless Dutch boys were swept away by the raging tide; the tide swept them right out of Texarkana to their country estates where they became unavailable for comment. Others remained at their posts and staunchly tried to plug new leaks. But the fall of certain isotopes in the wind created a universal byword, spoken on street corners and screamed by banner headlines: *LUCIFER IS FALLEN*.

The Minister of Defense, his uniform immaculate, his make-up unsmeared, and his equanimity unruffled, again faced the journalistic fraternity; this time the press conference was televised throughout the Christian Coalition.

LADY REPORTER: Your Lordship appears rather calm, in the face of the facts. Two violations of international law, both defined by treaty as warlike acts, have recently occurred. Doesn't that worry the War Ministry at all?

DEFENSE MINISTER: Madam, as you very well know, we do not have a *War* Ministry here; we have a *Defense* Ministry. And as far as I know, only *one* violation of international law has occurred. Would you mind acquainting me with the other?

LADY REPORTER: Which one are you *not* acquainted with —the disaster in Itu Wan, or the warning shot over the far South Pacific?

DEFENSE MINISTER (*suddenly stern*): Surely Madam intends nothing seditious, but your question seems to give comfort, if not credence, to the utterly false Asian charges that the so-called Itu Wan disaster was the result of a weapon test by us and not by them!

LADY REPORTER: If it does, I invite you to throw me in jail. The question was based on a Near East neutralist account, which reported that the Itu Wan disaster was the result of an Asian weapon test, underground, which broke free. The same account said that the Itu Wan test was sighted from our satellites and immediately answered by a space-to-earth warning shot southeast of New Zealand. But now that you suggest it, *was* the Itu Wan disaster also the result of a weapon test by us?

DEFENSE MINISTER (*with forced patience*): I recognize the journalistic requirement of objectivity. But to suggest that His Supremacy's government would deliberately violate—

LADY REPORTER: His Supremacy is an eleven-year-old boy, and to call it *his* government is not only archaic, but a highly dishonorable—even cheap!—attempt to shift the responsibility for a full denial from your own—

MODERATOR: Madam! Please restrain the tenor of your—

DEFENSE MINISTER: Overlook it, overlook it! Madam, you have my full denial if you must dignify the fantastic charges. The so-called Itu Wan disaster was not the result of a weapon test by us. Nor do I have any knowledge of any other recent nuclear detonation.

LADY REPORTER: Thank you.

MODERATOR: I believe the editor of the *Texarkana Star-Insight* has been trying to speak.

EDITOR: Thank you. I should like to ask, Your Lordship: What *did* happen in Itu Wan?

DEFENSE MINISTER: We have no nationals in that area; we have had no observers there since diplomatic relations were broken during the last world crisis. I can, therefore, only rely upon indirect evidence, and the somewhat conflicting neutralist accounts.

EDITOR: That is to be understood.

DEFENSE MINISTER: Very well, then, I gather there was a sub-surface nuclear detonation—in the megaton range—and it got out of hand. It was rather obviously a test of some sort. Whether it was a weapon or, as some Asia-fringe "neutrals" claim, an attempt to divert an underground river —it was clearly illegal, and adjoining countries are preparing a protest to the World Court.

EDITOR: Is there any risk of war?

DEFENSE MINISTER: I foresee none. But as you know, we have certain detachments of our armed forces which are subject to conscription by the World Court to enforce its decisions, if needed. I foresee no such need, but I cannot speak for the court.

FIRST REPORTER: But the Asian coalition has threatened an immediate all-out strike against our space installations if the court does not take action *against us*. What if the court is slow in acting?

DEFENSE MINISTER: No ultimatum has been delivered. The threat was for Asian home consumption, as I see it; to cover their blunder in Itu Wan.

LADY REPORTER: How is your abiding faith in Motherhood today, Lord Ragelle?

DEFENSE MINISTER: I hope Motherhood has at least as much abiding faith in me as I have in Motherhood.

LADY REPORTER: You deserve at least that much, I'm sure.

The news conference, radiated from the relay satellite twenty-two thousand miles from Earth, bathed most of the Western Hemisphere with the flickering VHF signal which carried such intelligence to the panelescent wall screens of the multitudes. One among the multitudes, Abbot Dom Zerchi switched off the set.

He paced for a while, waiting for Joshua, trying not to think. But "not thinking" proved impossible.

Listen, are we helpless? Are we doomed to do it again and again and again? Have we no choice but to play the Phoenix in an unending sequence of rise and fall? Assyria, Babylon, Egypt, Greece, Carthage, Rome, the Empires of Charlemagne and the Turk. Ground to dust and plowed with salt. Spain, France, Britain, America—burned into the oblivion of the centuries. And again and again and again.

Are we doomed to it, Lord, chained to the pendulum of our own mad clockwork, helpless to halt its swing?

This time, it will swing us clean to oblivion, he thought.

The feeling of desperation passed abruptly when Brother Pat brought him the second telegram. The abbot ripped it open, read it at a glance and chuckled. "Brother Joshua here yet, Brother?"

"Waiting outside, Reverend Father."

"Send him in."

"Ho, Brother, shut the door and turn on the silencer. Then read this."

Joshua glanced at the first telegram. "An answer from New Rome?"

"It came this morning. But turn on that silencer first. We've got things to discuss."

Joshua closed the door and flipped a wall switch. Concealed loudspeakers squealed a brief protest. When the squealing stopped, the room's acoustic properties seemed suddenly changed.

Dom Zerchi waved him toward a chair, and he read the first telegram in silence.

". . . no action whatever to be taken by you in connection with *Quo peregrinatur grex*," he read aloud.

"You'll have to shout with that thing on," said the abbot, indicating the silencer. "What?"

"I was just reading. So the plan is canceled?"

"Don't look so relieved. *That* came this morning. *This* came this afternoon." The abbot tossed him the second telegram:

IGNORE EARLIER MESSAGE OF THIS DATE. "QUO PEREGRINATUR" TO BE REACTIVATED IMMEDIATELY BY REQUEST OF HOLY FATHER. PREPARE CADRE TO LEAVE WITHIN THREE DAYS. WAIT FOR CONFIRMING WIRE BEFORE DEPARTURE. REPORT ANY VACANCIES IN CADRE ORGANIZATION. BEGIN CONDITIONAL IMPLEMENTATION OF PLAN. ERIC CARDINAL HOFFSTRAFF, VICAR APOST. EXTRATERR. PROVINCIAE

The monk's face lost color. He replaced the telegram on the desk and sat back in his chair, lips tight together.

"You know what *Quo peregrinatur* is?"

"I know *what* it is, Domne, but not in detail."

"Well, it started as a plan to send a few priests along with a colony group heading for Alpha Centauri. But that didn't work out, because it takes bishops to ordain priests, and after the first generation of colonists, more priests would have to be sent, and so on. The question boiled down to an argument about whether the colonies would last, and if so, should provision be made to insure the apostolic succession on colony planets without recourse to Earth? You know what that would mean?"

"Sending at least three bishops, I imagine."

"Yes, and that seemed a little silly. The colony groups have all been rather small. But during the last world crisis, *Quo peregrinatur* became an emergency plan for perpetuating the Church on the colony planets if the worst came to pass on Earth. We have a ship."

"A *starship*?"

"No less. And we have a crew capable of managing it."

"Where?"

"We have the crew right here."

"Here at the abbey? But who—?" Joshua stopped. His face grew even grayer than before. "But, Domne, my experience in space has been entirely in orbital vehicles, not in starships! Before Nancy died and I went to the Cisterc—"

"I know all about that. There are others with starship experience. You know who they are. There are even jokes about the number of ex-spacers that seem to feel a vocation to our Order. It's no accident, of course. And you remember when you were a postulant, how you were quizzed about your experience in space?"

Joshua nodded.

"You must also remember being asked about your willingness to go to space again, if the Order asked it of you."

"Yes."

"Then you were not wholly unaware that you were conditionally assigned to *Quo peregrinatur*, if it ever came to pass?"

"I—I guess I was afraid it was so, m'Lord."

"Afraid?"

"*Suspected*, rather. Afraid too, a little, because I've always hoped to spend the rest of my life in the Order."

"As a priest?"

"That—well, I haven't yet decided."

"*Quo peregrinatur* will not involve releasing you from your vows or mean abandoning the Order."

"The Order goes *too*?"

Zerchi smiled. "And the Memorabilia with it."

"The whole kit-and— Oh, you mean on microfilm. Where to?"

"The Centaurus Colony."

"How long would we be gone, Domne?"

"If you go, you'll never come back."

The monk breathed heavily and stared at the second telegram without seeming to see it. He scratched his beard and appeared bemused.

"Three questions," said the abbot. "Don't answer now, but start thinking about them, and think hard. First, are you willing to go? Second, do you have a vocation to the priesthood? Third, are you willing to lead the group? And by *willing*, I don't mean 'willing under obedience'; I mean enthusiastic, or willing to get that way. Think it over; you have three days to think—maybe less."

Modern change had made but few incursions upon the buildings and the grounds of the ancient monastery. To protect the old buildings against the encroachment of a more impatient architecture, new additions had been made outside the walls and even across the highway—sometimes at the expense of convenience. The old refectory had been condemned because of a buckling roof, and it was necessary to cross the highway in order to reach the new refectory. The inconvenience was somewhat mitigated by the culvert walkunder through which the brothers marched daily to meals.

Centuries old, but recently widened, the highway was the same road used by pagan armies, pilgrims, peasants, donkey carts, nomads, wild horsemen out of the East, artillery, tanks, and ten-ton trucks. Its traffic had gushed or trickled or dripped, according to the age and season. Once before, long ago, there had been six lanes and robot traffic. Then the traffic had stopped, the paving had cracked, and sparse grass grew in the cracks after an occasional rain. Dust had covered it. Desert dwellers had dug up its broken concrete for the building of hovels and barricades. Erosion made it a desert trail, crossing wilderness. But now there were six lanes and robot traffic, as before.

"Traffic's light tonight," the abbot observed as they left the old main gate. "Let's hike across. That tunnel can be suffocating after a dust storm. Or don't you feel like dodging buses?"

"Let's go," Brother Joshua agreed.

Low-slung trucks with feeble headlights (useful only for warning purposes) sped mindlessly past them with whining tires and moaning turbines. With dish antennae they watched the road, and with magnetic feelers they felt at the guiding strips of steel in the roadbed and were given guidance thereby, as they rushed along the pink, fluorescent river of oiled concrete. Economic corpuscles in an artery of Man, the behemoths charged heedlessly past the two monks who dodged them from lane to lane. To be felled by one of them was to be run over by truck after truck until a safety cruiser found the flattened imprint of a man on the pavement and stopped to clean it up. The autopilots' sensing mechanisms were better at detecting masses of metal than masses of flesh and bone.

"This was a mistake," Joshua said as they reached the center island and paused for breath. "Look who's standing over there."

The abbot peered for a moment, then clapped his forehead. "Mrs. Grales! I clean forgot: it's her night to prowl me down. She's sold her tomatoes to the sisters' refectory, and now she's after me again."

"After you? She was there last night, and the night before too. I thought she was waiting for a ride. What does she want from you?"

"Oh, nothing really. She's finished gypping the sisters on the price of tomatoes, and now she'll donate the surplus profit to me for the poor box. It's a little ritual. I don't mind the ritual. It's what comes afterwards that's bad. You'll see."

"Shall we go back?"

"And hurt her feelings? Nonsense. She's seen us by now. Come on."

They plunged into the thin stream of trucks again.

The two-headed woman and her six-legged dog waited with an empty vegetable basket by the new gate; the woman crooned softly to the dog. Four of the dog's legs were healthy legs, but an extra pair dangled uselessly at its sides. As for the woman, one head was as useless as the extra legs of the dog. It was a small head, a cherubic head, but it never opened its eyes. It gave no evidence of sharing in her breathing or her understanding. It lolled uselessly on one shoulder, blind, deaf, mute, and only vegetatively alive. Perhaps it lacked a brain, for it showed no sign of independent consciousness or personality. Her other face had aged, grown wrinkled, but the superfluous head retained the features of infancy, although it had been toughened by the gritty wind and darkened by the desert sun.

The old woman curtsied at their approach, and her dog drew back with a snarl. "Evenin', Father Zerchi," she drawled, "a most pleasant evenin' to yer—and to yer, Brother."

"Why, hello, Mrs. Grales—"

The dog barked, bristled, and began a frenzied dance, feinting toward the abbot's ankles with fangs bared for slashing. Mrs. Grales promptly struck her pet with the vegetable basket. The dog's teeth slashed the basket; the dog turned on its mistress. Mrs. Grales kept it away with the basket; and after receiving a few resounding whacks, the dog retired to sit growling in the gateway.

"What a fine mood Priscilla's in," Zerchi observed pleasantly. "Is she going to have pups?"

"Beg shriv'ness, yer honors," said Mrs. Grales, "but's not the pup's motherful condition as makes her so, devil fret her! but 'tis 'at man of mine. He's witched the piteous pup, he has—for love of witchin'—and it makes her 'feared of all. I beg yer honors' shriv'ness for her naughties."

"It's all right. Well, good night, Mrs. Grales."

But escape proved not that easy. She caught at the abbot's sleeve and smiled her toothlessly irresistible smile.

"A minute, Father, only a minute for 'n old tumater woman, if ye have it to spare."

"Why, of course! I'd be glad—"

Joshua gave the abbot a sidelong grin and went over to negotiate with the dog concerning right of way. Priscilla eyed him with plain contempt.

"Here, Father, here," Mrs. Grales was saying. "Take a little something for yer box. Here—" Coins rattled while Zerchi protested. "No, here, take of it, take of it," she insisted. "Oh, I know as how ye always say, by fret! but I be not so poor's ye might think on me. And ye do good work. If ye don't take of it, that no-good man of mine'll have it from me, and do him the Devil's work. Here—I sold my tumaters, and I got my price, near, and I bought my feed for the week and even a play-pretty for Rachel. I want ye to have of it. Here."

"It's very kind . . ."

"Grryumpf!" came an authoritative bark from the gateway. "Grryumpf! Rowf! rowf! RrrrrrrOWWFF!"—followed by a rapid sequence of yaps, yeeps, and Priscilla's howling in full retreat.

Joshua came wandering back with his hands in his sleeves.

"Are you wounded, man?"

"Grryumpf!" said the monk.

"What on earth did you *do* to her?"

"Grryumpf!" Brother Joshua repeated. "Rowf! Rowf! RrrrrOWWFF!"—then explained: "Priscilla believes in werewolves. The yelping was hers. We can get past the gate now."

The dog had vanished; but again Mrs. Grales caught at the abbot's sleeve. "Only a minute more of yer, Father, and I'll keep ye no longer. It's little Rachel I wanted to see yer about. There's the baptism and the christenin' to be thought of, and I wished to ask yer if ye'd do the honor of—"

"Mrs. Grales," he put in gently, "go see your own parish priest. He should handle these matters, not I. I have no parish—only the abbey. Talk to Father Selo at Saint Michael's. Our church doesn't even have a font. Women aren't permitted, except in the tribune—"

"The sister's chapel has a font, and women can—"

"It's for Father Selo, not for me. It has to be recorded in your own parish. Only as an emergency could I—"

"Ay, ay, that I know, but I saw Father Selo. I brought Rachel to his church and the fool of a man would not touch her."

"He refused to baptize Rachel?"

"That he did, the fool of a man."

"It's a priest you're talking of, Mrs. Grales, and no fool, for I know him well. He must have his reasons for refusing. If you don't agree with his reasons, then see someone else—but not a monastic priest. Talk to the pastor at Saint Maisie's perhaps."

"Ay, and that too have I done. . . ." She launched into what promised to be a prolonged account of her skirmishings on behalf of the unbaptized Rachel. The monks listened patiently at first, but while Joshua was watching her, he seized the abbot's arm above the elbow; his fingers gradually dug into Zerchi's arm until the abbot winched in pain and tore the fingers away with his free hand.

"What *are* you doing?" he whispered, but then noticed the monk's expression. Joshua's eyes were fixed on the old woman as if she were a cockatrice. Zerchi followed his gaze, but saw nothing stranger than usual; her extra head was half concealed by a sort of veil, but Brother Joshua had certainly seen *that* often enough.

"I'm sorry, Mrs. Grales," Zerchi interrupted as soon as she fell short of breath. "I really must go now. I'll tell you what: I'll call Father Selo for you, but that's all I can do. We'll see you again, I'm sure."

"Thank yer kindly, and beg yer shriv'ness for keeping yer."

"Good night, Mrs. Grales."

They entered the gate and walked toward the refectory. Joshua thumped the heel of his hand against his temple several times as if to jar something back into place.

"Why were you staring at her like that?" the abbot demanded. "I thought it rude."

"Didn't you notice?"

"Notice what?"

"Then you *didn't* notice. Well . . . let it pass. But who is Rachel? Why won't they baptize the child? Is she the woman's daughter?"

The abbot smiled without humor. "That's what Mrs. Grales contends. But there's some question as to whether Rachel is her daughter, her sister—or merely an excrescence growing out of her shoulder."

"Rachel!—*her other head?*"

"Don't shout so. She'll hear you yet."

"And she wants it baptized?"

"Rather urgently, wouldn't you say? It seems to be an obsession."

Joshua waved his arms. "How do they settle such things?"

"I don't know, and I don't want to know. I'm grateful to Heaven that it's not up to me to figure it out. If it were a simple case of Siamese twins, it would be easy. But it isn't. The old-timers say Rachel wasn't there when Mrs. Grales was born."

"A farmers' fable!"

"Perhaps. But some are willing to tell it under oath. How many souls has an old lady with an extra head—a head that 'just grew'? Things like that cause ulcers in high places, my son. Now, what was it you noticed? Why were you staring at her and trying to pinch my arm off like that?"

The monk was slow to answer. "It smiled at me," he said at last.

"What smiled?"

"Her extra, uh— Rachel. She smiled. I thought she was going to wake up."

The abbot stopped him in the refectory's entranceway and peered at him curiously.

"She smiled," the monk repeated very earnestly.

"You imagined it."

"Yes, m'Lord."

"Then *look* like you imagined it."

Brother Joshua tried. "I can't," he admitted.

The abbot dropped the old woman's coins in the poor box. "Let's go on inside," he said.

The new refectory was functional, chromium befixtured, acoustically tailored, and germicidally illuminated. Gone were the smoke-blackened stones, the tallow lamps, the wooden bowls and cellar-ripened cheeses. Except for the cruciform seating arrangement and a rank of images along one wall, the place resembled an industrial lunchroom. Its atmosphere had changed, as had the atmosphere of the entire abbey. After ages of striving to preserve remnants of culture from a civilization long dead, the monks had watched the rise of a new and mightier civilization. The old tasks had been completed; new ones were found. The past was venerated and exhibited in glass cases, but it was no longer the present. The Order conformed to the times, to an age of uranium and steel and flaring rocketry, amid the growl of heavy industry and the high thin whine of star drive converters. The Order conformed—at least in superficial ways.

"*Accedite ad eum,*" the Reader intoned.

The robed legions stood restlessly at their places during the reading. No food had yet appeared. The tables were bare of dishes. Supper had been deferred. The organism, the community whose cells were men, whose life had flowed through seventy generations, seemed tense tonight, seemed to sense a note amiss tonight, seemed aware, through the connaturality of its membership, of what had been told to only a few. The organism lived as a body, worshiped and worked as a body, and at times seemed dimly conscious as a mind that infused its members and whispered to itself and to Another in the lingua prima, baby tongue of the species. Perhaps the tension was increased as much by faint snortgrowl of practice rocketry from the distant anti-missile missile range as by the unexpected postponement of the meal.

The abbot rapped for silence, then gestured his prior, Father Lehy, toward the lectern. The prior looked pained for a moment before speaking.

"We all regret the necessity," he said at last, "of sometimes disturbing the quiet of contemplative life with news from the outside world. But we must remember too that we are here to pray for the world and its salvation, as for our own. Especially now, the world could use some praying for." He paused to glance at Zerchi.

The abbot nodded.

"Lucifer is fallen," said the priest, and stopped. He stood there looking down at the lectern as if suddenly struck dumb.

Zerchi arose. "That is Brother Joshua's inference, by the way," he interposed. "The Regency Council of the Atlantic Confederacy has said nothing to speak of. The dynasty has issued no statements. We know little more than we knew yesterday, except that The World Court is meeting in emergency session, and that the Defense Interior people are moving fast. There is a defense alert, and we'll be affected, but don't be disturbed. Father—?"

"Thank you, Domne," said the prior, seeming to regain his voice as Dom Zerchi was seated again. "Now, Reverend Father Abbot asked me to make the following announcements:

"First, for the next three days we shall sing the Little Office of Our Lady before Matins, asking her intercession for peace.

"Second, general instructions for civil defense in the event of a space-strike or missile-attack alert are available on the table by the entrance. Everybody take one. If you've read it, read it again.

"Third, in the event that an attack warning is sounded, the following brothers are to report immediately to Old Abbey courtyard for special instructions. If no attack warning comes, the same brothers will report there anyway day after tomorrow morning right after Matins and Lauds. Names—Brothers Joshua, Christopher, Augustin, James, Samuel—"

The monks listened with quiet tension, betraying no emotion. There were twenty-seven names in all, but no novices were among them. Some were eminent scholars, there were a janitor and a cook as well. At first hearing, one might assume that the names had been drawn from a box. By the time Father Lehy had finished the list, some of the brothers were eying each other curiously.

"And this same group will report to the dispensary for a complete physical examination tomorrow after Prime," the prior finished. He turned to look questioningly at Dom Zerchi. "Domne?"

"Yes, just one thing," said the abbot, approaching the lectern. "Brothers, let us *not* assume that there is going to be war. Let's remind ourselves that Lucifer has been with us—this time—for nearly two centuries. And was dropped only twice, in sizes smaller than megaton. We all know what *could* happen, if there's war. The genetic festering is still with us from the last time Man tried to eradicate himself. Back then, in the Saint Leibowitz' time, maybe they didn't know what would happen. Or perhaps they did know, but could not quite believe it until they tried it—like a child who knows what a loaded pistol is supposed to do, but who never pulled a trigger before. They had not yet seen a billion corpses. They had not seen the still-born, the monstrous, the dehumanized, the blind. They had not yet seen the madness and the murder and the blotting out of reason. Then they did it, and then they saw it.

"Now—*now* the princes, the presidents, the praesidiums, now they know—with dead certainty. They can know it by the children they beget and send to asylums for the deformed. They know it, and they've kept the peace. Not Christ's peace, certainly, but peace, until lately—with only two warlike incidents in as many centuries. Now they have the bitter certainty. My sons, they cannot do it again. Only a race of madmen could do it again—"

He stopped speaking. Someone was smiling. It was only a small smile, but in the midst of a sea of grave faces it stood out like a dead fly in a bowl of cream. Dom Zerchi frowned. The old man kept on smiling wryly. He sat at the "beggar's table" with three other transient tramps—an old fellow with a brushy beard, stained yellow about the chin. As a jacket, he wore a burlap bag with armholes. He continued to smile at Zerchi. He looked old as a rain-worn crag, and a suitable candidate for a Maundy laving. Zerchi wondered if he were about to stand up and make an announcement to his hosts—or blow a ramshorn at them, perhaps?— but that was only an illusion generated by the smile. He quickly dismissed the feeling that he had seen the old man before, somewhere. He concluded his remarks.

On his way back to his place, he paused. The beggar nodded pleasantly at his host. Zerchi came nearer.

"Who are you, if I may ask. Have I seen you somewhere before?"

לאצאר שמי

"What?"

"*Latzar shemi,*" the beggar repeated.

"I don't quite—"

"Call me Lazarus, then," said the old one, and chuckled.

Dom Zerchi shook his head and moved on. *Lazarus?* There was, in the region, an old wives' tale to the effect that—but what a shoddy sort of *myth* that was. Raised up by Christ but still not a Christian, they said. And yet he could not escape the feeling that he had seen the old man somewhere.

"Let the bread be brought for blessing," he called, and the deferment of supper was at an end.

After the prayers, the abbot glanced toward the beggars' table again. The old man was merely fanning his soup with a sort of basket hat. Zerchi dismissed it with a shrug, and the meal began in solemn silence.

Compline, the Church's night prayer, seemed especially profound that night.

But Joshua slept badly afterwards. In a dream he met Mrs. Grales again. There was a surgeon who sharpened a knife, saying, "This deformity must be removed before it becomes malignant." And the Rachel face opened its eyes and tried to speak to Joshua, but he could hear her only faintly, and understand her not at all.

"Accurate am I the exception," she seemed to be saying, "I commensurate the deception. Am."

He could make nothing of it, but he tried to reach through to save her. There seemed to be a rubbery wall of glass in the way. He paused and tried to read her lips. I am the, I am the—

"I am the Immaculate Conception," came the dream whisper.

He tried to tear his way through the rubbery glass to save her from the knife, but it was too late, and there was a great deal of blood afterwards. He awoke from the blasphemous nightmare with a shudder and prayed for a time; but as soon as he slept, there was Mrs. Grales again.

It was a troubled night, a night that belonged to Lucifer. It was the night of the Atlantic assault against the Asian space installations.

In swift retaliation, an ancient city died.

26 "This is your Emergency Warning Network," the announcer was saying when Joshua entered the abbot's study after Matins of the following day, "bringing you the latest bulletin on the pattern of fallout from the enemy missile assault on Texarkana. . . ."

"You sent for me, Domne?"

Zerchi waved him to silence and toward a seat. The priest's face looked drawn and bloodless, a steel-gray mask of icy self-control. To Joshua, he seemed to have shrunk in size, to have aged since nightfall. They listened gloomily to the voice which waxed and waned at four-second intervals as the broadcasting stations were switched on and off the air as an impediment to enemy direction-finding equipment:

". . . but first, an announcement just released by the Supreme Command. The royal family is safe. I repeat: the royal family is known to be safe. The Regency Council is said to have been absent from the city when the enemy struck. Outside of the disaster area, no civil disorders have been reported, and none is expected.

"A cease-fire order has been issued by the World Court of Nations, with a suspended proscription, involving the death sentence, against the responsible heads of government of both nations. Being suspended, the sentence becomes applicable only if the decree is disobeyed. Both governments cabled to the court their immediate acknowledgment of the order, and there is, therefore, a strong probability that the clash is at an end, a few hours after it began as a preventative assault against certain illegal space installations. In a surprise attack, the space forces of the Atlantic Confederacy last night struck at three concealed Asian missile sites located on the far side of the moon, and totally destroyed one enemy space station known to be involved in a guidance system for space-to-earth missiles. It was expected that the enemy would retaliate against our forces in space, but the barbarous assault on our capital city was an act of desperation which no one anticipated.

"*Special bulletin*: Our government has just announced its intention to honor the cease-fire for ten days if the enemy agrees to an immediate meeting of foreign ministers and military commanders on Guam. The enemy is expected to accept."

"Ten days," the abbot groaned. "It doesn't give us enough time."

"The Asian radio, however, is still insisting that the recent thermonuclear disaster in Itu Wan, causing some eighty thousand casualties, was the work of an errant Atlantic missile, and the destruction of the city of Texarkana was therefore retaliation in kind. . . ."

The abbot snapped off the set. "Where's the truth?" he asked quietly. "What's to be believed? Or does it matter at all? When mass murder's been answered with mass murder, rape with rape, hate with hate, there's no longer much meaning in asking whose ax is the bloodier. Evil, on evil, piled on evil. Was there any justification in our 'police action' in space? How can *we* know? Certainly there was no justification for what *they* did—or was there? We only know what *that* thing says, and *that* thing is a captive. The Asian radio has to say what will least displease its government; *ours* has to say what will least displease our fine patriotic opinionated rabble, which is what, coincidentally, the government wants it to say anyhow, so where's the difference? Dear God, there must be half a million dead, if they hit Texarkana with the real thing. I feel like saying words I've never even heard. Toad's dung. Hag pus. Gangrene of the soul. Immortal brain-rot. Do you understand me, Brother? And Christ breathed the same carrion air with us; how meek the Majesty of our Almighty God! What an Infinite Sense of Humor—for Him to become one of us!—King of the Universe, nailed on a cross as a Yiddish Schlemiel by the likes of us. They say Lucifer was cast down for refusing to adore the Incarnate Word; the Foul One must totally lack a sense of humor! God of Jacob, God even of *Cain!* Why do they do it all again?

"Forgive me, I'm raving," he added, less to Joshua than to the old woodcarving of Saint Leibowitz that stood in one corner of the study. He had paused in his pacing to glance up at the face of the image. The image was old, very old. Some earlier ruler of the abbey had sent it down to a basement storeroom to stand in dust and gloom while a dry-rot etched the wood, eating away the spring grain and leaving the summer grain so that the face seemed deeply lined. The saint wore a slightly satiric smile. Zerchi had rescued it from oblivion because of the smile.

"Did you see that old beggar in the refectory last night?" he asked irrelevantly, still peering curiously at the statue's smile.

"I didn't notice, Domne. Why?"

"Never mind, I guess I'm just imagining it." He fingered the mound of faggots where the wooden martyr stood. *That's where all of us are standing now*, he thought. On the fat kindling of past sins. And some of them are mine. Mine, Adam's, Herod's, Judas's, Hannegan's, mine. Everybody's. Always culminates in the colossus of the State, somehow, drawing about itself the mantle of godhood, being struck down by wrath of Heaven. Why? We shouted it loudly enough—God's to be obeyed by nations as by men. Caesar's to be God's policeman, not His plenipotentiary successor, nor His heir. To all ages, all peoples—"Whoever exalts a race or a State of a particular form of State or the depositories of power . . . whoever raises these notions above their standard value and divinizes them to an idolatrous level, distorts and perverts an order of the world planned and created by God. . . ." Where had *that* come from? Eleventh Pius, he thought, without certainty—eighteen centuries ago. But when Caesar got the means to destroy the world, wasn't he already divinized? Only by the consent of the people—same rabble that shouted: *"Non habomus regem nisi caesarem,"* when confronted by Him—God Incarnate, mocked and spat upon. Same rabble that martyred Leibowitz. . . .

"Caesar's divinity is showing again."

"Domne?"

"Let it pass. Are the brothers in the courtyard yet?"

"About half of them were when I passed. Shall I go see?"

"Do. Then come back here. I have something to say to you before we join them."

Before Joshua returned, the abbot had got the *Quo peregrinatur* papers out of the wall safe.

"Read the précis," he told the monk. "Look at the table of organization, read the procedural outline. You'll have to study the rest in detail, but later."

The communicator buzzed loudly while Joshua was reading.

"Reverend Father Jethrah Zerchi, Abbas, please," droned the voice of a robot operator.

"Speaking."

"Urgent priority wire from Sir Eric Cardinal Hoffstraff, New Rome. There is no courier service at this hour. Shall I read?"

"Yes, read the text of it. I'll send someone down later to pick up a copy."

"The text is as follows: *'Grex peregrinus erit. Quam primum est factum suscipiendum vobis, jussu Sactae Sedis. Suscipite ergo operis partem ordini vestro propriam . . .'*"

"Can you read that back in Southwest translation?" the abbot asked.

The operator complied, but in neither did the message seem to contain anything unexpected. It was a confirmation of the plan and a request for speed.

"Receipt acknowledged," he said at last.

"Will there be a reply?"

"Reply as follows: *Eminentissimo Domino Eric Cardinali Hoffstraff obsequitur Jethra Zerchius, A.O.L., Abbas. Ad has res disputandas iam coegi discessuros fratres ut hodie parati dimitti Roman primā aerisnave possint.* End of text."

"I read back: *'Eminentissimo . . .'*"

"All right, that's all. Out."

Joshua had finished ready the précis. He closed the portfolio and looked up slowly.

"Are you ready to get nailed on it?" Zerchi asked.

"I—I'm not sure I understand." The monk's face was pale.

"I asked you three questions yesterday. I need the answers now."

"I'm willing to go."

"That leaves two to be answered."

"I'm not sure about the priesthood, Domne."

"Look, you'll have to decide. You have less experience with starships than any of the others. None of the others is ordained. Someone has to be partially released from technical duties for pastoral and administrative duties. I told you this will not mean abandoning the Order. It won't, but your group will become an independent daughter house of the Order, under a modified rule. The Superior will be elected by secret ballot of the professed, of course—and you are the most obvious candidate, if you have a vocation to the priesthood as well. Have you, or haven't you? There's your inquisition, and the time's now, and a brief now it is too."

"But Reverend Father, I'm not through studying—"

"That doesn't matter. Besides the twenty-seven-man crew —all our people—others are going too: six sisters and twenty children from the Saint Joseph school, a couple of scientists, and three bishops, two of them newly consecrated. They can ordain, and since one of the three is a delegate of the Holy Father, they will even have the power to consecrate bishops. They can ordain you when they feel you're ready. You'll be in space for years, you know. But we want to know whether you have a vocation, and we want to know it now."

Brother Joshua stammered for a moment, then shook his head. "I don't know."

"Would you like half an hour? Would you like a glass of water? You go so gray. I tell you, son, if you're to lead the flock, you'll have to be able to decide things here-and-now. *You* need to *now*. Well, can you speak?"

"Domne, I'm not—certain—"

"You can *croak* anyhow, eh? Are you going to submit to the yoke, son? Or aren't you broken yet? You'll be asked to be the ass He rides into Jerusalem, but it's a heavy load, and it'll break your back, because He's carrying the sins of the world."

"I don't think I'm able."

"Croak and wheeze. But you *can* growl too, and that's well for the leader of the pack. Listen, none of us has been really able. But we've tried, and we've been tried. It tries you to destruction, but you're here for that. This Order has had abbots of gold, abbots of cold tough steel, abbots of corroded lead, and none of them was able, although some were abler than others, some saints even. The gold got battered, the steel got brittle and broke, and the corroded lead got stamped into ashes by Heaven. Me, I've been lucky enough to be quicksilver; I spatter, but I run back together somehow. I feel another spattering coming on, though, Brother, and I think it's for keeps this time. What are you made of, son? What's to be tried?"

"Puppy dog tails. I'm meat, and I'm scared, Reverend Father."

"Steel screams when it's forged, it gasps when it's quenched. It creaks when it goes under load. I think even steel is scared, son. Take half an hour to think? A drink of water? A drink of wind? Totter off awhile. If it makes you seasick, then prudently vomit. If it makes you terrified, scream. If it makes you anything, *pray*. But come into the church before Mass, and tell us what a monk is made of.

The Order is fissioning, and the part of us that goes into space goes forever. Are you called to be its shepherd, or are you not? Go and decide."

"I guess there's no way out."

"Of *course* there is. You have only to say, 'I'm not called to it.' Then somebody else will be elected, that's all. But go, calm down, and then come to us in church with a yes or a no. That's where I'm going now." The abbot arose and nodded a dismissal.

The darkness in the courtyard was nearly total. Only a thin sliver of light leaked from under the church doors. The faint luminosity of starlight was blurred by a dust haze. No hint of dawn had appeared in the east. Brother Joshua wandered in silence. Finally he sat on a curbing that enclosed a bed of rose bushes. He put his chin in his hands and rolled a pebble around with his toe. The buildings of the abbey were dark and sleeping shadows. A faint slice of cantaloupe moon hung low in the south.

The murmur of chanting came from the church: *Excita, Domine, potentiam tuam, et veni, ut salvos*—Stir up thy might indeed, O Lord, and come to save us. That breath of prayer would go on and on, as long as there was breath to breathe it. Even if the brethren thought it futile . . .

But they couldn't know it to be futile. Or could they? If Rome had any hope, why send the starship? Why, if they believed that prayers for peace on earth would ever be answered? Was not the starship an act of despair? . . . *Retrahe me, Satanus, et discede!* he thought. The starship is an act of hope. Hope for Man elsewhere, peace somewhere, if not here and now, then someplace: Alpha Centauri's planet maybe, Beta Hydri, or one of the sickly straggling colonies on that planet of What's-its-name in Scorpius. Hope, and not futility, is sending the ship, thou foul Seductor. It is a weary and dog-tired hope, maybe, a hope that says: Shake the dust off your sandals and go preach Sodom to Gomorrha. But it is hope, or it wouldn't say *go* at all. It isn't hope for Earth, but hope for the soul and substance of Man somewhere. With Lucifer hanging over, *not* sending the ship would be an act of presumption, as you, dirtiest one, tempted Our Lord: If thou be the Son of God, cast thyself down from the pinnacle. For angels will bear thee up.

Too much hope for Earth had led men to try to make it

Eden, and of that they might well despair until the time toward the consumption of the world—

Someone had opened the abbey doors. Monks were leaving quietly for their cells. Only a dim glow spilled from the doorway into the courtyard. The light was dim in the church. Joshua could see only a few candles and the dim red eye of the sanctuary lamp. The twenty-six of his brethren were just visible where they knelt, waiting. Someone closed the doors again, but not quite for through a crack he could still see the red dot of the sanctuary lamp. Fire kindled in worship, burning in praise, burning gently in adoration there in its red receptacle. Fire, loveliest of the four elements of the world, and yet an element too in Hell. While it burned adoringly in the core of the Temple, it had also scorched the life from a city, this night, and spewed its venom over the land. How strange of God to speak from a burning bush, and of Man to make a symbol of Heaven into a symbol of Hell.

He peered up again at the dusty stars of morning. Well, there would be no Edens found out there, they said. Yet there were men out there now, men who looked up to strange suns in stranger skies, gasped strange air, tilled strange earth. On worlds of frozen equatorial tundra, worlds of steaming Arctic jungle, a little like Earth perhaps, enough like Earth so that Man might live somehow, by the same sweat of his brow. They were but a handful, these celestial colonists of *Homo loquax nonnumquam sapiens,* a few harassed colonies of humanity that had had small help from Earth thus far; and now they might expect no help at all, there in their new non-Edens, even less like Paradise than Earth had been. Fortunately for them, perhaps. The closer men came to perfecting for themselves a paradise, the more impatient they seemed to become with it, and with themselves as well. They made a garden of pleasure, and became progressively more miserable with it as it grew in richness and power and beauty; for then, perhaps, it was easier for them to see that something was missing in the garden, some tree or shrub that would not grow. When the world was in darkness and wretchedness, it could believe in perfection and yearn for it. But when the world became bright with reason and riches, it began to sense the narrowness of the needle's eye, and that rankled for a world no longer willing to believe or yearn. Well, they were going to destroy it again, were they—this garden Earth, civilized and knowing, to be torn apart again that Man might hope again in wretched darkness.

And yet the Memorabilia was to go with the ship! Was it a curse? . . . *Discede, Seductor informis!* It was no curse, this knowledge, unless perverted by Man, as fire had been, this night. . . .

Why do I have to leave, Lord? he wondered. Must I go? And what am I trying to decide: to go, or to refuse to go? But that was already decided; there had been a summons to that—long ago. *Egrediamur tellure,* then, for it was commanded by a vow I pledged. So I go. But to lay hands on me and call me a priest, to call me *abbas* even, to set me to watch over the souls of my brethren? Must Reverend Father insist on that? But he isn't insisting on that; he is only insisting on knowing whether God insists on that. But he is in such a terrible hurry. Is he really so sure of me as all that? To drop it on me this way, he must be more certain of me than I am of myself.

Speak up, destiny, speak up! Destiny always seems decades away, but suddenly it's not decades away; it's right *now.* But maybe destiny is always right now, right here, right this very instant, maybe.

Isn't it enough that *he's* sure of me? But no, that is not nearly enough. Got to be sure myself, somehow. In half an hour. Less than half, now. *Audi me, Domine*—please, Lord— It's only one of your vipers of this generation, begging for something, begging to know, begging a sign, a sign, a portent, an omen. I've not enough time to decide.

He started nervously. Something—*slithering?*

He heard it as a quiet rustling in the dry leaves under the rose bushes behind him. It stopped, rustled, and slithered again. Would a sign from Heaven slither? An omen or a portent might. The Psalmist's *negotium perambulans in tenebris* might. A sidewinder might.

A cricket, perhaps. It was only rustling. Brother Hegan had killed a sidewinder in the courtyard once, but . . . Now it slithered again!—a slow dragging in the leaves. Would it be an appropriate sign if it slithered out and stung him in the backside?

The sound of prayer came from the church again: *Reminiscentur et convertentur ad Dominum universi fines terrae. Et adorabunt in conspectu universae familiae gentium. Quoniam Domini est regnum; et ipse dominabitur. . . .* Strange words for tonight: All the ends of the Earth shall remember and turn unto the Lord . . .

The slithering stopped suddenly. Was it right behind him? Really, Lord, a sign isn't absolutely essential. Really, I . . .

Something nudged at his wrist. He shot upward with a yelp and leaped away from the rose bushes. He seized a loose rock and threw it into the bushes. The crash was louder than he had expected. He scratched at his beard and felt sheepish. He waited. Nothing emerged from the bushes. Nothing slithered. He tossed a pebble. It too rattled offensively in the darkness. He waited, but nothing stirred in the bushes. Ask for an omen, then stone it when it comes—*de essentia hominum.*

A pink tongue of dawn was beginning to lick the stars from the sky. Soon he would have to go tell the abbot. And tell him what?

Brother Joshua brushed gnats from his beard and started toward the church, because someone had just come to the door and looked out—looking for him?

Unus panis, et unum corpus multi sumus, came the murmur from the church, *omnes qui de uno* . . . One bread and one body, though many, are we, and of one bread and one chalice have partaken. . . .

He paused in the doorway to look back toward the rose bushes. It was a trap, wasn't it? he thought. You'd send it, knowing I'd throw stones at it, wouldn't you?

A moment later, he slipped inside and went to kneel with the others. His voice joined theirs in the entreaty; for a time he ceased to think, amid the company of monastic spacegoers assembled there. *Annuntiabitur Domino generatio ventura* . . . And there shall be declared to the Lord a generation to come; and the heavens shall show forth His justice. To a people that shall be born, which the Lord hath made . . .

When he became aware again, he saw the abbot motioning to him. Brother Joshua went to kneel next to him.

"Hoc officium, Fili—tibine imponemus oneri?" he whispered.

"If they want me," the monk answered softly, *"honorem accipiam."*

The abbot smiled. "You heard me badly. I said 'burden,' not 'honor.' *Crucis autem onus si audisti ut honorem, nihilo errasti auribus."*

"*Accipiam,*" the monk repeated.

"You're certain?"

"If they choose me, I shall be certain."

"Well enough."

Thus it was settled. While the sun rose, a shepherd was elected to lead the flock.

Afterward, the conventual Mass was a Mass for Pilgrims and Travelers.

It had not been easy to charter a plane for the flight to New Rome. Even harder was the task of winning clearance for the flight after the plane had been chartered. All civil aircraft had come under the jurisdiction of the military for the duration of the emergency, and a military clearance was required. It had been refused by the local ZDI. If Abbot Zerchi had not been aware of the fact that a certain air marshal and a certain cardinal archbishop happened to be friends, the ostensible pilgrimage to New Rome by twenty-seven bookleggers with bindlestiffs might well have proceeded on shank's mare, for lack of permission to use rapid transport jet. By midafternoon, however, clearance had been granted. Abbot Zerchi boarded the plane briefly before takeoff—for last farewells.

"You are the continuity of the Order," he told them. "With you goes the Memorabilia. With you also goes the apostolic succession, and, perhaps—the Chair of Peter.

"No, no," he added in response to the murmur of surprise from the monks. "Not His Holiness. I had not told you this before, but if the worst comes on Earth, the College of Cardinals—or what's left of it—will convene. The Centaurus Colony may then be declared a separate patriarchate, with full patriarchal jurisdiction going to the cardinal who will accompany you. If the scourge falls on us here, to him, then, will go the Patrimony of Peter. For though life on Earth may be destroyed—God forbid—as long as Man lives elsewhere, the office of Peter cannot be destroyed. There are many who think that if the curse falls on Earth, the papacy would pass to him by the principle of *Epikeia* if there were no survivors here. But that is not your direct concern, brothers, sons, although you will be subject to your patriarch under special vows as those which bind the Jesuits to the Pope.

"You will be years in space. The ship will be your monastery. After the patriarchal see is established at the Centaurus Colony, you will establish there a mother house of the Visitationist Friars of the Order of Saint Leibowitz of Tycho. But the ship will remain in your hands, and the Memorabilia. If civilization, or a vestige of it, can maintain itself on Centaurus, you will send missions to the other colony worlds, and perhaps eventually to the colonies of their colonies. Wherever Man goes, you and your successors will go. And with you, the records and remembrances of four thousand years and more. Some of you, or those to come after you, will be mendicants and wanderers, teaching the chronicles of Earth and the canticles of the Crucified to the peoples and the cultures that may grow out of the colony groups. For some may forget. Some may be lost for a time from the Faith. Teach them, and receive into the Order those among them who are called. Pass on to them the continuity. Be for Man the memory of Earth and Origin. Remember this Earth. Never forget her, but—*never come back*." Zerchi's voice went hoarse and low. "If you ever come back, you might meet the Archangel at the east end of Earth, guarding her passes with a sword of flame. I feel it. Space is your home hereafter. It's a lonelier desert than ours. God bless you, and pray for us."

He moved slowly down the aisle, pausing at each seat to bless and embrace before he left the plane. The plane taxied onto the runway and roared aloft. He watched until it disappeared from view in the evening sky. Afterward, he drove back to the abbey and to the remainder of his flock. While aboard the plane, he had spoken as if the destiny of Brother Joshua's group were as clear-cut as the prayers prescribed for tomorrow's Office; but both he and they knew that he had only been reading the palm of a plan, had been describing a hope and not a certainty. For Brother Joshua's group had only begun the first short lap of a long and doubtful journey, a new Exodus from Egypt under the auspices of a God who must surely be very weary of the race of Man.

Those who stayed behind had the easier part. Theirs was but to wait for the end and pray that it would not come.

27 "The area affected by local fallout remains relatively stationary," said the announcer, "and the danger of further windspread has nearly vanished. . . ."

"Well, at least nothing *worse* has happened yet," remarked the abbot's guest. "So far, we've been safe from it here. It looks like we'll stay safe, unless the conference falls apart."

"Will we now," Zerchi grunted. "But listen a moment."

"The latest death toll estimate," the announcer continued, "on this ninth day after the destruction of the capital, gives two million, eight hundred thousand dead. More than half of this figure is from the population of the city proper. The rest is an estimate based on the percentage of the population in the fringe and fallout areas known to have received critical doses of radiation. Experts predict that the estimate will rise as more radiation cases are reported.

"This station is required by law to broadcast the following announcement twice daily for the duration of the emergency: 'The provisions of Public Law 10-WR-3E *in no way* empower private citizens to administer euthanasia to victims of radiation poisoning. Victims who have been exposed, or who think they have been exposed, to radiation far in excess of the critical dosage must report to the nearest Green Star Relief Station, where a magistrate is empowered to issue a writ of *Mori Vult* to anyone properly certified as a hopeless case, if the sufferer desires euthanasia. Any victim of radiation who takes his own life in any manner other than that prescribed by law will be considered a suicide, and will jeopardize the right of his heirs and dependents to claim insurance and other radiation relief benefits under the law. Moreover, any citizen who assists such a suicide may be prosecuted for murder. The Radiation Disaster Act authorizes euthanasia *only* after due process of law. Serious cases of radiation sickness must report to a Green Star Relief—'"

Abruptly, and with such force that he twisted the dial-knob free of its shaft, Zerchi switched off the receiver. He swung himself out of his chair and went to stand at the window and look down on the courtyard where a crowd of refugees were milling around several hastily built wooden tables. The abbey, old and new, was overrun by people of all ages and stations whose homes had been in the blighted regions. The abbot had temporarily readjusted the "cloistered" areas of the abbey to give the refugees access to virtually everything except the monks' sleeping quarters. The sign outside the old gate had been removed, for there were women and children to be fed, clothed, and given shelter.

He watched two novices carrying a steaming cauldron out of the emergency kitchen. They hoisted it onto a table and began ladling out soup.

The abbot's visitor cleared his throat and stirred restlessly in his chair. The abbot turned.

"Due process, they call it," he growled. "Due process of mass, state-sponsored suicide. With all of society's blessings."

"Well," said the visitor, "it's certainly better than letting them die horribly, by degrees."

"Is it? Better for whom? The street cleaners? Better to have your living corpses walk to a central disposal station while they can still walk? Less public spectacle? Less horror lying around? Less disorder? A few million corpses lying around might start a rebellion against those responsible. That's what you and the government mean by better, isn't it?"

"I wouldn't know about the government," said the visitor, with only a trace of stiffness in his voice. "What I meant by *better* was 'more merciful.' I have no intention of arguing your moral theology with you. If you think you have a soul that God would send to Hell if you chose to die painlessly instead of horribly, then go ahead and think so. But you're in a minority, you know. I disagree, but there's nothing to argue about."

"Forgive me," said Abbot Zerchi. "I wasn't getting ready to argue moral theology with you. I was speaking only of this spectacle of mass euthanasia in terms of human motivation. The very *existence* of the Radiation Disaster Act, and like laws in other countries, is the plainest possible evidence that governments were *fully* aware of the consequences of another war, but instead of trying to make the crime impossible, they tried to provide in advance for the consequences of the crime. Are the implications of that fact meaningless to you, Doctor?"

"Of course not, Father. Personally, I am a pacifist. But for the present we're stuck with the world as it is. And if they couldn't agree on a way to make an act of war impossible, then it is better to have *some* provisions for coping with the consequences than to have *no* provisions."

"Yes and no. Yes, if it's in anticipation of somebody else's crime. No, if it's in anticipation of one's own. And especially *no* if the provision to soften the consequences are criminal too."

The visitor shrugged. "Like euthanasia? I'm sorry, Father, I feel that the laws of society are what makes something a crime or not a crime. I'm aware that you don't agree. And there can be bad laws, ill-conceived, true. But in this case, I think we have a good law. If I thought I had such a thing as a soul, and that there was an angry God in Heaven, I might agree with you."

Abbot Zerchi smiled thinly. "You don't *have* a soul, Doctor. You *are* a soul. You *have* a body, temporarily."

The visitor laughed politely. "A semantic confusion."

"True. But which of us is confused? Are you sure?"

"Let's not quarrel, Father. I'm not with the Mercy Cadre. I work on the Exposure Survey Team. We don't kill anybody."

Abbot Zerchi gazed at him in silence for a moment. The visitor was a short muscular man with a pleasant round face and a balding pate that was sunburned and freckled. He wore a green serge uniform, and a cap with the Green Star insignia lay in his lap.

Why quarrel, indeed? The man was a medical worker, not an executioner. Some of the Green Star's relief work was admirable. Occasionally it was even heroic. That in some instances it wrought evil, according to Zerchi's belief, was no reason to regard its *good* works as tainted. The bulk of society favored it, and its workers were in good faith. The doctor had tried to be friendly. His request had seemed simple enough. He had been neither demanding nor officious about it. Still, the abbot hesitated before saying yes.

"The work you want to do here—will it take long?"

The doctor shook his head. "Two days at most, I think. We have two mobile units. We can bring them into your courtyard, hitch the two trailers together, and start right to work. We'll take the obvious radiation cases, and the wounded, first. We treat only the most urgent cases. Our job is clinical testing. The sick ones will get treatment at an emergency camp."

"And the sickest ones get something else at a mercy camp?"

The worker frowned. "Only if they want to go. Nobody makes them go."

"But you write out the permit that lets them go."

"I've given some red tickets, yes. I may have to this time.

Here—" He fumbled in his jacket pocket and brought out a red cardboard form, something like a shipping label with a loop of wire for attaching it to a buttonhole or a belt loop. He tossed it on the desk. "A blank 'crit-dose' form. There it is. Read it. It tells the man he's sick, very sick. And here— here's a green ticket too. It tells him he's well and has nothing to worry about. Look at the red one carefully! 'Estimated exposure in radiation units.' 'Blood count.' 'Urinalysis.' On one side, it's just like the green one. On the other side, the green one's blank, but look at the back of the red one. The fine print—it's directly quoted from Public Law 10-WR-3E. It has to be there. The law requires it. It has to be read to him. He has to be told his rights. What he does about it is his own affair. Now, if you'd rather we parked the mobile units down the highway, we can—"

"You just read it to him, do you? Nothing else?"

The doctor paused. "It has to be explained to him, if he doesn't understand it." He paused again, gathering irritation. "Good Lord, Father, when you tell a man he's a hopeless case, what are you going to say? Read him a few paragraphs of the law, show him the door, and say: 'Next, please!'? 'You're going to die, so good day'? *Of course* you don't read him that and nothing else, not if you have any human feeling at all!"

"I understand that. What I want to know is something else. Do you, as a physician, advise hopeless cases to go to a mercy camp?"

"I—" The medic stopped and closed his eyes. He rested his forehead on his hand. He shuddered slightly. "Of course I do," he said finally. "If you'd seen what I've seen, you would too. Of course I do."

"You'll not do it here."

"Then we'll—" The doctor quenched an angry outburst. He stood up, started to put on his cap, then paused. He tossed the cap on the chair and walked over to the window. He looked gloomily down at the courtyard, then out at the highway. He pointed. "There's the roadside park. We can set up shop there. But it's two miles. Most of them will have to walk." He glanced at Abbot Zerchi, then looked broodingly down into the courtyard again. "Look at them. They're sick, hurt, fractured, frightened. The children too. Tired, lame, and miserable. You'd let them be herded off down the highway to sit in the dust and the sun and—"

"I don't want it to be that way," said the abbot. "Look—

you were just telling me how a man-made law made it mandatory for you to read and explain *this* to a critical radiation case. I offered no objection to that in itself. Render unto Caesar to *that* extent, since the law demands it of you. Can you not, then, understand that *I* am subject to another law, and that it forbids me to allow you or anyone else on this property, under my rule, to counsel anyone to do what the Church calls evil?"

"Oh, I understand well enough."

"Very well. You need only make me one promise, and you may use the courtyard."

"What promise?"

"Simply that you won't advise anyone to go to a 'mercy camp.' Limit yourself to diagnosis. If you find hopeless radiation cases, tell them what the law forces you to tell them, be as consoling as you wish, but don't tell them to go kill themselves."

The doctor hesitated. "I think it would be proper to make such a promise with respect to patients who belong to your Faith."

Abbot Zerchi lowered his eyes. "I'm sorry," he said finally, "but that's not enough."

"*Why?* Others are not bound by your principles. If a man is not of your religion, why should you refuse to allow—" He choked off angrily.

"Do you *want* an explanation?"

"Yes."

"Because if a man is ignorant of the fact that something is wrong, and acts in ignorance, he incurs no guilt, provided natural reason was not enough to show him that it was wrong. But while ignorance may excuse the man, it does not excuse the *act*, which is wrong in itself. If I permitted the *act* simply because the *man* is ignorant that it is wrong, then I would incur guilt, because I *do* know it to be wrong. It is really that painfully simple."

"Listen, Father. They sit there and they look at you. Some scream. Some cry. Some just sit there. All of them say, 'Doctor, what can I do?' And what am I supposed to answer? Say nothing? Say, 'You can die, that's all.' What would you say?"

" 'Pray.' "

"Yes, you would, wouldn't you? Listen, pain is the only evil I know about. It's the only one I can fight."

"Then God help you."

"Antibiotics help me more."

Abbot Zerchi groped for a sharp reply, found one, but swiftly swallowed it. He searched for a blank piece of paper and a pen and pushed them across the desk. "Just write: 'I will not recommend euthanasia to any patient while at this abbey,' and sign it. Then you can use the courtyard."

"And if I refuse?"

"Then I suppose they'll have to drag themselves two miles down the road."

"Of all the merciless—"

"On the contrary. I've offered you an opportunity to do your work as required by the law you recognize, without overstepping the law I recognize. Whether they go down the road or not is up to you."

The doctor stared at the blank page. "What is so magic about putting it in writing?"

"I prefer it that way."

He bent silently over the desk and wrote. He looked at what he had written, then slashed his signature under it and straightened. "All right, there's your promise. Do you think it's worth any more than my spoken word?"

"No. No indeed." The abbot folded the note and tucked it into his coat. "But it's here in my pocket, and you know it's here in my pocket, and I can look at it occasionally, that's all. Do you *keep* promises, by the way, Doctor Cors?"

The medic stared at him for a moment. "I'll keep it." He grunted, then turned on his heel and stalked out.

"Brother Pat!" Abbot Zerchi called weakly. "Brother Pat, are you there?"

His secretary came to stand in the doorway. "Yes, Reverend Father?"

"You heard?"

"I heard some of it. The door was open, and I couldn't help hearing. You didn't have the silencer—"

"You heard him say it? 'Pain's the only evil I know about.' You heard that?"

The monk nodded solemnly.

"And that society is the only thing which determines whether an act is wrong or not? That too?"

"Yes."

"Dearest God, how did those two heresies get back into the world after all this time? Hell has limited imaginations down there. 'The serpent deceived me, and I did eat.' Brother Pat, you'd better get out of here, or I'll start raving."

"Domne, I—"

"What's keeping you? What's that, a letter? All right, give it here."

The monk handed it to him and went out. Zerchi left it unopened and glanced at the doctor's pledge again. Worthless, perhaps. But still the man was sincere. And dedicated. He'd have to be dedicated to work for the kind of salary the Green Star paid. He had looked underslept and overworked. He'd probably been living on benzedrine and doughnuts since the shot that killed the city. Seeing misery everywhere and detesting it, and sincere in wanting to do something about it. Sincere—that was the hell of it. From a distance, one's adversaries seemed fiends, but with a closer view, one saw the sincerity and it was as great as one's own. Perhaps Satan was the sincerest of the lot.

He opened the letter and read it. The letter informed him that Brother Joshua and the others had departed from New Rome for an unspecified destination in the West. The letter also advised him that information about *Quo peregrinatur* had leaked to the ZDI, who had sent investigators to the Vatican to ask questions about the rumored launching of an unauthorized starship. . . . Evidently the starship was not yet in space.

They'd learn soon enough about *Quo peregrinatur*, but with the help of Heaven, they'd find out too late. What then? he wondered.

The legal situation was tangled. The law forbade starship departures without commission approval. Approval was hard to get and slow in coming. Zerchi was certain that the ZDI and the commission would consider the Church was breaking the law. But a State-Church concordat had existed for a century and a half now; it clearly exempted the Church from licensing procedures, and it guaranteed to the Church the right to send missions to "whatever space installations and/or planetary outposts shall not have been declared by the aforesaid Commission to be ecologically critical or closed to unregulated enterprise." Every installation in the solar system was "ecologically critical" and "closed" at the time of the concordat, but the concordat further asserted the Church's right to "own space vessels and travel unrestricted to *open* installations or outposts." The concordat was very old. It had been signed in the days when the Berkstrun starship drive was only a dream in the wide imagination of some who thought that interstellar travel would open up the universe to an unrestricted outflow of population.

Things had turned out otherwise. When the first starship was born as an engineering drawing, it became plain that no institution except government had the means or the funds to build them; that no profit was to be derived from transporting colonies to extrasolar planets for purposes of "interstellar mercantilism." Nevertheless, the Asian rulers had sent the first colony ship. Then in the West the cry was heard: "Are we to let the 'inferior' races inherit the stars?" There had been a brief flurry of starship launchings as colonies of black people, brown, white, and yellow people were hurled into the sky toward the Centaur, in the name of racism. Afterwards, geneticists had wryly demonstrated that —since each racial group was so small that unless their descendants intermarried, each would undergo deteriorative genetic drift due to inbreeding on the colony planet—the racists had made cross-breeding necessary to survival.

The only interest the Church had taken in space had been concern for the colonists who were sons of the Church, cut off from the flock by interstellar distances. And yet she had not taken advantage of that provision of the concordat which permitted the sending of missions. Certain contradictions existed between the concordat and the laws of the State which empowered the commission, at least as the latter law might in theory affect the sending of missions. The contradiction had never been adjudicated by the courts, since there had never been cause for litigation. But now, if the ZDI intercepted Brother Joshua's group in the act of launching a starship without a commission permit or charter, there would be cause. Zerchi prayed that the group would get away without a test in the courts, which might take weeks or months. Of course there would be a scandal afterwards. Many would charge not only that the Church had violated Commission rulings but charity too, by sending ecclesiastical dignitaries and a bunch of rascal monks, when she might have used the ship as refuge for poor colonists, hungry for land. The conflict of Martha and Mary always recurred.

Abbot Zerchi suddenly realized that the tenor of his thinking had changed during the previous day or two. A few days ago, everyone had been waiting for the sky to burst asunder. But nine days had passed since Lucifer had prevailed in space and scorched a city out of existence. Despite the dead, the maimed, and the dying, there had been nine days of silence. Since the wrath had been stayed thus far, perhaps the worst could be averted. He had found himself thinking of things that might happen next week or next month, as if—after all—there might really *be* a next week or a next month. And why not? Examining conscience, he found that he had not altogether abandoned the virtue of hope.

A monk returned from an errand in the city that afternoon and reported that a camp for refugees was being set up at the park two miles down the highway. "I think it's being sponsored by Green Star, Domne," he added.

"Good!" the abbot said. "We're overflowing here, and I've had to turn three truckloads of them away."

The refugees were noisy in the courtyard, and the noise jangled overwrought nerves. The perpetual quiet of the old abbey was shattered by strange sounds: the boisterous laughter of men telling jokes, the cry of a child, the rattle of pots and pans, hysterical sobbing, a Green Star medic shouting: "Hey, Raff, go fetch an enema hose." Several times the abbot suppressed an urge to go to the window and call to them for silence.

After bearing it as long as he could, he picked up a pair of binoculars, an old book, and a rosary, and went up to one of the old watchtowers where a thick stone wall cut off most of the sounds from the courtyard. The book was a slim volume of verse, really anonymous, but by legend ascribed to a mythical saint, whose "canonization" was accomplished only in fable and the folklore of the Plains, and not by any act of the Holy See. No one, indeed, had ever found evidence that such a person as Saint Poet of the Miraculous Eyeball had ever lived: the fable had probably arisen out of the story that one of the early Hannegans had been given a glass eyeball by a brilliant physical theorist who was his protégé—Zerchi could not remember whether the scientist had been Esser Shon or Pfardentrott—and who told the prince that it had belonged to a poet who had died for the Faith. He had not specified which faith the poet had died for—that of Peter or that of the Texarkanan schismatics—but evidently the Hannegan had valued it, for he had mounted the eyeball in the clutch of a small golden hand which was still worn upon certain state occasions by princes of the Harq-Hannegan dynasty. It was variously called the *Orbis Judicans Conscientias* or the *Oculus Poetae Judicis,* and the remnants of the Texarkana Schism still revered it as a relic. Someone a few years back had proposed the rather silly hypothesis that Saint Poet was the same person as the "scurrilous versificator" once mentioned in the Journals of the Venerable Abbot Jerome, but the only substantiating "evidence" for this notion was that Pfardentrott—or. was it Esser Shon?—had visited the abbey during the reign of Venerable Jerome at about the same date as the "scurrilous versificator" entry in the Journal, and that the gift of the eyeball to Hannegan had occurred at some date after that visit to the abbey. Zerchi suspected that the thin book of verse had been penned by one of the secular scientists who had visited the abbey to study the Memorabilia at about that time, and that one of them could probably be identified with the "scurrilous versificator" and possibly with the Saint Poet of folklore and fable. The anonymous verses were a bit too daring, Zerchi thought, to have been written by a monk of the Order.

The book was a satirical dialogue in verse between two agnostics who were attempting to establish by natural reason alone that the existence of God could not be established by natural reason alone. They managed only to demonstrate that the mathematical limit of an infinite sequence of "doubting the certainty with which something doubted is known to be unknowable when the 'something doubted' is still a preceding statement of 'unknowability' of something doubted," that the limit of this process at infinity can only be equivalent to a statement of *absolute certainty,* even though phrased as an infinite series of negations of certainty. The text bore traces of St. Leslie's theological calculus, and even as a poetic dialogue between an agonostic identified only as "Poet" and another only as "Thon," it seemed to suggest a proof of the existence of God by an epistemological method, but the versifier had been a satirist; neither poet nor don relinquished his agnostic premises after the conclusion of absolute certainty had been reached, but concluded instead that: *Non cogitamus, ergo nihil sumus.*

Abbot Zerchi soon tired of trying to decide whether the book was high intellectual comedy or more epigrammatic buffoonery. From the tower, he could see the highway and the city as far as the mesa beyond. He focused the binocu-

lars on the mesa and watched the radar installation for a
time, but nothing unusual appeared to be happening there.
He lowered the glasses slightly to watch the new Green
Star encampment down at the roadside park. The area of the
park had been roped off. Tents were being pitched. Utility
crews worked at tapping the gas and power lines. Several
men were engaged in hoisting a sign at the entrance to the
park, but they held it edgewise to his gaze and he could
not read it. Somehow the boiling activity reminded him of a
nomad "carnival" coming to town. There was a big red
engine of some sort. It seemed to have a firebox and something like a boiler, but he could not at first guess its purpose. Men in Green Star uniforms were erecting something
that looked like a small carousel. At least a dozen trucks
were parked on the side road. Some were loaded with lum-
ber, others with tents and collapsible cots. One seemed
to be hauling firebricks, and another was burdened with pottery and straw.

Pottery?

He studied the last truck's cargo carefully. A slight frown
gathered on his forehead. It was a load of urns or vases,
all alike, and packed together with cushioning wads of
straw. Somewhere, he had seen the like of them, but could
not remember where.

Still another truck carried nothing but a great "stone"
statue—probably made of reinforced plastic—and a square
slab upon which the statue was evidently to be mounted.
The statue lay on its back, supported by a wooden frame-
work and a nest of packing material. He could see only its
legs and one outstretched hand that thrust up through the
packing straw. The statue was longer than the bed of the
truck; its bare feet projected beyond tailgate. Someone had
tied a red flag to one of its great toes. Zerchi puzzled over
it. Why waste a truck on a statue, when there was probable
need of another truckload of food?

He watched the men who were erecting the sign. At last
one of them lowered his end of the board and climbed a
ladder to perform some adjustment of the overhead brackets.
With one end resting on the ground, the sign tilted, and
Zerchi, by craning, managed to read its message:

MERCY CAMP NUMBER 18
GREEN STAR
DISASTER CADRE PROJECT

Hurridly, he looked again at the trucks. The pottery! Recognition came to him. Once he had driven past a crematorium and seen men unloading the same sort of urns from a truck with the same company markings. He swung the binoculars again, searching for the truck loaded with firebrick. The truck had moved. At last he located it, now parked inside the area. The bricks were being unloaded near the great red engine. He inspected the engine again. What had at first glance appeared to be a boiler, now suggested an oven or a furnace. "*Evenit diabolus!*" the abbot growled, and started for the wall stairs.

He found Doctor Cors in the mobile unit in the courtyard. The doctor was wiring a yellow ticket to the lapel of an old man's jacket, while telling him that he should go to a rest camp for a while and mind the nurses, but that he'd be all right if he took care of himself.

Zerchi stood with folded arms, munching at the edge of his lips and coldly watching the physician. When the old man was gone, Cors looked up warily.

"Yes?" His eyes took note of the binoculars and re-examined Zerchi's face. "*Oh,*" he grunted. "Well, I have nothing to do with that end of it, nothing at all."

The abbot gazed at him for a few seconds, then turned and stalked out. He went to his office and had Brother Patrick call the highest Green Star official. . . .

"I want it moved out of our vicinity."

"I'm afraid the answer is emphatically no." . . .

"Brother Pat, call the workshop and get Brother Lufter up here."

"He's not there, Domne."

"Then have them send me a carpenter and a painter. Anybody will do."

Minutes later, two monks arrived.

"I want five lightweight signs made at once," he told them. "I want them with good long handles. They're to be big enough to be read from a block away, but light enough for a man to carry for several hours without getting dog-tired. Can you do that?"

"Surely, m'Lord. What do you want them to say?"

Abbot Zerchi wrote it for them. "Make it big and make it bright," he told them. "Make it scream at the eye. That's all."

When they were gone, he called Brother Patrick again. "Brother Pat, go find me five good, young, healthy novices, preferably with martyr complexes. Tell them they may get what Saint Stephen got."

And I may get even worse, he thought, when New Rome hears about it.

28

Compline had been sung, but the abbot stayed on in the church, kneeling alone in the gloom of evening.

Domine, mundorum omnium Factor, parsurus esto imprimis eis filiis aviantibus ad sideria caeli quorum victus dificilior . . .

He prayed for Brother Joshua's group—for the men who had gone to take a starship and climb the heavens into a vaster uncertainty than any uncertainty faced by Man on Earth. They'd want much praying for; none was more susceptible than the wanderer to the ills that afflict the spirit to torture faith and nag a belief, harrowing the mind with doubts. At home, on Earth, conscience had its overseers and its exterior taskmasters, but abroad the conscience was alone, torn between Lord and Foe. Let them be incorruptible, he prayed, let them hold true to the way of the Order.

Doctor Cors found him in the church at midnight and beckoned him quietly outside. The physician looked haggard and wholly unnerved.

"I just broke my promise!" he stated challengingly.

The abbot was silent. "Proud of it?" he asked at last.

"Not especially."

They walked toward the mobile unit and stopped in the bath of bluish light that spilled out its entrance. The medic's lab-jacket was soaked with sweat, and he dried his forehead on his sleeve. Zerchi watched him with that pity one might feel for the lost.

"We'll leave at once, of course," said Cors. "I thought I'd tell you." He turned to enter the mobile unit.

"Wait a minute," the priest said. "You'll tell me the rest."

"Will I?" The challenging tone once again. "Why? So you can go threaten hell-fire? She's sick enough now, and so's the child. I'll tell you nothing."

"You already have. I know who you mean. The child, too, I suppose?"

Cors hesitated. "Radiation sickness. Flash burns. The woman has a broken hip. The father's dead. The fillings in the woman's teeth are radioactive. The child almost glows in the dark. Vomiting shortly after the blast. Nausea, anemia, rotten follicles. Blind in one eye. The child cries constantly because of the burns. How they survived the shock wave is hard to understand. I can't do anything for them except the Eucrem team."

"I've seen them."

"Then you know why I broke the promise. I have to *live* with myself afterwards, man! I don't want to live as the torturer of that woman and that child."

"Pleasanter to live as their murderer instead?"

"You're beyond reasonable argument."

"What did you tell her?"

" 'If you love your child, spare her the agony. Go to sleep mercifully as quick as you can.' That's all. We'll leave immediately. We've finished with the radiation cases and the worst of the others. It won't hurt the rest of them to walk a couple of miles. There aren't any more critical-dosage cases."

Zerchi stalked away, then stopped and called back. "Finish," he croaked. "Finish and then get out. If I see you again —I'm afraid of what I'll do."

Cors spat. "I don't like being here any better than you like having me. We'll go now, thanks."

He found the woman lying on a cot with the child in the corridor of the overcrowded guesthouse. They huddled together under a blanket and both were crying. The building smelled of death and antiseptic. She looked up at his vague silhouette against the light.

"Father?" Her voice was frightened.

"Yes."

"We're done for. See? See what they gave me?"

He could see nothing, but he heard her fingers pick at the edge of paper. The red ticket. He could find no voice to speak to her. He came to stand over the cot. He fished in his pocket and brought out a rosary. She heard the rattle of the beads and groped for it.

"You know what it is?"

"Certainly, Father."

"Then keep it. Use it."

"Thank you."

"Bear it and pray."

"I know what I have to do."

"Don't be an accomplice. For the love of God, child, don't—"

"The doctor said—"

She broke off. He waited for her to finish; she kept silent.

"Don't be an accomplice."

She still said nothing. He blessed them and left as quickly as possible. The woman had handled the beads with fingers that knew them; there was nothing he could say to her that she didn't already know.

"The conference of foreign ministers on Guam has just ended. No joint policy statement has yet been issued; the ministers are returning to their capitals. The importance of this conference, and the suspense with which the world awaits the results, cause this commentator to believe that the conference is not yet ended, but only recessed so that the foreign ministers may confer with their governments for a few days. An earlier report which alleged that the conference was breaking up amid bitter invective has been denied by the ministries. First Minister Rekol had only one statement for the press: 'I'm going back to talk to the Regency Council. But the weather's been pleasant here; I may come back later to fish.'

"The ten-day waiting period ends today, but it is generally held that the cease-fire agreement will continue to be observed. Mutual annihilation is the alternative. Two cities have died, but it is to be remembered that neither side answered with a saturation attack. The Asian rulers contend that an eye was taken for an eye. Our government insists that the explosion in Itu Wan was not an Atlantic missile. But for the most part, there is a weird and brooding silence from both capitals. There has been little waving of the bloody shirt, few cries for wholesale vengeance. A kind of dumb fury, because murder has been done, because lunacy reigns, prevails, but neither side wants total war. Defense remains at battle alert. The General Staff has issued an announcement, almost an appeal, to the effect that we will not use the worst if Asia likewise refrains. But the announcement says further: 'If they use dirty fallout, we shall reply in kind, and in such force that no creature will live in Asia for a thousand years.'

"Strangely, the least hopeful note of all comes not from Guam but from the Vatican at New Rome. After the Guam conference ended, it was reported that Pope Gregory ceased to pray for peace in the world. Two special Masses were sung in the basilica: the *Exsurge quare obdormis*, Mass against the Heathen, and the *Reminiscere*, Mass in Time of War; then, the report says His Holiness retired to the mountains to meditate and pray for justice.

"And now a word from—"

"Turn it off!" Zerchi groaned.

The young priest who was with him snapped off the set and stared wide-eyed at the abbot. "I don't believe it!"

"What? About the Pope? I didn't either. But I heard it earlier, and New Rome has had time to deny it. They haven't said a word."

"What does it mean?"

"Isn't that obvious? The Vatican diplomatic service is on the job. Evidently they sent in a report on the Guam conference. Evidently it horrified the Holy Father."

"What a warning! What a gesture!"

"It was more than a gesture, Father. His Holiness isn't chanting Battle Masses for dramatic effect. Besides, most people will think he means 'against the heathen' on the other side of the ocean, and 'justice' for our side. Or if they know better, they'll still mean that themselves." He buried his face in his hands and rubbed them up and down. "Sleep. What's sleep, Father Lehy? Do you remember? I haven't seen a human face in ten days that didn't have black circles under its eyes. I could hardly doze last night for somebody screaming over in the guesthouse."

"Lucifer's no sandman, that's true."

"What are you staring at out that window?" Zerchi demanded sharply. "That's another thing. Everybody keeps looking at the sky, staring up and wondering. If it's coming, you won't have time to see it until the flash, and then you'd better *not* be looking. Stop it. It's unhealthy."

Father Lehy turned away from the window. "Yes, Reverend Father. I wasn't watching for that though. I was watching the buzzards."

"Buzzards?"

"There've been lots of them, all day. Dozens of buzzards —just circling."

"Where?"

"Over the Green Star camp down the highway."

"That's no omen, then. That's just healthy vulture appetite. Agh! I'm going out for some air."

In the courtyard he met Mrs. Grales. She carried a basket of tomatoes which she lowered to the ground at his approach.

"I brought ye somewhat, Father Zerchi," she told him. "I saw yer sign being down, and some poor girl inside the gate, so I reckoned ye'd not mind a visit by yer old tumater woman. I brought ye some tumaters, see?"

"Thank you, Mrs. Grales. The sign's down because of the refugees, but that's all right. You'll have to see Brother Elton about the tomatoes, though. He does the buying for our kitchen."

"Oh, not for buying, Father. He-he! I brought 'em to yer for free. Ye've got lots to feed, with all the poor things yer putting up. So they're for free. Where'll I put 'em?"

"The emergency kitchen's in the—but no, leave them there. I'll get someone to carry them to the guesthouse."

"Port 'em myself. I ported them this far." She hoisted the basket again.

"Thank you, Mrs. Grales." He turned to go.

"Father, wait!" she called. "A minute, yer honor, just a minute of your time—"

The abbot suppressed a groan. "I'm sorry, Mrs. Grales, but it's as I told you—" He stopped, stared at the face of Rachel. For a moment, he had imagined— Had Brother Joshua been right about it? But surely, no. "It's—it's a matter for your parish and diocese, and there's nothing I can—"

"No, Father, not that!" she said. "It be somewhat else I wanted to ask of ye." (There! It *had* smiled! He was certain of it!) "Would ye hear my confession, Father? Beg shriv'ness for bothering ye, but I'm sad for my naughties, and I would it were you as shrives me."

Zerchi hesitated. "Why not Father Selo?"

"I tell ye truthful, yer honor, it's that the man is an occasion of sin for me. I go meanin' well for the man, but I look once on his face and forget myself. God love him, but I can't."

"If he's offended you, you'll have to forgive him."

"Forgive, that I do, that I do. But at a goodly distance. He's an occasion of sin for me, I'll tell, for I go losing my temper with him on sight."

Zerchi chuckled. "All right, Mrs. Grales. I'll hear your

confession, but I've got something I have to do first. Meet me in the Lady Chapel in about half an hour. The first booth. Will that be all right?"

"Ay, and bless ye, Father!" She nodded profusely. Abbot Zerchi could have sworn that the Rachel head mirrored the nods, ever so slightly.

He dismissed the thought and walked over to the garage. A postulant brought out the car for him. He climbed in, dialed his destination, and sank back wearily into the cushions while the automatic controls engaged the gears and nosed the car toward the gate. In passing the gate, the abbot saw the girl standing at the roadside. The child was with her. Zerchi jabbed at the CANCEL button. The car stopped. "Waiting," said the robot controls.

The girl wore a cast that enclosed her hips from the waist to left knee. She was leaning on a pair of crutches and panting at the ground. Somehow she had got out of the guesthouse and through the gate, but she was obviously unable to go any farther. The child was holding on to one of her crutches and staring at the traffic on the highway.

Zerchi opened the car door and climbed out slowly. She looked up at him, but turned her glance quickly away.

"What are you doing out of bed, child?" he breathed. "You're not supposed to be up, not with that hip. Just where did you think you were going?"

She shifted her weight, and her face twisted with pain. "To town," she said. "I've got to go. It's urgent."

"Not so urgent that somebody couldn't go do it for you. I'll get Brother—"

"No, Father, no! Nobody else can do it for me. I've got to go to town."

She was lying. He felt certain she was lying. "All right, then," he said. "I'll take you to town. I'm driving in anyway."

"No! I'll walk! I'm—" She took a step and gasped. He caught her before she fell.

"Not even with Saint Christopher holding your crutches could you walk to town, child. Come on, now, let's get you back to bed."

"I've got to get to town, I tell you!" she shrieked angrily.

The child, frightened by its mother's anger, began crying monotonously. She tried to calm its fright, but then wilted:

"All right, Father. Will you drive me to town?"

"You shouldn't be going at all."

"I tell you, I've got to go!"

"All right, then. Let's help you in . . . the baby . . . now you."

The child screamed hysterically when the priest lifted it into the car beside the mother. It clung to her tightly and resumed the monotonous sobbing. Because of the loose moist dressings and the singed hair, the child's sex was difficult to determine at a glance, but Abbot Zerchi guessed it to be a girl.

He dialed again. The car waited for a break in the traffic, then swerved onto the highway and into the mid-speed lane. Two minutes later, as they approached the Green Star encampment, he dialed for the slowest lane.

Five monks paraded in front of the tent area, in a solemn hooded picket line. They walked to and fro in procession beneath the Mercy Camp sign, but they were careful to stay on the public right-of-way. Their freshly painted signs read:

> *ABANDON EVERY HOPE*
> *YE*
> *WHO ENTER HERE*

Zerchi had intended to stop to talk to them, but with the girl in the car he contented himself with watching as they drifted past. With their habits and their hoods and their slow funereal procession, the novices were indeed creating the desired effect. Whether the Green Star would be sufficiently embarrassed to move the camp away from the monastery was doubtful, especially since a small crowd of hecklers, as it had been reported to the abbey, had appeared earlier in the day to shout insults and throw pebbles at the signs carried by the pickets. There were two police cars parked at the side of the highway, and several officers stood nearby to watch with expressionless faces. Since the crowd of hecklers had appeared quite suddenly, and since the police cars had appeared immediately afterwards, and just in time to witness a heckler trying to seize a picket's sign, and since a Green Star official had thereupon gone huffing off to get a court order, the abbot suspected that the heckling had been as carefully staged as the picketing, to enable the Green Star officer to get his writ. It would probably be granted, but until it was served, Abbot Zerchi meant to leave the novices where they were.

He glanced at the statue which the camp workers had erected near the gate. It caused a wince. He recognized it as one of the composite human images derived from mass psychological testing in which subjects were given sketches and photographs of unknown people and asked such questions as: "Which would you most like to meet?" and "Which do you think would make the best parent?" or "Which would you want to avoid?" or "Which do you think is the criminal?" From the photographs selected as the "most" or the "least" in terms of the questions, a series of "average faces," each to evoke a first-glance personality judgment had been constructed by computer from the mass test results.

This statue, Zerchi was dismayed to notice, bore a marked similarity to some of the most effeminate images by which mediocre, or worse than mediocre, artists had traditionally misrepresented the personality of Christ. The sweet-sick face, blank eyes, simpering lips, and arms spread wide in a gesture of embrace. The hips were broad as a woman's, and the chest hinted at breasts—unless those were only folds in the cloak. Dear Lord of Golgotha, Abbot Zerchi breathed, is that all the rabble imagine You to be? He could with effort imagine the statue saying: "Suffer the little children to come unto me," but he could not imagine it saying: "Depart from me into everlasting fire, accursed ones," or flogging the money-changers out of the Temple. What question, he wondered, had they asked their subjects that conjured in the rabble-mind this composite face? It was only anonymously a *christus*. The legend on the pedestal said: *COMFORT*. But surely the Green Star must have seen the resemblance to the traditional pretty *christus* of poor artists. But they stuck it in the back of a truck with a red flag tied to its great toe, and the intended resemblance would be hard to prove.

The girl had one hand on the door handle; she was eying the car's controls. Zerchi swiftly dialed FAST LANE. The car shot ahead again. She took her hand from the door.

"Lots of buzzards today," he said quietly, glancing at the sky out the window.

The girl sat expressionless. He studied her face for a moment. "Are you in pain, daughter?"

"It doesn't matter."

"Offer it to Heaven, child."

She looked at him coldly. "You think it would please God?"

"If you offer it, yes."

"I cannot understand a God who is pleased by my baby's hurting!"

The priest winced. "No, no! It is not the pain that is pleasing to God, child. It is the soul's endurance in faith and hope and love *in spite* of bodily afflictions that pleases Heaven. Pain is like negative temptation. God is not pleased by temptations that afflict the flesh; He is pleased when the soul rises above the temptation and says, 'Go, Satan.' It's the same with pain, which is often a temptation to despair, anger, loss of faith—"

"Save your breath, Father. I'm not complaining. The baby is. But the baby doesn't understand your sermon. She can hurt, though. She can hurt, but she can't understand."

What can I say to that? the priest wondered numbly. Tell her again that Man was given preternatural impassibility once, but threw it away in Eden? That the child was a cell of Adam, and therefore— It was true, but she had a sick baby, and she was sick herself, and she wouldn't listen.

"Don't do it, daughter. Just don't do it."

"I'll think about it," she said coldly.

"I had a cat once, when I was a boy," the abbot murmured slowly. "He was a big gray tomcat with shoulders like a small bulldog and a head and neck to match, and that sort of slouchy insolence that makes some of them look like the Devil's own. He was pure cat. Do you know cats?"

"A little."

"Cat lovers don't know cats. You can't love *all* cats if you know cats, and the ones you can love if you know them are the ones the cat lovers don't even like. Zeke was that kind of cat."

"This has a moral, of course?" She was watching him suspiciously.

"Only that I killed him."

"Stop. Whatever you're about to say, stop."

"A truck hit him, crushed his back legs. He dragged himself under the house. Once in a while he'd make a noise like a cat fight and thrash around a little, but mostly he just lay quietly and waited. 'He ought to be destroyed,' they kept telling me. After a few hours he dragged himself from under the house. Crying for help. 'He ought to be destroyed,' they said. I wouldn't let them do it. They said it was cruel to let him live. So finally I said I'd do it myself, if it had to be done. I got a gun and a shovel and took him out to the edge of the woods. I stretched him out on the ground while I dug a hole. Then I shot him through the head. It was a small-bore rifle. Zeke thrashed a couple of times, then got up and started dragging himself toward some bushes. I shot him again. It knocked him flat, so I thought he was dead, and put him in the hole. After a couple of shovels of dirt, Zeke got up and pulled himself out of the hole and started for the bushes again. I was crying louder than the cat. I had to kill him with the shovel. I had to put him back in the hole and use the blade of the shovel like a cleaver, and while I was chopping with it, Zeke was still thrashing around. They told me later it was just spinal reflex, but I didn't believe it. I knew that cat. He wanted to get to those bushes and just lie there and wait. I wished to God that I had only let him get to those bushes, and die the way a cat would if you just let it alone—with *dignity*. I never felt right about it. Zeke was only a cat, but—"

"Shut up!" she whispered.

"—but even the ancient pagans noticed that Nature imposes nothing on you that Nature doesn't prepare you to bear. If that is true even of a cat, then is it not more perfectly true of a creature with rational intellect and will—whatever you may believe of Heaven?"

"Shut up, damn you shut up!" she hissed.

"If I am being a little brutal," said the priest, "then it is to you, not to the baby. The baby, as you say, can't understand. And you, as you say, are not complaining. Therefore—"

"Therefore you're asking me to let her die slowly and—"

"No! I'm not asking you. As a priest of Christ I am *commanding* you by the authority of Almighty God not to lay hands on your child, not to offer her life in sacrifice to a false god of expedient mercy. I do not advise you, I adjure and command you in the name of Christ the King. Is that clear?"

Dom Zerchi had never spoken with such a voice before, and the ease with which the words came to his lips surprised even the priest. As he continued to look at her, her eyes fell. For an instant he had feared that the girl would laugh in his face. When Holy Church occasionally hinted that she still considered her authority to be supreme over all nations and superior to the authority of states, men in these times tended to snicker. And yet the authenticity of the command could still be sensed by a bitter girl with a dying child. It *had* been brutal to try to reason with her, and he regretted it. A simple direct command might accomplish what persuasion could not. She needed the voice of authority now, more than she needed persuasion. He could see it by the way she had wilted, although he had spoken the command as gently as his voice could manage.

They drove into the city. Zerchi stopped to post a letter, stopped at Saint Michael's to speak for a few minutes with Father Selo about the refugee problem, stopped again at ZDI for a copy of the latest civil defense directive. Each time he returned to the car, he half expected the girl to be gone, but she sat quietly holding the baby and absently stared toward infinity.

"Are you going to tell me where you wanted to go, child?" he asked at last.

"Nowhere. I've changed my mind."

He smiled. "But you were so urgent about getting to town."

"Forget it, Father. I've changed my mind."

"Good. Then we'll go back home. Why don't you let the sisters take care of your daughter for a few days?"

"I'll think about it."

The car sped back along the highway toward the abbey. As they approached the Green Star camp, he could see that something was wrong. The pickets were no longer marching their tour. They had gathered in a group and were talking, or listening, to the officers and a third man that Zerchi could not identify. He switched the car over to the slow lane. One of the novices saw the car, recognized it, and began waving his sign. Dom Zerchi had no intention of stopping while the girl was in the car, but one of the officers stepped out into the slow lane just ahead of them and pointed his traffic baton at the vehicle's obstruction detectors; the autopilot reacted automatically and brought the car to a stop. The officer waved the car off the road. Zerchi could not disobey. The two police officers approached, paused to note license numbers and demand papers. One of them glanced in curiously at the girl and the child, took note of the red tickets. The other waved toward the now-stationary picket line.

"So you're the bejeezis behind all this, are you?" He grunted at the abbot. "Well, the gentleman in the brown tunic over there has a little news for you. I think you'd better listen." He jerked his head toward a chubby courtroom type who came pompously toward them.

The child was crying again. The mother stirred restlessly.

"Officers, this girl and baby aren't well. I'll accept the process, but please let us drive on back to the abbey now. Then I'll come back alone."

The officer looked at the girl again. "Ma'am?"

She stared toward the camp and looked up at the statue towering over the entrance. "I'm getting out here," she told them tonelessly.

"You'll be better off, ma'am," said the officer, eying the red tickets again.

"No!" Dom Zerchi caught her arm. "Child, I forbid you—"

The officer's hand shot out to seize the priest's wrist. "Let go!" he snapped, then softly: "Ma'am, are you his ward or something?"

"No."

"Where do you get off forbidding the lady to get out?" the officer demanded. "We're just a little impatient with you, *mister,* and it had better be—"

Zerchi ignored him and spoke rapidly to the girl. She shook her head.

"The baby, then. Let me take the baby back to the sisters. I insist—"

"Ma'am, is that your child?" the officer asked. The girl was already out of the car, but Zerchi was holding the child.

The girl nodded. "She's mine."

"Has he been holding you prisoner or something?"

"No."

"What do you want to do, ma'am?"

She paused.

"Get back in the car," Dom Zerchi told her.

"*You cut that tone of voice, mister!*" the officer barked. "Lady, what about the kid?"

"We're both getting out here," she said.

Zerchi slammed the door and tried to start the car, but the officer's hand flashed in through the window, hit the CANCEL button, and removed the key.

"Attempted kidnapping?" one officer grunted to the other.

"Maybe," said the other, and opened the door. "Now let go of the woman's baby!"

"To let it be murdered here?" the abbot asked. "You'll have to use force."

"Go around to the other side of the car, Fal."

"*No!*"

"Now, just a little baton under the armpit. That's it, *pull!* All right, lady—there's your kid. No, I guess you can't, not with those crutches. *Cors?* Where's Cors? Hey, Doc!"

Abbot Zerchi caught a glimpse of a familiar face coming through the crowd.

"Lift the kid out while we hold this nut, will you?"

Doctor and priest exchanged a silent glance, and then the baby was lifted from the car. The officers released the abbot's wrists. One of them turned and found himself hemmed in by novices with upraised signs. He interpreted the signs as potential weapons, and his hand dropped to his gun. "Back up!" he snapped.

Bewildered, the novices moved back.

"Get out."

The abbot climbed out of the car. He found himself facing the chubby court official. The latter tapped him on the arm with a folded paper. "You have just been served with a restraining order, which I am required by the court to read and explain to you. Here is your copy. The officers are witnesses that you have been confronted with it, so you cannot resist service—"

"Oh, give it here."

"That's the right attitude. Now you are directed by the court as follows: 'Whereas the plaintiff alleges that a great public nuisance has been—' "

"Throw the signs in the ash barrel over there," Zerchi instructed his novices, "unless somebody objects. Then climb in the car and wait." He paid no attention to the reading of the order, but approached the officers while the process server trailed behind, reading in monotonous staccato. "Am I under arrest?"

"We're thinking about it."

" '—and to appear before this court on the aforesaid date to show cause why an injunction—' "

"Any particular charge?"

"We could make four or five charges stick, if you want it that way."

Cors came back through the gate. The woman and her child had been escorted into the camp area. The doctor's expression was grave, if not guilty.

"Listen, Father," he said, "I know how you feel about all this, but—"

Abbot Zerchi's fist shot out at the doctor's face in a straight right jab. It caught Cors off balance, and he sat down hard in the driveway. He looked bewildered. He snuffled a few times. Suddenly his nose leaked blood. The police had the priest's arms pinned behind him.

"'—and herein fail not,'" the process server jabbered on, "'lest a decree pro confesso—'"

"Take him over to the car," said one of the officers.

The car toward which the abbot was led was not his own but the police cruiser. "The judge will be a little disappointed in you," the officer told him sourly. "Now stand still right there and be quiet. One move and you go in the locks."

The abbot and the officer waited by the cruiser while the process server, the doctor, and the other officer conferred in the driveway. Cors was pressing a handkerchief to his nose.

They talked for five minutes. Thoroughly ashamed, Zerchi pressed his forehead against the metal of the car and tried to pray. It mattered little to him at the moment what they might decide to do. He could think only of the girl and the child. He was certain she had been ready to change her mind, had needed only the command, *I, a priest of God, adjure thee*, and the grace to hear it—if only they had not forced him to stop where she could witness "God's priest" summarily overruled by "Caesar's traffic cop." Never to him had Christ's Kingship seemed more distant.

"All right, mister. You're a lucky nut, I'll say that."

Zerchi looked up. "What?"

"Doctor Cors refuses to file a complaint. He says he had one coming. Why did you hit him?"

"Ask him."

"We did. I'm just trying to decide whether we take you in or just give you the summons. The court officer says you're well known hereabouts. What do you do?"

Zerchi reddened. "Doesn't this mean anything to you?" He touched his pectoral cross.

"Not when the guy wearing it punches somebody in the nose. What do you do?"

Zerchi swallowed the last trace of his pride. "I am the abbot of the Brothers of Saint Leibowitz at the abbey you see down the road."

"That gives you a license to commit assault?"

"I'm sorry. If Doctor Cors will hear me, I'll apologize. If you give me a summons, I promise to appear."

"Fal?"

"The jail's full of D.P.s."

"Listen, if we just forget the whole thing, will you stay away from this place, and keep your gang out there where they belong?"

"Yes."

"All right. Get moving. But if you so much as drive past here and spit, that'll be *it*."

"Thank you."

A calliope was playing somewhere in the park as they drove away; and looking back, Zerchi saw that the carousel was turning. One officer mopped his face, clapped the process server on the back, and they all went to their cars and drove away. Even with five novices in the car, Zerchi was alone with his shame.

29 "I believe you've been warned about that temper before?" Father Lehy demanded of the penitent.

"Yes, Father."

"You realize that the intent was relatively murderous?"

"There was no intent to kill."

"Are you trying to excuse yourself?" the confessor demanded.

"No, Father. The intent was to hurt. I accuse myself of violating the spirit of the Fifth Commandment in thought and deed, and of sinning against charity and justice. And bringing disgrace and scandal upon my office."

"You realize that you have broken a promise never to resort to violence?"

"Yes, Father. I deeply regret it."

"And the only mitigating circumstance is that you just saw red and swung. Do you often let yourself abandon reason like that?"

The inquisition continued, with the ruler of the Abbey on his knees, and the prior sitting in judgment over his master.

"All right," Father Lehy said at last, "now for your penance, promise to say—"

Zerchi was an hour and a half late getting to the chapel, but Mrs. Grales was still waiting. She was kneeling in a pew near the confessional, and she seemed half asleep. Embarrassed within himself, the abbot had hoped that she would not be there. He had his own penance to say before he could hear her. He knelt near the altar and spent twenty minutes finishing the prayers Father Lehy had assigned him as penance for that day, but when he moved back toward the confessional, Mrs. Grales was still there. He spoke to her twice before she heard him, and when she rose, she stumbled a little. She paused to feel at the Rachel face, exploring its eyelids and lips with withered fingers.

"Is something wrong, daughter?" he asked.

She looked up at the high windows. Her eyes wandered about the vaulted ceiling. "Ay, Father," she whispered. "I feel the Dread One about, I do. The Dread One's close, very close about us here. I feel need of shriv'ness, Father—and something else as well."

"Something else, Mrs. Grales?"

She leaned close to whisper behind her hand. "I need be giving shriv'ness to Him, as well."

The priest recoiled slightly. "To whom? I don't understand."

"Shriv'ness—to Him who made me as I am," she whimpered. But then a slow smile spread her mouth. "I—I never forgave Him for it."

"Forgive God? How can you—? He is just. He is Justice, He is Love. How can you say—?"

Her eyes pleaded with him. "Mayn't an old tumater woman forgive Him just a little for His Justice? Afor I be asking His shriv'ness on me?"

Dom Zerchi swallowed a dry place. He glanced down at her bicephalous shadow on the floor. It hinted at a terrible Justice—this shadow shape. He could not bring himself to reprove her for choosing the word *forgive*. In her simple world, it was conceivable to forgive justice as well as to forgive injustice, for Man to pardon God as well as for God to pardon Man. So be it, then, and bear with her, Lord, he thought, adjusting his stole.

She genuflected toward the altar before they entered the confessional, and the priest noticed that when she crossed herself, her hand touched Rachel's forehead as well as her own. He brushed back the heavy curtain, slipped into his half of the booth, and whispered through the grille.

"What do you seek, daughter?"

"Blessings, Father, for I have sinned—"

She spoke haltingly. He could not see her through the mesh that covered the grille. There was only the low and rhythmic whimper of a voice of Eve. The same, the same, everlastingly the same, and even a woman with two heads could not contrive new ways of courting evil, but could only pursue a mindless mimicry of the Original. Still feeling the shame of his own behavior with the girl and the officers and Cors, he found it hard to concentrate. Still, his hands shook as he listened. The rhythm of the words came dull and muffled through the grille, like the rhythm of distant hammering. Spikes driven through palms, piercing timber. As *alter Christus* he sensed the weight of each burden for a moment before it passed on to the One who bore them all. There was the business about her mate. There were the murky and secret things, things to be wrapped in dirty newspaper and buried by night. That he could only make sense of a little of it, seemed to make the horror worse.

"If you are trying to say that you are guilty of abortion," he whispered, "I must tell you that the absolution is reserved to the bishop and I can't—"

He paused. There was a distant roaring, and the faint snort-growl of missiles being fired from the range.

"The Dread One! The Dread One!" whined the old woman.

His scalp prickled: a sudden chill of unreasonable alarm. "Quickly! An act of contrition!" he muttered. "Ten Aves, ten Pater Nosters for your penance. You'll have to repeat the confession again later, but now an Act of Contrition."

He heard her murmuring from the other side of the grille. Swiftly he breathed an absolution: *"Te absolvat Dominus Jesus Christus; ego autem eius auctoritate te absolvo ab omni vinculo. . . . Denique, si absolvi potes, ex peccatis tuis ego te absolvo in Nomine Patris . . ."*

Before he had finished, a light was shining through the thick curtain of the confessional door. The light grew brighter and brighter until the booth was full of bright noon. The curtain began to smoke.

"Wait, *what!*" he hissed. "Wait till it dies."

"wait wait wait till it dies," echoed a strange soft voice from beyond the grille. It was not the voice of Mrs. Grales.

"Mrs. Grales? Mrs. Grales?"

She answered him in a thick-tongued, sleepy murmur. "I never meant to . . . I never meant to . . . never love

. . . Love . . ." It trailed away. It was not the same voice that had answered him a moment ago.

"Now, quickly, *run!*"

Not waiting to see that she heeded him, he bounded out of the confessional and ran down the aisle toward the altar of reservation. The light had dimmed, but it still roasted the skin with noon sunglare. *How many seconds remained?* The church was full of smoke.

He vaulted into the sanctuary, stumbled over the first step, called it a genuflection, and went to the altar. With frantic hands, he removed the Christ-filled ciborium from the tabernacle, genuflected again before the Presence, grabbed up the Body of his God and ran for it.

The building fell in on him.

When he awoke, there was nothing but dust. He was pinned to the ground at the waist. He lay on his belly in the dirt and tried to move. One arm was free, but the other was caught under the weight that held him down. His free hand still clutched the ciborium, but he had tipped it in falling, and the top had come off, spilling several of the small Hosts.

The blast had swept him clean out of the church, he decided. He lay in sand, and saw the remains of a rose bush caught in a rockfall. A rose remained attached to a branch of it—one of the Salmon Armenians, he noticed. The petals were singed.

There was a great roaring of engines in the sky, and blue lights kept winking through the dust. He felt no pain at first. He tried to crane his neck so as to get a look at the behemoth that sat on him, but then things started hurting. His eyes filmed. He cried out softly. He would not look back again. Five tons of rock had tucked him in. It held whatever remained of him below the waist.

He began recovering the little Hosts. He moved his free arm gingerly. Cautiously he picked each of them out of the sand. The wind threatened to send the small flakes of Christ wandering. Anyway, Lord, I tried, he thought. Anyone needing the last rites? Viaticum? They'll have to drag themselves to me, if they do. Or is anybody left?

He could hear no voices above the terrible roaring.

A trickle of blood kept seeping into his eyes. He wiped at it with his forearm so as to avoid staining the wafers with gory fingers. Wrong blood, Lord, mine, not Yours. *Dealba me.*

He returned most of the scattered Victim to the vessel, but a few fugitive flakes eluded his reach. He stretched for them, but blacked out again.

"JesusMaryJoseph! Help!"

Faintly he heard an answer, distant and scarcely audible under the howling sky. It was the soft strange voice he had heard in the confessional, and again it echoed his words:

"jesus mary joseph help"

"What?" he cried.

He called out several times, but no further answer came. The dust had begun sprinkling down. He replaced the lid of the ciborium to keep the dust from mingling with the Wafers. He lay still for a time with his eyes closed.

The trouble with being a priest was that you eventually had to take the advice you gave to others. *Nature imposes nothing that Nature hasn't prepared you to bear.* That's what I get for telling her what the Stoic said before I told her what God said, he thought.

There was little pain, but only a ferocious itching that came from the captive part of him. He tried to scratch; his fingers encountered only bare rock. He clawed at it for a moment, shuddered, and took his hand away. The itch was maddening. Bruised nerves flashed foolish demands for scratching. He felt very undignified.

Well, Doctor Cors, how do you know that the itch is not the more basic evil than the pain?

He laughed a little at that one. The laugh caused a sudden blackout. He clawed his way out of the blackness to the accompaniment of someone screaming. Suddenly the priest knew that the screaming was his own. Zerchi was suddenly afraid. The itch had been transmuted into agony, but the screams had been those of raw terror, not of pain. There was agony now even in breathing. The agony persisted, but he could bear that. The dread had arisen from that last taste of inky blackness. The blackness seemed to brood over him, covet him, await him hungrily—a big black appetite with a yen for souls. Pain he could bear, but not that Awful Dark. Either there was something in it that should not be there, or there was something here that remained to be done. Once he surrendered to that darkness, there would be nothing he could do or undo.

Ashamed of his fright, he tried to pray, but the prayers seemed somehow unprayerful—like apologies, but not petitions—as if the last prayer had already been said, the last canticle already sung. The fear persisted. *Why?* He tried to reason with it. You've seen people die, Jeth. Seen many people die. It looks easy. They taper off, and then there's a little spasm, and it's over. That inky Dark—gulf between *aham* and *Asti*—blackest Styx, abyss between Lord and Man. Listen, Jeth, you really believe there's Something on the other side of it, don't you? Then why are you shaking so?

A verse from the *Dies Irae* drifted into mind, and it nagged at him:

> *Quid sum miser tunc dicturus?*
> *Quem patronum rogaturus,*
> *Cum vix justus sit securus?*

"What am I, who am wretched, then to say? Whom shall I ask to be my protector, since even the *just* man is scarcely safe?" *Vix securus?* Why "scarcely safe"? Surely He would not damn the just? Then why are you shaking so?

Really, Doctor Cors, the evil to which even you should have referred was not suffering, but the unreasoning fear of suffering. *Metus doloris.* Take it together with its positive equivalent, the craving for worldly security, for Eden, and you might have your "root of evil," Doctor Cors. To minimize suffering and to maximize security were natural and proper ends of society and Caesar. But then they became the only ends, somehow, and the only basis of law—a perversion. Inevitably, then, in seeking only them, we found only their opposites: maximum suffering and minimum security.

The trouble with the world is *me.* Try that on yourself, my dear Cors. Thee me Adam Man we. No "worldly evil" except that which is introduced into the world by Man—me thee Adam us—with a little help from the father of lies. Blame anything, blame God even, but oh don't blame *me.* Doctor Cors? The only evil in the world *now,* Doctor, is the fact that the world no longer is. What pain hath wrought?

He laughed weakly again, and it brought the ink.

"Me us Adam, but Christ, Man me; Me us Adam, but Christ, Man me," he said aloud. "You know what, Pat?— they'd . . . together . . . rather get nailed on it, but not alone . . . when they bleed . . . want company. Because . . . Because why it is. Because why it is the same as Satan wants Man full of Hell. I mean the same as Satan wants Hell full of Man. Because Adam . . . And yet Christ . . . But still me . . . Listen, Pat—"

This time it took longer to drive the inky Dark away, but he had to make it clear to Pat before he went into it all the way. "Listen, Pat, because . . . why it is I told her the baby had to . . . is why I. I mean. I mean Jesus never asked a man to do a damn thing that Jesus didn't do. Same as why I. Why I can't let go. Pat?"

He blinked several times. Pat vanished. The world congealed again and the blackness was gone. Somehow he had discovered what he was afraid of. There was something he had yet to fulfill before that Dark closed over him forever. *Dear God, let me live long enough to fulfill it.* He was afraid to die before he had accepted as much suffering as that which came to the child who could not comprehend it, the child he had tried to save for further suffering—no, not *for* it, but in spite of it. He had commanded the mother in the name of Christ. He had not been wrong. But now he was afraid to slide away into that blackness before he had endured as much as God might help him endure.

> *Quem patronum rogaturus,*
> *Cum vix justus sit securus?*

Let it be for the child and her mother, then. What I impose, I must accept. *Fas est.*

The decision seemed to diminish the pain. He lay quietly for a time, then cautiously looked back at the rock heap again. *More* than five tons back there. Eighteen centuries back there. The blast had broken open the crypts, for he noticed a few bones caught between the rocks. He groped with his free hand, encountered something smooth, and finally worked it free. He dropped it in the sand beside the ciborium. The jawbone was missing, but the cranium was intact except for a hole in the forehead from which a sliver of dry and half-rotten wood protruded. It looked like the remains of an arrow. The skull seemed very old.

"Brother," he whispered, for none but a monk of the Order would have been buried in those crypts.

What did you do for them, Bone? Teach them to read and write? Help them rebuild, give them Christ, help restore a culture? Did you remember to warn them that it could never be Eden? Of course you did. Bless you, Bone, he thought, and traced a cross on its forehead with his thumb. For all your pains, they paid you with an arrow between the eyes. Because there's more than five tons and eighteen centuries of rock back there. I suppose there's about two million years of it back there—since the first of *Homo inspiratus*.

He heard the voice again—the soft echo-voice that had answered him a little while ago. This time it came in a kind of childish singsong: "la la la, la-la-la—"

Although it seemed to be the same voice he had heard in the confessional, surely it could not be Mrs. Grales. Mrs. Grales would have forgiven God and run for home, if she had got out of the chapel in time—and please forgive the reversal, Lord. But he was not even sure that it was a reversal. Listen, Old Bone, should I have told that to Cors? Listen, my dear Cors, why don't you forgive God for allowing pain? If He didn't allow it, human courage, bravery, nobility, and self-sacrifice would all be meaningless things. Besides, you'd be out of a job, Cors.

Maybe that's what we forgot to mention, Bone. Bombs and tantrums, when the world grew bitter because the world fell somehow short of half-remembered Eden. The bitterness was essentially against God. Listen, Man, you have to give up the bitterness—"be granting shriv'ness to God," as she'd say—before anything; before love.

But bombs and tantrums. They didn't forgive.

He slept awhile. It was natural sleep and not that ugly mind-seizing nothingness of the Dark. A rain came, clearing the dust. When he awoke, he was not alone. He lifted his cheek out of the mud and looked at them crossly. Three of them sat on the rubble heap and eyed him with funereal solemnity. He moved. They spread black wings and hissed nervously. He flipped a bit of stone at them. Two of them took wing and climbed to circle, but the third sat there doing a little shuffle-dance and peering at him gravely. A dark and ugly bird, but not like that Other Dark. This one coveted only the body.

"Dinner's not quite ready, brother bird," he told it irritably. "You'll have to wait."

It would not have many meals to look forward to, he noticed, before the bird itself became a meal for another. Its feathers were singed from the flash, and it kept one eye closed. The bird was soggy with rain, and the abbot guessed that the rain itself was full of death.

"la la la, la-la-la wait wait wait till it dies la . . ."

The voice came again. Zerchi had feared that it might have been a hallucination. But the bird was hearing it too. It kept peering at something out of Zerchi's range of vision. At last it hissed raucously and took wing.

"Help!" he shouted weakly.

"help," parroted the strange voice.

And the two-headed woman wandered into sight around a heap of rubble. She stopped and looked down at Zerchi.

"Thank God! Mrs. Grales! See if you can find Father Lehy—"

"thank god mrs. grales see if you can . . ."

He blinked away a film of blood and studied her closely. "Rachel," he breathed.

"rachel," the creature answered.

She knelt there in front of him and settled back on her heels. She watched him with cool green eyes and smiled innocently. The eyes were alert with wonder, curiosity, and —perhaps something else—but she could apparently not see that he was in pain. There was something about her eyes that caused him to notice nothing else for several seconds. But then he noticed that the head of Mrs. Grales slept soundly on the other shoulder while Rachel smiled. It seemed a young shy smile that hoped for friendship. He tried again.

"Listen, is anyone else alive? Get—"

Melodious and solemn came her answer: "listen is anyone else alive—" She savored the words. She enunciated them distinctly. She smiled over them. Her lips reframed them when her voice was done with them. It was more than reflexive imitation, he decided. She was trying to communicate something. By the repetition, she was trying to convey the idea: *I am somehow like you.*

But she had only just now been born.

And you're somehow different, too, Zerchi noticed with a trace of awe. He remembered that Mrs. Grales had arthritis in both knees, but the body which had belonged to her was now kneeling there and sitting back on its heels in that limber posture of youth. Moreover, the old woman's wrinkled skin seemed less wrinkled than before, and it seemed to glow a little, as if horny old tissue were being revivified. Suddenly he noticed her arm.

"You're hurt!"

"you're hurt."

Zerchi pointed at her arm. Instead of looking where he pointed, she imitated his gesture, looking at his finger and extending her own to touch it—using the wounded arm. There was very little blood, but there were at least a dozen cuts and one looked deep. He tugged at her finger to bring her arm closer. He plucked out five slivers of broken glass. Either she had thrust her arm through a window, or, more likely, had been in the path of an exploding windowpane when the blast had come. Only once when he removed an inch-long lance of glass did a trace of blood appear. When he pulled the others free, they left tiny blue marks, with no bleeding. The effect reminded him of a demonstration of hypnosis he had once witnessed, of something he had dismissed as a hoax. When he looked up at her face again, his awe increased. She was still smiling at him, as if the removal of the glass splinters had caused her no discomfort.

He glanced again at the face of Mrs. Grales. It had grown gray with the impersonal mask of coma. The lips seemed bloodless. Somehow he felt certain it was dying. He could imagine it withering and eventually falling away like a scab or an umbilical cord. Who, then, was Rachel? And what?

There was still a little moisture on the rain-wet rocks. He moistened one fingertip and beckoned for her to lean closer. Whatever she was, she had probably received too much radiation to live very long. He began tracing a cross on her forehead with the moist fingertip.

"Nisi baptizata es et nisi baptizari nonquis, te baptizo. . . ."

He got no farther than that. She leaned quickly away from him. Her smile froze and vanished. *No!* her whole countenance seemed to shout. She turned away from him. She wiped the trace of moisture from her forehead, closed her eyes, and let her hands lie limply in her lap. An expression of complete passivity came over her face. With her head bowed that way, her whole attitude seemed suggestive of prayer. Gradually, out of the passivity, a smile was reborn. It grew. When she opened her eyes and looked at him again, it was with the same open warmth as before. But she glanced around as if searching for something.

Her eyes fell on the ciborium. Before he could stop her, she picked it up. *"No!"* he coughed hoarsely, and made a grab for it. She was too quick for him, and the effort cost him a blackout. As he drifted back to consciousness and lifted his head again, he could see only through a blur. She was still kneeling there facing him. Finally he could make out that she was holding the golden cup in her left hand, and in her right, delicately between thumb and forefinger, a single Host. She was offering it to *him*, or was he only imagining it, as he had imagined awhile ago that he was talking to Brother Pat?

He waited for the blur to clear. This time it wasn't going to clear, not completely. *"Domine, non sum dignus . . ."* he whispered, *"sed tantum dic verbo . . ."*

He received the Wafer from her hand. She replaced the lid of the ciborium and set the vessel in a more protected spot under a jutting rock. She used no conventional gestures, but the reverence with which she had handled it convinced him of one thing: *she sensed the Presence under the veils*. She who could not yet use words nor understand them, had done what she had as if by *direct instruction*, in response to his attempt at conditional baptism.

He tried to refocus his eyes to get another look at the face of this being, who by gestures alone had said to him: I do not need your *first* Sacrament, Man, but I am worthy to convey to you *this* Sacrament of Life. Now he knew what she was, and he sobbed faintly when he could not again force his eyes to focus on those cool, green, and untroubled eyes of one born free.

"Magnificat anima mea Dominum," he whispered. "My soul doth magnify the Lord, and my spirit hath rejoiced in God my Saviour; for He hath regarded the lowliness of His handmaid. . . ." He wanted to teach her these words as his last act, for he was certain that she shared something with the Maiden who first had spoken them.

"Magnificat anima mea Dominum et exultavit spiritus meus in Deo, salutari meo, quia respexit humilitatem . . ."

He ran out of breath before he had finished. His vision went foggy; he could no longer see her form. But cool fingertips touched his forehead, and he heard her say one word:

"Live."

Then she was gone. He could hear her voice trailing away in the new ruins. "la la la, la-la-la . . ."

The image of those cool green eyes lingered with him as long as life. He did not ask *why* God would choose to raise up a creature of primal innocence from the shoulder of Mrs. Grales, or why God gave to it the preternatural gifts of Eden—those gifts which Man had been trying to seize by brute force again from Heaven since first he lost them. He had seen primal innocence in those eyes, and a promise of resurrection. One glimpse had been a bounty, and he wept in gratitude. Afterwards he lay with his face in the wet dirt and waited.

Nothing else ever came—nothing that he saw, or felt, or heard.

30 They sang as they lifted the children into the ship. They sang old space chanteys and helped the children up the ladder one at a time and into the hands of the sisters. They sang heartily to dispel the fright of the little ones. When the horizon erupted, the singing stopped. They passed the last child into the ship.

The horizon came alive with flashes as the monks mounted the ladder. The horizons became a red glow. A distant cloudbank was born where no cloud had been. The monks on the ladder looked away from the flashes. When the flashes were gone, they looked back.

The visage of Lucifer mushroomed into hideousness above the cloudbank, rising slowly like some titan climbing to its feet after ages of imprisonment in the Earth.

Someone barked an order. The monks began climbing again. Soon they were all inside the ship.

The last monk, upon entering, paused in the lock. He stood in the open hatchway and took off his sandals. "*Sic transit mundus,*" he murmured, looking back at the glow. He slapped the soles of his sandals together, beating the dirt out of them. The glow was engulfing a third of the heavens. He scratched his beard, took one last look at the ocean, then stepped back and closed the hatch.

There came a blur, a glare of light, a high thin whining sound, and the starship thrust itself heavenward.

The breakers beat monotonously at the shores, casting up driftwood. An abandoned seaplane floated beyond the breakers. After a while the breakers caught the seaplane and threw it on the shore with the driftwood. It tilted and fractured a wing. There were shrimp carousing in the breakers, and the whiting that fed on the shrimp, and the shark that munched the whiting and found them admirable, in the sportive brutality of the sea.

A wind came across the ocean, sweeping with it a pall of fine white ash. The ash fell into the sea and into the breakers. The breakers washed dead shrimp ashore with the driftwood. Then they washed up the whiting. The shark swam out to his deepest waters and brooded in the cold clean currents. He was very hungry that season.

A SELECTION OF FINE READING
AVAILABLE IN CORGI BOOKS

Novels

War

Romance

Horror

Science Fiction

☐ YS	1349	THE ILLUSTRATED MAN	Ray Bradbury 3/-
☐ YS	1367	FAHRENHEIT 451	Ray Bradbury 3/-
☐ YS	1383	NEEDLE	Hal Clement 3/-
☐ YS	1300	A FOR ANDROMEDA	Hoyle & Elliot 3/-
☐ SS	1334	A SWORD ABOVE THE NIGHT	John Lymington 2/6

General

☐ FG	988	BORSTAL BOY	Brendan Behan 5/-
☐ GG	1214	THE BRIDAL BED	Joseph Braddock 3/6
☐ GG	1285	GREAT WAR SPEECHES	Winston Churchill 3/6
☐ GG	1319	SINATRA	Robin Douglas-Home 3/6
☐ GG	1137	THE FIFTY MINUTE HOUR	Robert Lindner 3/6
☐ SG	1353	FOUR FAMOUS TRIALS	Maurice Moiseiwitsch 2/6
☐ GG	1366	MY LIFE WITH CLEOPATRA	Wanger & Hyams 3/6

Westerns

☐ GW	1174	THE LOG OF A COWBOY	Andy Adams 3/6
☐ F	683	BLOOD BROTHER	Elliott Arnold 5/-
☐ GW	1363	FROM WHERE THE SUN NOW STANDS	Will Henry 3/6
☐ SW	1380	CATLOW	Louis L'Amour 2/6
☐ S	558	SHANE	Jack Schaefer 2/6
☐ GW	1310	CARRINGTON	Michael Straight 3/6
☐ SW	924	SUDDEN—OUTLAWED	Oliver Strange 2/6
☐ SW	1050	SUDDEN MAKES WAR	Oliver Strange 2/6

Crime

☐ SC	1103	PSYCHO	Robert Bloch 2/6
☐ SC	1385	THE COUNT OF NINE	A. A. Fair 2/6
☐ SC	1361	AN AXE TO GRIND	A. A. Fair 2/6
☐ SC	1305	THE DEEP	Mickey Spillane 2/6
☐ SC	1306	I, THE JURY	Mickey Spillane 2/6
☐ SC	1307	KISS ME, DEADLY	Mickey Spillane 2/6
☐ SC	1308	MY GUN IS QUICK	Mickey Spillane 2/6
☐ SC	1369	ME, HOOD!	Mickey Spillane 2/6
☐ SC	1346	THE LONG WAIT	Mickey Spillane 2/6
☐ SC	1344	VENGEANCE IS MINE	Mickey Spillane 2/6
☐ SC	1345	ONE LONELY NIGHT	Mickey Spillane 2/6
☐ SC	1347	THE BIG KILL	Mickey Spillane 2/6

All these great books are available at your local bookshop or newsagent; or can be ordered direct from the publisher. Just tick the titles you want and fill in the form below.

CORGI BOOKS, Department OC, Park Royal Road, London, N.W.10.
Please send cheque or postal order. No currency, PLEASE. Allow 6d. per book to cover the cost of postage on orders of less than 6 books.

NAME ....

ADDRESS ....

....